War Clouds on the Horn of Africa

War Clouds on the Horn of Africa: The Widening Storm

Second, Revised Edition

Tom J. Farer

CARNEGIE ENDOWMENT FOR INTERNATIONAL PEACE
NEW YORK   WASHINGTON, D.C.

©1979. Carnegie Endowment for International Peace. All rights reserved, including the right to reproduce this book or portions thereof in any form, except for the inclusion of brief quotations in a review. Inquiries should be addressed to the Carnegie Endowment for International Peace, 11 Dupont Circle, Washington, D.C. 20036 or 30 Rockefeller Plaza, New York, New York 10020.

I.S.B.N. 0-87003-014-0 cloth; 0-87003-013-2 paper.

Library of Congress Catalog Card Number: 78-75279.

Printed in the United States of America.

To my Mother who keeps a liberal's faith; to Mika, who also felt on the Horn's sere plains a glorious freedom of the heart; and to my children, Dima and Paola, who, by their way of being in the world, help me to sustain the fragile belief that it is worth struggling to shape the future.

Contents

List of Maps

Foreword to the Second Edition

This book is the revised edition of a study originally published in 1976 under the auspices of the Endowment's New York-based International Fact-Finding Center. This center provides an opportunity for foreign affairs professionals to undertake anticipatory research on pre-crisis issues that carry significant threats to peaceful international relations.

Even in mid-1974, as the Fact-Finding Center got under way, the Horn of Africa seemed to be a prototype pre-crisis situation. Haile Selassie was an old man whose advanced age posed a major succession problem for his brittle regime. The leader of Kenya was equally advanced in years. The opening of the Suez Canal was soon to take place. The French presence in Djibouti was certain to undergo change. The rebellion in Eritrea continued to flare. Great-power interest in the area was increasing. Therefore the Endowment asked Professor Tom J. Farer, who had studied the politics and society of the Horn for many years, to assess the prospects for conflict and the policies for avoiding it. The result was *War Clouds on the Horn of Africa*. Its title was taken from a memorandum distributed by the Ethiopian government to African chiefs of state meeting in Addis Ababa. Farer's study was received enthusiastically, reviewed widely, and used across the country in international relations courses.

Since the publication of the first edition, convulsive changes in the Horn seemed to justify a second look at the region's poignant political dramas. The long-standing friendly relationship between the United States and Ethiopia gradually crumbled. The Soviet Union switched sides dramatically from Somalia to Ethiopia. Somalis fought and lost a bitter war in the Ogaden against Ethiopian troops aided by both the Cubans and the Soviets. The Eritrean problem persisted. Through it all the Horn remained a flashpoint for potential conflict. In this revised edition of *War Clouds*, Farer re-evaluates the significance of these changes for regional security and for relations between the United States and the Soviet Union.

Farer anticipated in his first edition that the Somali-Ethiopian conflict would help to undermine detente, but he does not accept two of the conventional explanations for this outcome, and he explains why in this edition. First, he rejects the thesis that deeper Soviet involvement is explicable only in terms of a matured conspiracy to threaten vital Western interests, and second, he questions whether Soviet behavior in the Horn constitutes a radical challenge to the rules of the geopolitical game.

In 1979 the most plausible future on the Horn, according to Farer, is the confirmation of central authority in Ethiopia and the country's successful transformation along the revolutionary lines envisioned by the military government. He addresses the vital questions that arise. To what degree would the confirmation of central authority be dependent on forces and developments outside the Horn? For neighboring states, both African and Arab, what is the likely impact of a re-integrated Ethiopia—governed by a regime without effective internal opposition, enjoying the benefits of a radically more productive agricultural sector, and allied with the Soviet Union? Is a peaceful solution in Eritrea possible?

Farer argues that U.S. policy for the Horn is inadequate because it will achieve neither our humanitarian nor our strategic goals. But in his judgment, given a more co-operative and imaginative approach to the Horn's problems by interested outside parties, a peace of accommodation can be achieved. For the Horn possesses the human resources for self-transformation. Both Ethiopia and Somalia are real nations with governments that function and leaders who are making serious efforts to solve problems of poverty and underdevelopment. The Eritrean liberation movement has also managed to build the foundations of a new society. Farer's analysis suggests why accommodation will require governments in the region and outside powers alike to re-orient their objectives and to rethink their policies.

As always, Endowment publication of this report implies a belief only in the importance of the subject. The views expressed are those of the author.

Comments or inquiries on this and other work of the Endowment may be addressed to the offices of the Carnegie Endowment for International Peace, 11 Dupont Circle, Washington, D.C. 20036 or 30 Rockefeller Plaza, New York, New York 10020.

Thomas L. Hughes
President
Carnegie Endowment for
International Peace

Acknowledgement

As I warned in the first edition's acknowledgement, expressions of gratitude are inevitably incomplete. But that conveniently tragic caveat could hardly justify my omitting a declaration of gratitude to Vivian Hewitt and Jane Lowenthal, who administer the Carnegie Endowment's library with grace, intelligence, and a wonderfully sensitive appreciation of how to assist research. I hope they will forgive an oversight stemming from the tumbling rush into print produced by the sensed imminence of violence on the Horn.

In preparing this second edition I have multiplied conceptual and data-gathering debts owed to my old friend Colin Legum, whose annual volume of the *Africa Contemporary Record* remains an indispensable Baedeker for anyone following political and economic developments in that continent. Colin and his colleague Bill Lee will very shortly bring out a second edition of their immensely useful work, *Conflict in the Horn of Africa*.

While a considerable number of other people assisted me in tracking and interpreting events on the Horn over the past two years, particular debts are owed to John Harbison of the University of Wisconsin (Parkside) and to Princeton Lyman, former director of USAID in Ethiopia and for years one of AID's most creative thinkers. I also want to express a general appreciation to officials in the State Department's Bureau of African Affairs and the Swedish Foreign Ministry for responding with clarity and candor to my quest for information.

Equally candid and helpful were the Eritrean patriot, Osman Saleh Sabbe, and Dr. Hussein Mohamed Adam, chairman of the social science faculty at the Somali National University and editor of the journal *Halgan*. I doubt that any of the above will agree entirely with my conclusions and proposals; certainly they cannot be held responsible for them. In the grand egoistic tradition established by infinite forebears I will say that the sole responsibility, at least for the demerits of my interpretations and recipes, should be imputed to me.

Once again Diane Bendahmane, my gracious and feisty editor at Carnegie, helped to restrain my congenital impulse to rhetorical excess and, however gently, to note points where I had been tempted to substitute ipse dixit for argument. Larry Fabian was another Endowment staff member whose astute comments helped me to spruce up some intellectually murky terrain.

Tom J. Farer

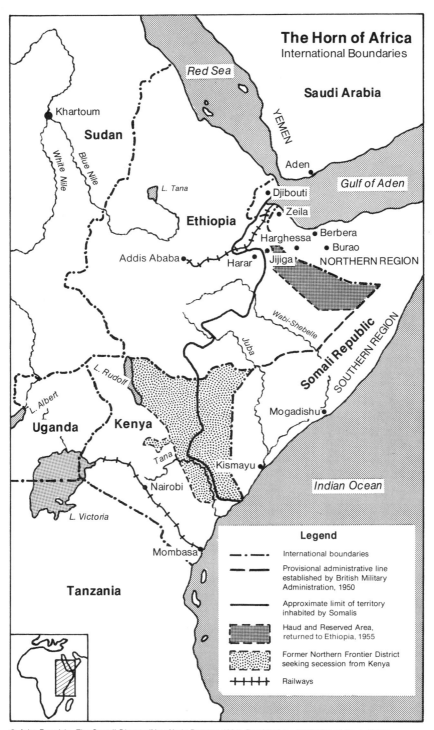

The Horn of Africa
International Boundaries

Saudi Arabia

Red Sea

YEMEN

Khartoum

Sudan

White Nile

Blue Nile

L. Tana

Aden

Gulf of Aden

Djibouti

Zeila

Ethiopia

Harghessa

Berbera

Burao

Addis Ababa

Harar

Jijiga

NORTHERN REGION

Wabi-Shebelle

Juba

Somali Republic

SOUTHERN REGION

L. Rudolf

L. Albert

Uganda

Kenya

Tana

Mogadishu

Kismayu

Nairobi

Indian Ocean

L. Victoria

Mombasa

Tanzania

Legend

— · — · — International boundaries

— — — — Provisional administrative line established by British Military Administration, 1950

———— Approximate limit of territory inhabited by Somalis

Haud and Reserved Area, returned to Ethiopia, 1955

Former Northern Frontier District seeking secession from Kenya

++++++ Railways

© John Drysdale. *The Somali Dispute* (New York: Praeger, 1964). Reprinted by permission of the publisher.

Introduction

Sir, to enable us to determine . . . with a firm and precise judgment, I think it may be necessary to consider distinctly the true nature and the peculiar circumstances of the object which we have before us. . . . I shall therefore endeavor, with your leave, to lay before you some of the most material of these circumstances in as full and as clear a manner as I am able to state them.

Edmund Burke. From a speech on moving resolutions for conciliation with the Colonies.

The Horn of Africa is roughly three-quarters of a million square miles in the northeast of the continent, consisting largely of eroding, ravine-slashed plateaus, seared bushland, and rubble-strewn volcanic desert, but with some biggish patches of fertile lowland particularly around its southwestern rim. Being a metaphor rather than a political entity, it has no precise boundaries; but it is conventionally thought of as embracing Ethiopia, the Somali Democratic Republic, and the Republic of Djibouti, the former French colony wedged in between the Eritrean and Somali coasts. The life of the vast bulk of its people is nasty, brutish, and short, with wars adding periodically to the chronic decimation by disease and malnutrition.

In the northern province of Eritrea, Ethiopia's outlet to the Red Sea, the land is bled by a brutal secessionist struggle. My Lais follow Guernicas in a random and revolting procession. The 1977 conflict between Somalia and Ethiopia simply added to the agony of a population that presses remorselessly on the area's exiguous resources and complicated the task of ameliorating poverty and famine, a task to which the revolutionary governments of both Ethiopia and the Somali Democratic Republic have formally consecrated themselves.

The present and potential destruction of human values on the Horn would be reason enough for international concern, even if the area's travail could be isolated. But, in fact, isolation is problematical

1

since the potential belligerents touch the larger international system at many sensitive points.

In the first place, there is the elementary matter of geography. Clinging to the northeast edge of the African continent, both Ethiopia and Somalia look as if they should be implicated in the geopolitics of the Middle East and the whole northwest quadrant of the Indian Ocean, including, of course, the Persian Gulf. Commerce from the gulf, East Africa, and Asia must pass near the Somali coast, maneuver through the narrow Strait of Bab el Mandeb within a few miles of Africa, and then debouch into the Red Sea and parallel the Ethiopian coast for 600 miles en route to the Strait of Tiran and the now tranquil Gulf of Aqaba or to the Mediterranean.

Geography is the force which has evoked varying degrees of superpower concern with the Horn. Under the terms of a mutual defense agreement signed in 1953, the United States supplied Ethiopia with over $200 million worth of military assistance, virtually one-half of all U.S. military aid to sub-Sahara Africa during the next two decades. Until 1977, the Ethiopian armed forces flew U.S. planes, fired U.S. rifles loaded with U.S. ammunition, and rolled on U.S. tanks and trucks. Most of the officer corps had gone through U.S. training programs. Dependence on the United States for spare parts was virtually total. In 1975, with much-reduced support levels reflecting a sharp slackening of U.S. interest, the U.S. Military Assistance Advisory Group (MAAG) based in Addis Ababa still numbered more than fifty men, roughly one-half of the MAAG personnel then in sub-Sahara Africa.

Before the Ogaden war of 1977, the tie between the Somali Democratic Republic and the Soviet armed forces, initiated by a 1963 assistance agreement, was equally close. In 1963, the Somali army was a rag-tag affair consisting of some 5,000 ill-trained men carrying World War I vintage rifles, without significant armor, and supported by a handful of moth-eaten planes superannuated out of the British and Egyptian air forces. According to the International Institute of Strategic Studies' respected survey of contemporary armed forces, by 1975 Somalia deployed approximately 23,000 men, 250 tanks and over 300 armored personnel carriers, and, by African standards, a respectably modern little air force. In armor and air power it compared favorably on paper with Ethiopia's military establishment. The net result was that, while in 1963 Ethiopia could have responded to Somali-inspired insurgency by marching to the sea, by 1975 U.S. military experts conceded to the Somalis the capacity not only for effective defensive operations but also for an offense which could penetrate deeply into the contested border areas of Ethiopia before losing its momentum.

Even more than in the case of Ethiopia, Somali military capability was and remains dependent on external support. The country's gross national product of $300 million is roughly one-tenth the size of Ethiopia's. It runs a permanent trade deficit, attracts trivial foreign investment, and has a currency virtually unrecognized outside the country's precincts.

In return for its not insubstantial services, the Soviet Union was rewarded with most of the substance, though apparently not all the forms, of base rights. The principal Soviet installation was at the port of Berbera, by supersonic aircraft an instant's distance from Bab el Mandeb. According to Western intelligence experts, by 1975 the Soviets were finishing off a 12,000 foot airstrip, having completed installations for moderate ship repairs, facilities for bunkering and ship-to-ship missile storage, and quarters for naval personnel—all protected by a SAM (surface to air missile) defense system. Certain areas of the port were under exclusive Soviet control. West of Berbera, near the small city of Harghessa, Soviet aircraft had access to a fighter base. Still a third airfield reportedly was under construction in the southern part of the country.

In the final paragraph of this book's first edition, completed in the summer of 1976, I stressed the risk to U.S.-Soviet relations coiled behind the then simmering border conflict between Ethiopia and Somalia:

> Crises, like beauty, exist not in the nature of things but in the minds of men. They arise at peculiar conjunctions of time, place, and circumstance. In the wake of Vietnam, the air is filled with tests of will looking for somewhere to settle. The Horn is not an especially hospitable setting for human habitation. But as a venue for confrontation by proxy, it now shows real promise.

Two years later, soldiers of the West Somali Liberation Front, equipped and trained, if not initially led, by the armed forces of the Somali Democratic Republic, stormed across Ethiopia's Ogaden region. The anticipated war had begun. In its wake came the anticipated blow to détente, arriving, however, in a form radically different from the one I had envisioned:

> If war comes to the Horn, the Russians cannot avoid the appearance of complicity. Unless public opinion is alerted to the parochial roots of the conflict and the limited influence the superpowers can reasonably exert on their "clients," the prevailing skepticism—and in certain sectors outright hostility—towards the incipient process of U.S.-Soviet accommodation and the compulsion to demonstrate U.S. willpower are likely to cement diverse American constituencies in a demand for aid to Ethiopia and coercive measures against Somalia's patron. They will, as well, conspire to obscure the distinctly local causes of the conflict and

the autonomous will of the belligerents, while bootlessly inflating the strategic value of the area. Advocates of intervention will caricature the Somalis as puppets dangling on Soviet strings and the Ethiopians as doughty underdogs defending a noble tradition and a sacred principle of international law. We can anticipate rhetorical invocation of the 1930s with Ethiopia playing again the improbable role of Western democracy's hero. And, as for détente, it will again be victimized by the inertial force of a global competition which neither superpower yet knows how to reduce.

Together, of course, the United States and the USSR altered that scenario, the former by rapidly distancing itself from Ethiopia's military government before the outbreak of war, the latter by switching sides with a vengeance, after failing in its efforts to reconcile the antagonists. Together, therefore, they stripped away the features of the prospective conflict most likely to inflame their mutual relations. When they finished, the United States had no sympathetic tie with either local belligerent, and the Soviet Union, together with its Cuban ally—whose 17,000 troops stiffened Ethiopia's defenses and then spearheaded its successful counterattack—had become defenders of the territorial status quo, champions of black Africa's most sacred norm: the inviolability of colonial boundaries.

Despite this dizzying exchange of partners and roles, war on the Horn seems to have contributed as much as any other single development to the souring of détente. Even though, in the process of transferring its support to Ethiopia, the Soviet Union has lost the use of its air and naval facilities in Somalia, spokesmen for influential segments of Western opinion voice unrelenting concern over the strategic consequences of the Soviet-Cuban presence on the Horn. Early in February, 1978, shortly before the Cuban-led counteroffensive smashed fading Somali hopes of hanging on to a piece of the Ogaden, William Buckley announced in the *International Herald Tribune* that "the Soviet Union guards the entrance to the Indian Ocean as decisively as Gibraltar dominates the Mediterranean Strait." Eight days later the West German daily, *Deutsche Zeitung,* called on "the Federal Republic . . . and its European partners, notably France, [to] urge Washington to take a firm stand: It is at the Horn that Europe's access to oil supplies will be defended."

Anxiety over the Soviet presence on the Horn dates back to the early part of the decade when units of the Soviet navy began to deploy in the Indian Ocean on a full-time basis. The deployment grew rapidly for several years before leveling off at a size somewhat less than the French Indian Ocean flotilla. In the West it catalyzed both a specific concern with the security of Western oil supplies and the sense of a less easily defined but broader strategic peril arising from the growing capacity of the USSR to exert an influence—by showing the flag, reassuring clients, threatening friends of the West, perhaps even intervening to preserve friendly regimes and to assist in displacing governments aligned with the West. This more diffuse, strategic threat was associated with the writings of Admiral S. G. Gorshkov, chief of Soviet naval forces and principal propagandist for their potential missions. In resuscitating the geopolitical doctrines popularized at the turn of the century by the American Admiral Alfred T. Mahan, Gorshkov touched a responsive chord among Western naval theorists who cited his writings as conclusive evidence of Soviet intentions and a compelling justification for enhancing U.S. capability to pour forces into the Indian Ocean.

In Western eyes, the shift of Soviet support transformed the president of the Somali Democratic Republic, Mohammed Siad Barre, from a dangerous accomplice of Soviet imperialism into a sort of African Solzhenitsyn delivering prescient warnings of the Soviet Union's insatiably aggressive designs. It similarly managed at least the partial redemption of the Eritrean liberation movements. Dismissed for years by Western pundits, diplomats, and, of course, the Israelis as the running dogs of Arab chauvinism, an intolerable threat to Israeli shipping, and potentially the last link in an Arab chain around the Red Sea, the movements were suddenly praised for their remarkable skill, tenacity, and courage. Consistent with this revision of images, Russians and Cubans suddenly found themselves pilloried in the Western press for assisting in Ethiopia's merciless pacification campaign. Although the major Eritrean group is genuinely Marxist, the liberation struggle has become respectable in the orthodox Western faith. Suddenly the Israelis find few associates to join them in worrying about the Red Sea's conversion into an Arab lake. And just as suddenly American officials and media pundits, once immovably opposed to any secessionist movement, discover the peculiar history of Eritrea and find grounds to distinguish it from ordinary cases of secessionist aspiration. Are they right now, or were they right before? Is it, in any event, too late to appreciate the merits of the Eritrean case?

Two years ago it seemed to me that the U.S. policy which best reconciled humanitarian and strategic interests was a major diplomatic effort to wrench concessions from the Ethiopians on behalf of both Somali and Eritrean claims to self-determination. I argued that if Ethiopia were unwilling to yield the substance of Eritrean independence, however dressed up in the garments of federalism, the United States should cut off arms supplies to the military government in Addis. That this might facilitate Somali seizure of the entire Ogaden seemed to me unimportant, if not an actual humanitarian bonus, given the undeniable will of the Ogaden population to secede. Behind my proposal lay two convictions: In strategic terms, what happened on the Horn mattered very little to the United States; but continued military assistance to an Ethiopian government determined to resist violently Somali and particularly Eritrean claims promised the worst humanitarian consequences.

Even before the fall of Haile Selassie, the United States had finally begun to equivocate about the strength of its commitment to the Ethiopian empire. Equivocation survived the Emperor's death. Washington would neither satisfy the revolutionary government's request for the additional aid it deemed necessary to defeat the Eritreans and deter the Somalis, nor choke off the existing modest flow of aid and, thereby, as it then appeared, open the door to Eritrean and Somali self-determination.

In the name of retaining influence with the Dergue, Secretary of State Henry Kissinger's State Department managed to antagonize every important local actor, including the Dergue, and to assist in prolonging a bloody and unstable status quo. Military assistance on a small scale and arms sales on a very much larger one continued until 1977 when the Dergue declared its intention to rely in the future on the Soviet bloc for military aid.

Forced to preside over the bankruptcy of a policy it had not made, the Carter administration soon fabricated a few problems of its very own. It sent the Somali government a feeler in terms sufficiently ambiguous to encourage Siad Barre's wishful imaginings that he might retain his freedom of action while substituting American for Soviet patronage. Only after the Somali armed forces were plainly engaged in occupying the Ogaden and Siad Barre was busily condemning Washington's allegedly perfidious failure to meet its commitments did the Carter administration declare publicly and unequivocally that it would not assist a government seeking to revise colonial borders. An earlier statement to that effect might very well *not* have deterred a Somali government driven by irredentist emotions that it had sedulously fostered among its troops and the general population, but it certainly would have avoided the appearance of indecision and incompetence.

The administration's next improvisation followed close on the first signs of a Somali military disaster. The United States warned the Cubans and Russians that prosecution of the Ethiopian counterattack across the Somali border would be deemed intolerable. Since the United States had not found intolerable Israel's retaliatory and prophylactic seizure and indefinite occupation of Arab territory after the 1967 war, the normative consistency of its position in this case was not self-evident. Be that as it may, Washington's rhetorical guarantee of Somalia's border pleased not only the Somalis, but also the Saudis, Ethiopians, and Iranians, all of whom were more interested in keeping the Soviets as far away as possible from the Red Sea and Indian Ocean than in nice questions of international law.

Since its northern territory was another focal point of Somali irridentism, Kenya, the West's one staunch East African ally, exhibited rather more ambivalence about the U.S. embrace of Somali interests. To satisfy Nairobi in particular and African sentiment in general, the administration demanded, as a condition of "defensive" military assistance, Somali renunciation of violent means for uniting the Somali people scattered about the Horn.

As far as one can tell, American and Somali negotiators, their efforts no doubt complicated by continued Somali support for anti-Dergue guerrillas in the Ogaden, have still not devised a mutually acceptable formula. So military assistance remains in the balance. Meanwhile, the United States has modestly increased its economic and diplomatic presence. At the same time, it has moved to calm Kenyan nerves—frazzled by the proximity of the unpredictably belligerent monster in Uganda, the irridentist Somalis, and the Marxist Ethiopians—by increased military aid and other expressions of support calculated to project a strong western commitment to Kenyan security. As for Ethiopia itself, equivocation, or should one say watchful waiting, is the Carter administration policy of the day, while it considers whether to maintain its slender presence or to compete strongly for influence, in part by helping to underwrite economic development.

What mix of policies will best advance the political, military, and humanitarian objectives of the United States? Any persuasive answer to that question must, of course, rest on an assessment of the area's strategic significance for the surrounding region. But it must also be informed by an understanding of the Horn's inner reality, an appreciation of the history, character, resources, and aspirations that drive the local actors on this bloodsoaked projection off Africa's eastern flank.

Part One

Ethiopia and Eritrea

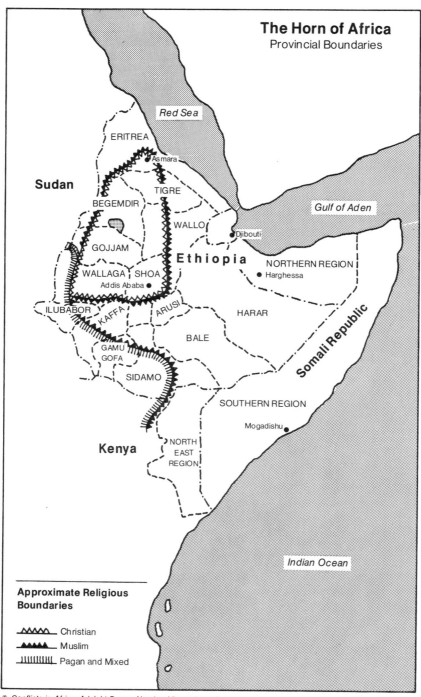

The Horn of Africa
Provincial Boundaries

Red Sea

ERITREA

Asmara

Gulf of Aden

Sudan

TIGRE

BEGEMDIR

WALLO

Djibouti

GOJJAM

Ethiopia

NORTHERN REGION

Harghessa

WALLAGA SHOA

Addis Ababa

ILUBABOR

KAFFA

ARUSI

HARAR

BALE

Somali Republic

GAMU
GOFA

SIDAMO

SOUTHERN REGION

Mogadishu

Kenya

NORTH
EAST
REGION

Indian Ocean

Approximate Religious Boundaries

⋀⋀⋀⋀ Christian

▲▲▲▲ Muslim

⊥⊥⊥⊥⊥⊥ Pagan and Mixed

© *Conflicts in Africa. Adelphi Papers Number Ninety-three.* (London: The International Institute for Strategic Studies, 1972). Reprinted by permission of the publisher.

Ethiopia 1

The Setting

Both geographically and politically, Ethiopia is dominated by a vast, thickly populated central highland, most of which is 6,000 to 8,000 feet above sea level. Frequent reference to the Ethiopian "tableland" obscures the real nature of the terrain, which is carved up by canyons and gorges thousands of feet deep. The net effect is captured in a remark attributed to one member of the 1867 British Expeditionary Force: "They tell us this is a tableland. If it is, they have turned the table upside down and we are scrambling up and down the legs."

The reality, then, is a network of plateaus varying enormously in size and degree of isolation. Some are almost inaccessible. The terrain alone could explain why effective central rule has been exceptional in the course of Ethiopian history.

In the northwest, the plateau folds down into undulating grasslands which extend over the Sudanese border. On the east, opposite the northern part of the Somali Democratic Republic, it falls, often precipitously, into the Great Rift Valley before rising again as the Somali Plateau and making its way over to the sea. As the Rift Valley pushes north where it will finally be transformed into the Red Sea, it expands progressively and incorporates at its center one of the world's harshest deserts, the Danakil Depression, a blistering, rubble-strewn wasteland where the temperature can reach 140 degrees Fahrenheit and there is no shade. To the south and southeast, the highlands drop down into poorly watered bush country, which presses deep into Kenya and the southern section of Somalia. And in the southwest, the plateau gives way to tropical forests from whose rich agricultural potential the curse of malaria is gradually being lifted.

Because of the altitude of its political heartland and also because of its historic remoteness, Ethiopia has often been compared to Switzerland or Tibet. During the just-concluded reign of Haile Selassie, however, the politically most revealing analogy was to Peter the

Great's Russia. The main features were remarkably similar: an ethnic mosaic ruled by a rigidly centralized monarchy; the monarch's legitimacy resting on an ancient tradition and a national church; and the monarch himself surrounded by a horde of more-or-less dependent nobles and docile bureaucrats, supported by a large army, and committed only to that degree of modernization which would enhance his power and dignity. In Haile Selassie's case the degree was not very great, since the twentieth-century brand of modernization could not be harnessed to the purposes of an ancient monarchal order.

In both Peter's Russia and Selassie's Ethiopia, the ethnic group with which the monarch was identified to some degree dominated the institutions of the state, but other groups were by no means unrepresented. And just as the highest stratum of the favored group shared room at the top, its masses participated in the general misery at the bottom.

The depth of Ethiopian misery is pretty much invulnerable to exaggeration. By virtually any measure of social welfare or economic development, Ethiopia is one of the world's poorest countries. Its per capita gross national product is somewhere in the vicinity of $90, which places it among the bottom twenty nation-states. It is one of the eight states with an average per capita daily caloric intake of less than 1,600. Literacy is estimated at five percent of the population in contrast, for example, to the neighboring state of Kenya, where between twenty and twenty-five percent of the population is literate. Its transportation network is so exiguous that the average peasant must walk eight hours in order to reach a road on which wheeled vehicles of any kind can move. That is one, but only one, reason why tens of thousands can die of starvation while their government exports grain.

Among the diverse peoples who now cluster within the frontiers of Ethiopia, three—the Amharas, the Tigres, and the Gallas (or Oromo, as they are often called)—have played the leading historic roles. The former two are Semitic in origin; speak related languages; live, respectively, in the central and northern highlands; and, with very few exceptions, are Coptic Christians. The Gallas, a Hamitic people who once preponderated along the Somali coast, pushed into the highlands during the sixteenth and seventeenth centuries. Although they arrived as a hostile force, they seem to have been domesticated rather rapidly. Substantial numbers converted to Christianity. Galla chiefs and Amhara nobles intermarried. In the twentieth century, there have been Galla soldiers, bureaucrats, and landholders, and Galla blood runs in the veins of many noble Christian families.

The process of assimilation proceeded with sufficient speed so that, from the eighteenth century onward, regional and provincial rather than ethnic rivalries appear to have predominated in Ethiopian politics. For all that, the process of assimilation has never been completed, in part perhaps because many Gallas embrace Islam, in part perhaps because there are areas where Galla peasants have seen their interests in land subordinated to Christian aristocrats and soldiers who were the beneficiaries of imperial patronage. The historian Richard Greenfield describes a trip taken in 1958 to a large area under military administration "because a police column had been annihilated there in the mid-1950s."

> The writer journeyed around that region . . . with a military escort. . . . The *mulu asir-alika* (Sergeant) of the escort displayed almost 'colonialist' attitudes and boasted, 'The Galla are Amhara's slaves—they do as they are told,' and he also remarked, 'Their old men say that where Amhara comes the grass does not grow.' In some areas of Wellegga, also, local people are liable to despise 'Amhara'—who may well be Shewan Gallas—and may even refuse them water until they get to know them.

"But," Greenfield concludes, "these are largely peasant attitudes and prejudices not unlike those to be found in many ancient countries. They are fading and differ from the attitudes of the educated and of the future. . . ."[1] Perhaps; yet at least once during the 1960s, the Emperor found it necessary to stamp on a senior establishment figure of Galla ancestry who championed the rights of the Galla peasantry. The ethnic distinction may be dying, but it seems likely that an obituary is premature.

In the course of Ethiopian history, the locus of any effectively centralized power had often been in the Tigre-dominated portion of the realm. But at the end of the nineteenth century, the title of King of Kings passed to Menelik II, an Amharic-speaking claimant from the central highlands province of Shoa. And in Shoa it remained until September, 1974, when the Lion of Judah was bundled into a police Volkswagen and hauled off to enforced seclusion. This traditional rivalry between Shoa and Tigre would survive the monarchy's demise.

The Present as History

Without some modest grip on the paramount themes of Ethiopia's past, one is likely to encounter the present and future as impenetrable riddles. But in its gorgeous diversity, that past tends to elude any facile summary. With its court intrigues and fraternal strife, its tales of torture, betrayal, and murder, there is material for a thousand Jacobean dramas. There is also the stuff of epic poetry: the rise and fall of great kings and intervening dark ages of chaos, foreign invasions forcing heroic wars of national defense, triumphs inevitably succeeded by decay in which the seeds of new triumphs eventually germinate. And through it all a culture—a vital though jagged sense of common identity—surviving over two millennia, resisting or assimilating invaders, comes at last, perhaps, to its rendezvous with the dissolving forces of modernization.

History shapes the present in part through the collective memory of its heirs. Today, as in the past, the Ethiopian elite is Christian. To be a Christian is to be a vicarious participant in thirteen centuries of intermittent conflict with the Islamic world. By A.D. 1000, the energies released by Mohammed's evangelism had catapulted Arabs across the Red Sea to wrench the African coast from Christian hands. In the subsequent centuries, the political frontier between Islam and Ethiopia has rolled back and forth in response to the shifting fortunes of war.

During the third decade of the sixteenth century, Ethiopian culture came close to the breaking point when the almost legendary Imam Ahmed Ibn Ibrahim Al-Ghazi, or Ahmed Gran ("The Left-Handed") as the Ethiopians called him, came storming up from the Somali coast in a *jihad* ("crusade"), which marked its passage by pillaged towns, burned churches, and new converts for Islam. In ten years of unremitting conflict, his ethnically mixed force—including a large contingent of Somalis and stiffened in one crucial battle by 900 Arab, Turkish, and Albanian mercenary musketeers—poured over the central highlands and streamed north into Christianity's Tigrean redoubt.

With the help of some 400 Portuguese musketeers sent in response to desperate appeals for aid, the Ethiopians gradually turned the tide. In 1542, during what proved to be the decisive battle, Gran was killed and his army forced to retreat. Although for some years the struggle continued spasmodically, Islam as an armed force gradually receded, leaving in its wake, however, a large though politically impotent body of believers.

Gran's *jihad* was the high-water mark but not the end of the Islamic threat. Even three centuries later, long after Islam's eclipse as a dynamic force in international politics, a morally regenerative eruption on its African periphery, the Mahdists* of the Sudan, was able to threaten Ethiopian national existence. And again at the cost of a dismembered emperor,** the lords of the nation and their teeming followers streamed out to meet and break the Islamic lance.

To this day, it is commonplace for educated Ethiopians to remark: "We are a Christian island in an Islamic sea." This rooted perception

* The Mahdists were the followers of a messianic religious leader (a Mahdi) named Mohammed Ahmed, who wrested Khartoum from General Charles George ("Chinese") Gordon and thereafter, until his defeat by Anglo-Egyptian forces under General Horatio Kitchener, dominated the Sudan.
** During the continuing struggle following Gran's death, Muslim forces killed the Ethiopian emperor Gahados and delivered his head to one of Gran's widows.

of an irremedial enmity can hardly facilitate amicable resolution of the Eritrean insurgency, which is sustained by Arab arms as well as by just grievances, or the confrontation with the Somali Democratic Republic, a nation of devout Muslims and a member of the Arab League.

A second feature of Ethiopian history which shadows the present is the tenuous nature of central authority. The Emperor's title, King of Kings, was not grandiloquence; it was literal, historic truth. There were many provincial dynasties; only occasionally did one succeed in coordinating all or most of the others. During his half-century reign, Haile Selassie faced and repeatedly crushed regionally-based challengers. Despite Selassie's efforts to extend the nerves of government into every region of the national body, the difficult terrain, the lilliputian road network, the shrunken educational system, the immensity of the land, the torpor of the government's bureaucracy, and the persistence of ethnic diversity all have conspired to limit the penetration of central authority and to sustain a centrifugal potential. Fearful of that potential, any central government, whether radical or conservative in its social policies, is likely—out of fear of the precedent's contagion—to resist demands for real regional autonomy, much less independence.

A third feature of Ethiopian history with contemporary resonance is the repeated use of the East African coast, particularly along the Red Sea, as a point of departure for Ethiopia's enemies when they invaded the Christian heartland. In 1868, Massawa was the port of disembarkation for Field Marshal Sir Robert Napier's extravagant force, complete with elephants and a brass band, which paraded into the highlands to release the British consul and a handful of other Europeans imprisoned by Emperor Tewodros, Ethiopia's version of Ivan the Terrible.[2] Napier's departure coincided with the revival of Egyptian power. Influenced, Greenfield suggests, by the suddenly enhanced significance of the Red Sea following the opening of the Suez Canal, Egypt seized control of the sea's entire western coast. By 1875, Egyptian troops were pressing on the Ethiopian highlands all along its curving periphery. But within a year, they were virtually annihilated by an Ethiopian army under the command of Emperor Yohannes IV. Egypt retained only a precarious toe-hold on the Red Sea coast. And even that was relinquished a few years later when the Mahdists raised the standard of rebellion against the Egyptians in the Sudan.

The Italians were next. Belated initiates of the Imperial Club, by the mid-1880s they had hacked out a 50,000-square-mile triangle with its apex in the Tigrean highlands. They called it Eritrea. During this first stage, progress was eased by a de facto alliance with Emperor Menelik II, who needed Italian weapons to consolidate his fissiparous empire. The alliance quickly shattered when it became apparent that the Italians regarded Eritrea merely as an hors d'oeuvre. Having no intention of constituting an entrée, Menelik moved decisively against his erstwhile Christian allies when they came knifing out of the Eritrean salient. The coming disaster was veiled by a series of inconclusive skirmishes with elements of the numerically superior forces rallying to Menelik from every part of the country. Finally, at Adowa in 1896, the Ethiopians fell en masse on the Italian army and tore it to shreds.

Four decades later, the Italians came back, this time with planes, poison gas, and a larger army, under Rodolfo Graziani, fleshed out with African units recruited in Eritrea and Somalia. While the Emperor retired, despite the vigorous opposition of some of his supporters, to plead Ethiopia's case abroad and to plot his return, guerrilla groups sprang up all over the country, first to bleed the occupying force and later to assist in its demolition by a British contingent one-tenth its size. Six years after the invasion, the Italians were prisoners in what they had conceived of as the fulcrum of their East African empire.

From Gran to Graziani, the record is constant: sooner or later the highlands expel foreign objects. The achievement has bred self-confidence; but its price, so frequently paid during the past century, can hardly encourage initiatives which would reduce Ethiopian control over the Red Sea coast.

After the Fall of the Lion

Revolutionary forces had been accumulating for years behind the dam of the Emperor's hardening opposition to change. Journalists, historians, and diplomats dutifully recorded the rising level of frustration, but few if any imagined that it might overwhelm the Lion of Judah, much less two thousand years of monarchal and theocratic government. Like his long-lived Spanish contemporary, Haile Selassie had spun around himself an aureole of invulnerability. It is doubtful that even the prospective agents of revolution imagined that their time would come round until the Emperor demonstrated that he was in fact mortal.

Events beyond the reach of this diminutive political genius conspired against a grand Wagnerian exit. The acute rise in the price of oil fueled inflationary pressures in the cities and traumatized the small but critically positioned middle class of industrial workers, civil servants, and soldiers. Meanwhile, in parts of the highlands, above all in the provinces of Wallo and Tigre, a murderous drought consumed the countryside.

From 1970 through 1972, almost no rain had fallen. With their plow oxen dead or dying, their seed grain largely consumed for food, their own bodies pathetically weakened, the peasants were powerless to exploit the long rains of 1973. The harvest was derisory. Having lost everything, those who could still move began to trek out of the countryside in search of help. Thousands of skeletal corpses marked their passage. Gradually, an army of scarecrows collected in the towns and cities or clotted along the few roads, halting with their bodies trucks bound for the coast with grain and vegetables for export.

As early as November, 1972, the first word of the disaster was trickling into the capital's torpid bureaucracy. The annual crop survey circulated that month by the Ministry of Agriculture accurately detailed the areas of crop failure and forecast "widespread food shortages."[3] The Council of Ministers responded early the following year by ordering the minister of agriculture to suppress the survey. That was the beginning of an official coverup, a conspiracy of silence that would implicate within twelve months every foreign embassy and bilateral and multilateral aid mission in Addis Ababa.

The imperial Ethiopian government was prepared to admit that there was a problem. What it would not concede through the whole of 1973 and into the early months of 1974 was the dimension of the problem and its own plain inability to cope. As late as March, 1974, with perhaps 100,000 peasants already dead, the government labeled descriptions of disaster then beginning to circulate freely in Europe as "wishful malice."[4]

The failure to act was a compound of arrogance, indifference, incompetence, and amour-propre—a compound, in short, of everything that was rotten in the state of Ethiopia. Drought and famine, some officials said privately, were immutably part of the cycle of existence in Ethiopia. From time to time, the rains failed. Peasants died. This had always been the case. It was nothing new. A major feeding program would set a dangerous precedent. Millions might become dependent on the government. And the government could not afford such largesse.

Above all, there was the question of "face." Ethiopia was not some crumbly little Sahelian country stamped out of French dough. It was a great and ancient empire with a history and culture to match that of any state. If it could not feed its own people, how could it claim equality of place in international councils?

And so while it was prepared to receive assistance, the imperial government, which in practice meant Haile Selassie, would not allow the aid and relief agencies to declare publicly the terrible need. As one minister put it, "If we can save the peasants only by confessing our failure to the world, it is better that they die."[5] Which they did.

Even without an accelerated international relief effort, many might have been saved if the government could only have organized its domestic resources. It essayed feeble gestures which served only to re-emphasize its ineffable corruption and incompetence. Money collected from civil servants ordered to tithe and from students who voluntarily abstained from breakfast simply disappeared.

Present failures were multiplied by past neglect. Wallo was the forgotten province. Its people had scorned the Emperor as an upstart. Retreating from the Italian armies in 1935, he had hastened through the province while its citizens gathered to spit upon him. The Emperor had a long memory. He had built few roads anywhere in the empire; but in Wallo there were virtually none at all, just as there were no hospitals, or schools, or any other earnest of imperial concern. So food could not be brought into the villages, and the villagers could not reach the feeding centers until, in tens of thousands of cases, it was too late.

Famine relief was not the only governmental function infected with incompetence and corruption. The infection was equally rampant in the army's supply system. And its ultimate victims were not peasants conditioned to stoic docility by history, the Emperor, and the church, but rather armed men who even in the lower ranks had, by virtue of their training, been in varying degrees detached from the traditional pieties. The main burden of corruption fell on common soldiers and their noncommissioned officers (NCOs). When a grain ration arrived mixed with sand to compensate for the amount diverted into commercial channels, they suffered. Maladministration aggravated the injury of meager salaries shrinking in the face of a suddenly galloping inflation. Discontent seems to have been particularly acute in the Second Division, which had borne the brunt of the endless conflict in Eritrea.

In retrospect, it now seems clear that revolt was also simmering in the ranks of the younger officers. These were educated men. More than a few had studied abroad. All of them must have been sensitive to their country's acute underdevelopment relative to African states only recently released from colonialism. As soldiers and Ethiopians, they were ardent nationalists. But their ties to the existing order of things were relatively loose.

The armed forces were the most democratic institution in the empire. Officers were drawn from every part of the country and only rarely from the aristocracy. They manned not only the most democratic but also the most effective institution. For all its corruption, most of it at the top, the army *functioned*. It had fought not without valor in Korea and the Congo. It had held on in Eritrea and thrashed the Somalis in a brief but bloody border skirmish in 1974. Until the beginning of the 1970s, many observers had rated it the best army in black Africa with the possible exception of Nigeria.

But now the balance seemed to be shifting toward Somalia where, in 1969, the army had overthrown its own corrupt civilian government and installed a junta committed to national strength and revolutionary reform. By 1974, it had doubled the number of men at arms, equipped them with the largest armored force between the Sahara and South Africa, and coincidentally begun to effect a genuine social revolution. It is doubtful that Ethiopian officers failed to appreciate either the precedent or the contrast with their own flaccid government which could neither feed its people nor even attract any longer the guns and tanks and planes which had assured Ethiopian pre-eminence on the Horn.

In late February of 1974, the combustible elements in the Ethiopian armed forces finally ignited. The flame of mutiny raced through the streets of Asmara. To this day, there are conflicting reports of who took the initiative in Asmara, and subsequently in Addis and Harar, among the three other divisions of the army, as well as the elite airborne unit and, finally, the air force. Some observers claim it was a revolt from the bottom, a mutiny of private soldiers and their sergeants. Others insist that the younger officers were deeply involved from the outset, though sometimes disguised as NCOs, so great was their initial fear of imperial retribution.

The locus of leadership was obscured, in part at least because of the apparent unanimity within the Second Division below the level of its general officers. Rejecting the authority of their commanders, the troops dispatched a series of demands to the Emperor. Wholly unrevolutionary in content, they sounded like nothing more than the manifesto of a soldier's trade union: a litany of better pay and higher fringe benefits. The government, carefully distinguished from His Imperial Majesty, was condemned for its failure to protect the interests of its men at arms.

In his response, the Emperor was equally careful to disclaim any threat to imperial authority. Alluding obliquely to fears that he might order mass punishments for the Second Division, he said that no one could condemn men who had simply exercised the right of all loyal subjects to petition their Emperor.

That was a nice gesture; but, even coupled with concessions on pay, it did not get the cork back into the bottle. Excitement and a kind of creative turmoil began rippling through all the units of the armed forces. Within days, the spark had leaped over to the organized civilian population, particularly in Addis. Workers struck, students marched, demands began to multiply and escalate.

Patently embarrassed by civilian condemnation of the parochial character of their demands and sensing, perhaps, that the dam really had begun to give way, the troops began to inject revolutionary political content into their manifestos. The government was condemned for corruption and the failure to alleviate the famine whose dimensions were now widely appreciated. And far more ominously, there came the demand for constitutional reform.

The Emperor remained an island of formal serenity amidst these oceanic emotions. If the politicians—all, of course, wholly his creatures, subordinate to imperial control in even their most minor acts—had failed, they had to be replaced. He accepted the resignation of Prime Minister Aklilu Habte-Wold and his colleagues who had presided over the coverup of the drought, then called on one of the cabinet members, Endalkachew Makonnen, to form a new government. An elegant, suave graduate of Oxford, linked to powerful aristocratic families, Endalkachew hardly mirrored the growing revolutionary spirit. Nevertheless he accepted the mandate, chose a cabinet, and with the Emperor's approval established a committee of experts to draft a new constitution.

Meanwhile, the Emperor maintained the elegant, stately ritual of his imperial rounds. But behind this facade of imperturbability, it is reported that he began the intricate, subtle maneuvers that had so often before preserved his position. No deep appreciation of the Ethiopian scene was required to detect deep rifts within the armed forces and between it and the civilian radicals, particularly the students. Haile Selassie had spent a lifetime balancing off against each other potential sources of opposition. The senior command structure was riven by personal, regional, and ethnic feuds. And there were few men of high position in the armed forces or the civil government who had not enjoyed forms of imperial favor which, being without legislative or other formal authorization, would in a modern government fall plainly under the rubric of "corruption." They were, therefore, sorely limited in their capacity to respond with enthusiasm to the crescendoing demands in the cantonments of the army, the university, and the streets to punish the corrupt. So even if the senior dignitaries of the empire had been playing an important role in the movement for reform, they could hardly have avoided trying to deflect it from any radical demarche. But, in fact, they were powerless.

By midspring, the armed forces—soldiers and officers acting as a single body—had elected representatives to an Armed Forces Coordinating Committee. No one above the rank of colonel was eligible; along with everyone else, generals could cast one vote for candidates. This limitation was necessary, the organizers said, for if senior officers served on the committee, either they would intimidate with their rank or they would lose their authority to command in the field. One hundred and twenty men were elected: sergeants, warrant officers, captains, majors from units scattered throughout the empire; anonymous men, called collectively the Dergue. And by slow and subtle degrees they began to gnaw away the throne of the Lion of Judah.

The arrests, which by September would vacuum up virtually the entire senior elite that had served as the eyes, ears, and arms of the Emperor, began early in Endalkachew Makonnen's brief tenure. The arrivistes went first, men like the deposed prime minister, Aklilu Habte-Wold, who had risen on the strength of the Emperor's favor, often extended to those of modest background who demonstrated loyalty and ability in his service. Virtually all of Endalkachew's colleagues in the prior cabinet were soon ensconced in the rough barracks of the Addis-based Fourth Division. Charged with corruption and criminal negligence in the matter of the drought, they awaited promised investigations and trial.

In the meantime, the capital played host to such prodigies as a four-day general strike, probably the first successful effort of its kind in the short history of independent black Africa, and a demonstration by an estimated 30,000 Muslims demanding equal rights. Concessions tumbled from the new government: wage increases for teachers and the lowest-paid civil servants; appointment of a committee to investigate corruption in the previous government; new proposals for land reform, that perennial of official rhetoric. Throughout the country, the cauldron of long-suppressed grievances continued to boil. Tax collectors, provincial administrators (notorious for their lassitude and corruption), and, in some parts of the empire, landlords found life increasingly perilous. Particularly in the south where the Gallas had been incorporated by conquest and their lands assigned to Shoan officers in the Imperial Army, latent peasant antagonism bubbled violently to the surface.

Endalkachew's government could concede, but it seemed incapable of dramatic action. There was, after all, no tradition of ministerial initiative. Indeed, for decades nothing had been better calculated to assure departure from the political scene than a show of independent judgment. Constitutions and cabinets had come and gone, while the Emperor remained the brains and the heart of real government. Endalkachew and his colleagues, having risen in the old system, could hardly have been disposed psychologically to break loose from its constraints. Moreover, it was by no means clear, on the one hand, how far the Emperor wanted them to go in meeting the demands for reform and, on the other, whether effective power had slipped definitively from his hands. The overriding impression one had visiting Addis in the summer of 1974 was the paralyzing fear which suffused the civil government. Torpid under the best of circumstances, trained to passivity by the Emperor's carrots and sticks, it was totally incapable of responding to the cascade of demands that poured down on it.

The Dergue rumbled its dissatisfaction with the pace of change. The pattern of arrests broadened. Judges, generals, provincial governors, and aristocrats were added to the guest list at the "Fourth Division Hilton." The Emperor's cadre of advisors and aids began to dwindle, although the daily ritual of consultation and supplication continued. Piece by piece, the Dergue was dismantling the *ancien régime.*

Not without internal tensions, to be sure. The worst threat to its cohesion arose early in the game, in March, when airborne troops swarmed over Debre Zeit Air Base, thirty miles from the capital, seized a covey of young officers, and locked up the ordnance. The action was justified by an alleged plot to bomb the Imperial Palace and precipitate Haile Selassie's removal, an allegation firmly denied by the air force which proceeded to sulk throughout the spring. One of the many rumors that slithered through the fevered city was that the real reason for the paratroopers' action was the corruption of their commanding officer by the Palace. Similar rumors of imperial funds being circulated discreetly undoubtedly stiffened and spread the conviction that the Emperor would never consent to a graceful transition to constitutional impotence.

The future of the Emperor was one of the issues reckoned by the diplomatic and journalistic communities and the Addis rumor-mill to divide Dergue members. Some officers, it was believed, favored his formal removal coincident with transformation of the monarchy into a strictly ceremonial position. Others seemed intimidated by the widely held belief that any move against the Emperor would galvanize the mass of Ethiopians into armed resistance to the Dergue.

Uncertainty about the true strength of the old order undoubtedly braked the momentum of revolutionary change and encouraged the Dergue to lurk behind the increasingly hollow forms of monarchal and parliamentary government. Foreign journalists wrote ominously that the Ethiopian populace was the world's most heavily armed, that there were nine million guns in private hands—300,000 in Addis alone—that you could purchase grenades and submachine guns in the market, that provincial aristocrats could mobilize well-armed private armies, and finally that, if threatened with the secularization of the state, the Coptic church could unleash this heavily armed mass of true believers, plunging the empire into a maelstrom of blood.

As spring gave way to summer, the suspicion began to spread that the lions of the old order were, in fact, toothless. Day after day, arrests shrunk their numbers both in Addis and in their provincial strongholds. At the end of June, the constitutional experts brought forth a set of concrete proposals. Their draft provided for a constitutional monarchy with merely ceremonial functions, parliamentary rule, and a secular state. The Patriarch of the Ethiopian Orthodox Church, Abune Teofilos,* denounced the proposal to transform religion into a matter of purely private conscience. But the capital remained quiet.

Frustrated by the paralysis of the civil government, emboldened by the passivity of the elite, and embittered by efforts to fracture their unity, the members of the Coordinating Committee began to move out from behind the scene.

In early August, they forced the resignation of Endalkachew's government, dispatched Endalkachew himself to the detention center, and appointed in his place an aristocrat, Michael Imru, who had for years languished in unwanted diplomatic sinecures because of his

---

* The Dergue arrested him in February, 1976.

unambiguous commitment to serious reform. The new government was also distinguished by its minister of defense, Gen. Aman Michael Andom, a favorite of the armed forces both because of his martial virtues and his reputation for incorruptibility.

The change in government did not, however, generate any noticeable momentum in the pace of reform. The Dergue wanted instant change. No civilian government could produce it, or at least so it now appeared to the leaders of the revolution. And so on September 12, 1974, they moved to fill the vacuum of authority and to break decisively with the old order. They drove to the Palace where Haile Selassie, after fifty years at the apex of government, waited utterly alone, already stripped of every instrument of power. He looked, it is said, with some disdain at the little blue Volkswagen, then stepped into the back seat and was driven out through the Palace gates, where a small, hostile crowd hurled epithets at the tiny, bearded ascetic who had finally lost his struggle with history.

With him went the last civilian government. At the request of the Dergue, General Aman assumed the prime ministership, while retaining the defense portfolio. In addition, he was named chief of staff. He would, moreover, serve as the ceremonial head of state pending the return of the Crown Prince, who was invited to assume the office of constitutional monarch; and, finally, the general was designated chairman of the Provisional Military Administrative Council, that is, of the Dergue now transformed by its own will into the formal agency of executive and legislative power. Despite the general's several titles, it was widely assumed that he remained an instrument rather than the leader of the revolutionary elite.

Having assumed the indicia as well as the substance of power, the new rulers of the ancient kingdom had at last to confront their differences. Several fundamental issues appeared to fracture opinion among these still largely anonymous men: Should there be a military or a civilian government? How should the old elite be treated? Should there be conciliation or more repression in Eritrea? How might government be decentralized? And what should be the character of land reform? Any one of these issues might have been the first to draw blood, mangling the quite extraordinary unity which the Dergue had maintained in the face of persistent efforts to play upon differences of ideology as well as of region, ethnicity, and rank. But if one had had to project the issue from which the first blood would gush, the choice would inevitably have fallen on Eritrea.

Notes

For information on the history and ethnology of Ethiopia, the author is particularly indebted to the works of Richard Greenfield, Donald N. Levine and Dame Margerie Perham: Greenfield, *Ethiopia: A New Political History* (New York: Praeger, 1965); Levine, *Wax and Gold* (Chicago: University of Chicago Press, 1965) and *Greater Ethiopia* (Chicago: University of Chicago Press, 1975); and Perham, *The Government of Ethiopia* (London: Faber & Faber, 1969). Also helpful was *Area Handbook for Ethiopia* (Washington, D.C.: American University Foreign Area Studies, 1971) by Kaplan, Faber *et al.*

1. Greenfield, p. 7.

2. For a brilliant account of this extravaganza, see Alan Moorehead, *The Blue Nile* (New York: Harper & Row, 1962), pp. 235–6.

3. Jack Shepherd, *The Politics of Starvation* (New York: Carnegie Endowment for International Peace, 1975), pp. 13–14.

4. Shepherd, p. 15.

5. *New York Times,* May 19, 1974.

Eritrea 2

The Making of a State

Eritrea is an accidental place, the remnant of Italian imperial dreams after the disaster of Adowa. Its two and one-half million people, forming an ethnic mosaic hardly less diverse than Ethiopia's, originally had nothing in common other than common domicile within a colony's arbitrary frontiers. The frontiers split several cultural communities, among which by far the largest were the Tigrinya-speaking* Christian Tigres of the northern highlands; roughly one-third were cut off in Eritrea from their brothers in the adjoining Ethiopian province of Tigre.

At the turn of the century, it must have seemed inevitable that the Tigre overlap, connecting more than a quarter of Eritrea's population to Ethiopia, would constitute a running sore on the body of Italian authority. In fact, during the colonial era, the Tigres proved no less tractable than other Christians or the Islamic segment of the native population. From the colony's founding until British occupa-

---

* Languages from both the Hamitic and Semitic families are spoken in Ethiopia: Gallinya, a Hamitic language of the Cushite group, is spoken in southern and northeastern Ethiopia and is related to Afar, Somali, and other languages spoken south of Ethiopia.

The relationship among the Semitic languages is somewhat complicated. In the north, there are Tigrinya and Tigre. These languages are spoken in Eritrea and in the Ethiopian province of Tigre. There, Tigrinya is the major language, Tigre being spoken by a relatively small number of people, all of them Muslims who live in the coastal plains and northern highlands of Eritrea. Although Tigre and Tigrinya are related languages, geographical barriers have long separated the Tigres so that their languages are now mutually unintelligible.

In the central area of Ethiopia they speak Amharic, the official language of the country. As French and Spanish spring from Latin, Amharic, Tigrinya and Tigre spring from a common root language (Geez) which survives only for certain ecclesiastical purposes.

25

tion in 1941, Italy ruled unchallenged. It was even able to recruit
Eritreans for service in the army which invaded Ethiopia in 1935.*

If the Italians did not provoke much open opposition to their rule,
they did not build a large reservoir of affection either. Once Italian
prestige was deflated by British victory, the "friendly" natives showed
signs of a well-nourished hostility which was sharply intensified by
gradually increasing head-to-head economic competition, in which
the Eritreans did not fare well, and by the inauguration of Ethiopia's
campaign to annex Eritrea as part of the postwar settlement.

With the fervent support of the Coptic Church, the traditional
bearer of Ethiopian nationalism whose clerical network covered the
Eritrean highlands, the Emperor fostered the growth of a unionist
party, which quickly became the dominant voice among Eritrean
Christians. This party was, however, opposed at all times by a small
minority of Christian separatists who recognized that the imperial impulse is not restricted to the white race. Initially favoring independence, following a massacre in August, 1946, of Christian Eritreans

---

* Success in avoiding internal opposition cannot be attributed to the peculiarly enlightened or liberal character of Italian rule for the simple reason that it was neither
enlightened nor liberal. Like the British in Kenya, the Italians had come not merely to
govern but to live. A thin stream of the Mezzogiorno's favorite export, people, was
directed south away from the main current flowing to the Western Hemisphere. By
the 1930s, the Italian element in a total population of perhaps one million had swollen
to roughly 40,000.

Goaded by their unassuageable hunger for the best land, best jobs, and superior
caste status, settlers inevitably demand crude discrimination against indigenous populations. The encouragement of immigration being a major purpose of colonial rule, the
Italian administration, even before it was envenomed by fascism, was bound to sympathize with settler priorities. Discrimination assumed the familiar pattern of carefully
limited educational opportunities, exclusion from middle and upper levels of the police, judicial, and administrative bureaucracies, preclusion of political activity, and denial of development-related goods and services.

Yet the population remained passive. Why? First, because fragmentation along the
fault lines of race, religion, vocation, region, and clan left few openings for cooperation
in pursuit of any purpose. Second, the Italian presence created relatively attractive
economic opportunities for a substantial number of impoverished Eritreans, benefits
which multiplied in the late 1920s and early 1930s when Italy began preparing the
infrastructure of its East African empire. However menial, the jobs provided benefits
in excess of very low pre-existing expectations. It would take some time for the base of
economic aspirations to rise above that which the Italians were willing to concede.
Third, the Italian administration did not attempt radical alteration of social and economic patterns in the countryside, where most Eritreans lived. Fourth, the fact that the
Italians were, after all, Christian and in that sense participants in the historic alliance
against the Islamic world may have helped to allay the antagonism of the Tigres who,
by virtue of their numbers, ties to Ethiopia, and relative preponderance in administrative jobs, were the most dangerous threat to the colony's tranquility. Finally, it would
be naive to overlook three strategic considerations: the large and growing army south
of Suez maintained by the Italians with an eye to eventual expansion; the territory's
modest size (50,000 square miles, only one-tenth the size of Ethiopia); and its accessi-
bility through the two ports of Massawa and, further south, Assab.

by Muslim soldiers from the Sudan Defense Force, the separatists effected a brief rapprochement with the unionists on the basis of joint support for an autonomous state within the framework of the Ethiopian empire. But rapprochement quickly shattered on the rock of Haile Selassie's distaste for a federal solution. The separatists thereupon reverted to their original position, festooned, however, with a claim for the "restoration" of Tigre Province to Eritrea, a development which would, of course, have had for them the happy consequence of guaranteeing a solid Christian majority in the new state.

The Muslim community, constituting about half the colony's population, reacted more slowly to the political opportunity created by Italy's defeat and her formal renunciation of all right and title to her colony. Its largest component, the Tegray tribes, ethnic cousins of the Christian Tigres, who spread from the tip of the predominantly Christian plateau to the western lowlands bordering the Sudan, was initially preoccupied with other matters. The attention of the lowland Tegrays was absorbed by a vicious little struggle between them and a tribe on the Sudanese side of the border. The highland Tegrays were convulsed by internal conflict: a threatened uprising of serfs, supported by merchants in the main north highland towns, against the traditional aristocratic families. During World War II the festering struggle of the serfs was restrained by an unstable British compromise. At the war's conclusion it intensified and spread to all Tegray tribes. Confronted, by the end of 1946, with a situation where ninetenths of the Tegray population was united in opposition to the aristocratic remainder, the British administration committed itself to a process of emancipation.

The emancipation struggle raised political consciousness throughout the Muslim community and honed leaders able to give it effective expression. In December, 1946, Ibrahim Sultan Ali, a townsman who had become the most prominent figure in the emancipation movement, organized a meeting of representatives from all the Muslim groups to consider the question of Eritrea's future. The meeting produced an organization (the Muslim League with Ibrahim Sultan as secretary-general), a negative program (opposition to union with Ethiopia), and a bundle of disagreements over the alternatives to union. After a long wrangle, the various factions coalesced loosely around independence, either immediately or "in case this is held to be impossible, . . . an international trusteeship . . . for ten years . . . with British control or such control as may be directed by the Trusteeship Council of the U.N.O."[1]

The unionist cause was strengthened, inadvertently, by both British and Italian policy. From the outset, British occupation policy was laissez faire in conception. Faced with an enthusiastically Fascist settler community, the British, determined to maintain control with a minimum commitment of men and resources and eager to use the colony as an entrepôt and arsenal for their North African campaign, simulated the snail more than the hare in altering the structure of Italian ascendancy. Acrid land disputes between Eritreans and settlers continued to be litigated before Italian judges who applied Italian colonial law. Although the British displaced Italians at the apex of the administration, just below it Italian functionaries remained at their desks, and Eritrean clerks at their disposal. Incentives for enhanced agricultural production were generally awarded, in the name of superior efficiency, to Italian farmers. Concerned with winning the war, not with promoting in Eritrea greater levels of social justice than those obtaining in English colonies, the British administration actually appropriated some Eritrean-owned land and transferred it to Italian hands.

A division of the social and economic spoils which seemed tolerable—or at any rate was tolerated—when the Italians were at the top of the heap quickly became intolerable after they had fallen a notch and become, like the Indians in the British colonies of East Africa, a buffer between the administrative heights and the indigenous population. The emergent hostility was not limited to harsh glances and nasty words. Particularly in the countryside, a number of Italians were put to the knife. Hostility was compounded when settler hopes for the restoration of Italian rule or at least de facto hegemony began to rise. Kindled originally by the retention of economic ascendancy and British insistence on treating Eritrea as occupied *Italian* territory, hostility ignited as Italy belatedly switched rulers and sides, then flared when the cold war produced suitors from both East and West for the Italian hand.

The postwar atmosphere, although friendlier than Italy might justifiably have hoped at the time of its surrender, was clearly inimical to the restoration of full colonial rule over Somalia, Eritrea, and Libya. Trusteeships, on the other hand, seemed within reach. In Somalia, reach and grasp coincided rather neatly despite harsh indigenous opposition. But in Eritrea, the Italians had also to contend with the astute diplomacy of Haile Selassie, whose canonization in the democracies as an anti-Fascist hero obscured the tough authoritarian nature of his own political enterprise.

Quickly recognizing that restoration of colonial status was unattainable, the settlers, with Italian government support, pressed first for Italian trusteeship and then, when that too began to drift out of reach, for independence. They apparently assumed, not implausibly, that an independent Eritrea would look to Italy for economic assistance and also for political support against Ethiopian imperialism and would, moreover, allow the settlers to play a mediating role between the Muslim and Christian parties. The swing toward independence by the settlers and their local clients led to the formation of a strong independence bloc incorporating the Muslim League, the Liberal

Progressive Party of Christian Separatists, and the settler-dominated organizations. With the aid of lavish Italian disbursements, the bloc began to eat away unionist support, including a corporal's guard of Muslim renegades.

The unionists responded with all the weapons at their disposal. Christian waverers were coerced by the church's threatened denial of access to the sacraments. Tegray tribesmen, who in the past had often roamed across the Ethiopian frontier in search of grazing during the dry months of winter and spring, suddenly found their way barred by the Ethiopian authorities unless they could produce Unionist party membership cards. For Christians or anyone else who supported independence, there was, finally, an ample supply of terror.

It had flared up before the bloc's formation in connection with a 1948 fact-finding visit by a commission representing the Big Four (France, Britain, the United States, and the USSR). Following a period of moderating violence, the bloc's formation and the prospective visit of a United Nations investigatory commission fueled a new wave of terror.

> Between October 1949 and the arrival of the United Nations Commission in February 1950, 9 Italians, an Indian, a Greek, 3 Christian supporters of the Bloc, and 4 Moslem tribesmen were assassinated. Italian cafes in Asmara and Addi Ugri were attacked with rifle fire and hand-grenades; hand-grenades were thrown at Italian and Eritrean supporters of the Bloc in Asmara, Massawa, and Decamere; an open assault was made on the village of a district chief . . . who supported the Bloc; Italian farms were raided and ransacked; and the livestock of Moslem tribesmen was looted. The climax came in February when, as the United Nations Commission was arriving, violent fighting broke out in Asmara between Moslems and Christians. It persisted for five days before order was restored and resulted in a long casualty list and wounded.[2]

Lest the purpose of an atrocity be misunderstood, the terrorists often left notes at the scene of the crime threatening death to other bloc supporters.

While the terror succeeded in re-converting virtually all the unionist apostates, it did not, surprisingly, have the coincident effect of firmly cementing the Muslim bloc. Rather, bloc members managed to subordinate their hatred of the unionists to fear, mistrust, and contempt for each other.

In early 1950, shortly after the arrival of the United Nations commission which would propose the colony's future, the bloc smashed itself into three pieces. The precipitating causes were Eritrean suspicion of the Italian connection, heightened by unionist propaganda and Italian exuberance, and a latent struggle for power between Tegray tribal leaders and Ibrahim Sultan who, though a townsman, was believed to harbor ambitions for the leadership of all the Tegrays. On these issues the Muslims split, with the western Tegrays going off on their own to demand, for their chunk of the colony, independence preceded by a period of British trusteeship. In the meantime, a portion of the Christian separatists broke away for a second attempt at accommodation with the unionists. Although the two Christian factions did not negotiate a formal alliance, the rebels, having apparently received modest encouragement from Addis Ababa, set up shop as the Liberal Unionist party with a platform of "conditional" or federal union.

Under the terms of the Italian peace treaty, the Big Four obligated themselves to seek agreement on the disposal of the former Italian colonies and, failing agreement, to refer the issue to the United Nations General Assembly and thereafter to implement its recommendations. Following three years of maneuvering worthy of a Byzantine court, the erstwhile allies achieved uniform agreement on one proposition only: their inability to agree. So, as provided in the treaty, the issue was bumped over to the General Assembly where, surrounded by the lesser states and joined by the two concerned parties—Ethiopia and Italy—they all persisted in denouncing each other's proposals.

Ignoring the prior exertions of the Big Four commission which had visited Eritrea in 1948 and found the population evenly divided between supporters of union and advocates of a transition to independence,* the United Nations sent out its own commission. Its members managed to develop a level of mutual hostility quite rivaling that of their Big Four predecessors and, in consequence of their cordial ill will, to produce two separate reports and three sets of proposals.

One report concluded that only a minority favored independence; the other report found a majority so disposed. The three proposals, reduced to their essence, were (1) union with Ethiopia, (2) federation with Ethiopia, and (3) independence preceded by a ten-year trusteeship under United Nations administration. Unaided even by a statement of the basic facts that commission members agreed on and no doubt weary of the perplexing struggles convulsing this distant and obscure place, the United Nations chose the nominal middle way. It resolved that Eritrea should "constitute an autonomous unit federated with Ethiopia under the sovereignty of the Ethiopian Crown." The Eritrean government was to have full "legislative, executive, and judicial powers in the field of domestic affairs"; an undefined entity designated the "Federal Government," which was to be directed by a federal legislature with proportionate Eritrean representation, was

---

* This finding was condemned on several dubious grounds by the French and Russians who, for various reasons, were in 1948 eager to impose an Italian trusteeship.

to have jurisdiction over defense, foreign affairs, finance, and foreign and interstate commerce and communications. The resolution provided finally for a two-year transition during which the British administration would assist a United Nations commissioner to fashion the new political structure.[3]

The Short, Unhappy Life of Federation

Eduardo Matienzo of Bolivia, the appointed commissioner, arrived in Eritrea on February 9, 1951, to find that communal hatred and the related resurgence of sheer banditry was cutting a swath of death and devastation across the face of the colony. His appearance had all the impact on the colony's hemorrhage of Canute's proclamation to the sea. It took over a year for the United Nations administration—with Ethiopian government support, terror no longer appearing useful—to reduce both mercenary and political banditry to manageable proportions. Only then was Matienzo able to begin the process of negotiating a constitutional framework.

Even assuming the greatest good will on all sides (an assumption wholly unwarranted by the facts), achievement of a viable federation seemed remote. It would exist at the Emperor's sufferance, and he had been opposed from the beginning. Given the nature of his government, a centralized autocracy, as well as the historic tension in Ethiopia between center and periphery, continued opposition was predictable.

No one could accuse the Emperor even of much transitional hypocrisy. Rather than quietly conceding the General Assembly a decent interval to forget that it had, in substance, consigned Eritrea to imperial whim, he reached immediately for control. His representative at the constitutional discussions opposed a federal constitution, insisting that federal authority be lodged in the existing imperial government. Since that government had no legislature, the demand was a little hard to reconcile with the provision in the General Assembly resolution that Eritreans be represented in a federal legislature "in the proportion that the population of Eritrea bears to the population of the Federation."[4] That little difficulty was avoided by the simple expedient of ignoring the reference to a legislature.

Perhaps one should not condemn Matienzo too harshly. He had no mandate to draft a federal constitution, only one for Eritrea. Moreover, he was required to obtain Ethiopian as well as Eritrean approval of his draft.

While deferring to the Emperor's will on the matter of a federal legislature, Matienzo held firm against other Ethiopian demands, which would have ripped out the barest essentials of local autonomy. The Emperor was not given the power he sought to appoint all executive officials and to approve or reject all local legislation, a demand which even a majority of the unionists opposed. The Emperor was also frustrated in his efforts to impose on Eritrea the official language of the empire—Amharic—in place of Arabic, preferred by the Muslims, and Tigrinya.

It was in the course of the constitutional negotiations that the first cracks began to appear in the imperial-unionist front. From its inception, the relationship must have been more one of convenience than love. The Emperor was, after all, an Amharic-speaking Shoan. Shoans predominated among his noble and bureaucratic favorites and were the leading recipients of his lavish patronage. He was not, therefore, the most attractive emperor the Christian Tigres could visualize. But Emperor he was and that made him the only available guarantor of Italian and Muslim subordination. The Tigres may have felt like the Polish communist who was asked whether he regarded the Russians as brothers or friends. "Brothers, of course!" he snapped. "One chooses one's friends."

After the guarantee of Christian ascendancy was, in effect, institutionalized by the United Nations resolution, the analogy became increasingly apt. Slowly, but not altogether imperceptibly, many unionists began to slide toward support of a genuine federation.

While the unionists were entertaining belated second thoughts about the merits of unconditional union, the two Muslim factions labored successfully to sustain their deep mutual hostility. Their division, their respective acceptance of the federal concept, and the shift of opinion in the unionist camp cumulatively produced opportunities for coalition politics. These opportunities were realized at the end of 1952 after the first—and as it turned out the last—election under the democratic constitution when the Muslim Tegrays from western Eritrea joined the unionists to form a majority coalition in the new assembly.

The alliance, bridging seven years of continuous and a millennium of intermittent hostility, created the basis for effective government. To no end. The Emperor, having failed in the constitutional negotiations to abort autonomy, set about suffocating it. Over the next ten years, through bribery, intimidation, and where necessary (as it often was) naked force, the Emperor stripped away the emblems and gutted the substance of democracy and autonomy, both of which he appeared to loathe. On November 14, 1962, following a rigged parliamentary vote, the chief administrator of Eritrea announced its unconditional union with Ethiopia. The charade was over. The rebellion had already begun.

It germinated during the late 1950s in Cairo where two veterans of the antiunionist campaign—Ibrahim Sultan Ali and Woldeab Woldemariam—had taken refuge. Before federation, Woldemariam had led a small trade union movement, the Christian separatists, and—as evidenced by the failure of six attempts to assassinate him—a charmed life. Following Britain's withdrawal, the environment for political activities became still less salubrious. The Ethiopian authorities banned formal political parties, and associations with political overtones were informally hamstrung.

Labor union activities became equally perilous. With an Ethiopian garrison on hand to work his will, the Emperor suppressed the Eritrean General Union of Labour Syndicates, which Woldemariam had directed. And when, in the post-federation depression, this proved insufficient to quell labor unrest, more direct measures were available. In February, 1958, a general strike in Asmara and Massawa was crushed by troops who killed and wounded dozens and arrested hundreds. Thus tranquility was restored.

Apparently unwilling to alter his line of work in ways which would attract imperial favor, Woldemariam left for Cairo where, with Ibrahim Sultan Ali, he founded the Eritrean Democratic Front.[5] Initially, its strategy may have been primarily political; Eritreans seem to have had some difficulty in annulling a touching faith in the United Nations' willingness to look after its progeny. At various low points of the cryptofederal experience, Eritreans had futilely petitioned the United Nations for assistance. The requisite third-party concern was unavailable. The United Nations, then as now, was generally insensitive to a member state's domestic peccadillos.

Despite the brutality of Italy's conquest and six-year occupation of Ethiopia, the Emperor left the settler community in peace. So Eritrea ceased to be an object of serious concern in Rome.

There was, of course, an abundance of concern in Washington once work went forth on the huge communications and intelligence-monitoring base complex, Kagnew Station, authorized by the 1953 military and economic assistance agreement between the United States and the imperial Ethiopian government. But Washington's concern was for order, not justice.

So whatever the original intention of its founders, the Eritrean Democratic Front soon went looking for guns. And it took a name appropriate to armed struggle: the Eritrean Liberation Front (ELF). Scrounging together £ 6500, the ELF purchased a consignment of superannuated Italian rifles and in late 1961 opened the conflict with a scattering of hit-and-run engagements.

Toward National Liberation

In order to trace the eighteen-year course of the insurrection to its present state, one must pass through a jungle of conflicting claims surrounded by marshy data. This is, of course, true in varying degrees for every civil war. The monopoly of violence being the most salient feature of public authority, "legitimate" or "constitutional" governments must minimize the insurgents' achievements or attribute them to the activities of foreign agents. The insurgents, conversely, must seek to enhance their charms and status by emphasizing their indigenous character and by magnifying their political and military operations. In this way, they attract domestic fence-straddlers and foreign support while discouraging external assistance to the incumbents.

Guerrilla tactics magnify a hundredfold these innate obstacles to an accurate account of civil armed conflict. Guerrillas live by mobility and secrecy. Their operational bases are hidden or remote. The nature of their operations—small, scattered units; difficult communications; a political leadership often compelled to operate far from the zone of combat—guarantees an operational diffusion of authority.

The historian's frustrations are further amplified when the rebellion erupts in a Third World state with an autocratic government, for in that case the local press is a mouth organ of officialdom and the foreign press is rarely there. In the case of Eritrea, the problem was additionally complicated by the phenomenon of endemic banditry and, in certain areas, inter-village looting which would have assured a certain level of violent incidents even if the ELF did not exist.

How much can confidently be said about the insurgency's evolution? Its launching was facilitated by the 1950s recession-bred migration of workers from Asmara and the port cities to Saudi Arabia and the Sudan. The workers, plus young Muslims who went to Cairo for a university education, formed a pool of latent militants who could be organized beyond the Emperor's reach. A second early asset was the 1962 eruption of civil war in the Yemen. Weapons from patrons poured into and overflowed the arsenals of the Yemeni belligerents. Some of these weapons filtered into the hands of the ELF.

By 1964–65, the movement began to receive a dribble of direct assistance. Its initial patrons were several Arab League states—particularly the Sudan and Syria—and perhaps the People's Republic of China. During this period of incipient external support, the ELF claimed for the first time to have moved beyond organizational activity and sporadic raids on government outposts to the actual administration of liberated areas. It also announced the division of Eritrea into five wilayat ("zones"), each under the control of a military commander. One sign of increased guerilla activity in 1965 was the Ethiopian government's accusation of Syrian intervention in the empire's internal affairs. Up to that point, the government had attempted to smother the movement with official indifference. All violent acts were attributed simply to shifta ("bandits").

Consistent with this public posture, the army was prevented from launching search-and-destroy operations. While officially ignoring the insurgency, the authorities continued the policy of currying support primarily among Christian Eritreans with doses of development funds and imperial patronage.

Despite the government's calm front, it apparently sensed the progressive deterioration of control over the province. One demon-stration of its concern was sub rosa discussions with the Sudanese government. In return for reduced support of the ELF, Ethiopia offered to curtail assistance which Israel was funneling through Ethiopia to the southern Sudanese insurrectionists, the Anya'nya. This diplomatic initiative bore fruit in 1967 at roughly the same time that the Emperor unleashed his troops. Air and ground forces swept through suspected ELF areas—all of which were populated predominantly by Muslims—burning villages and generating refugees. One authority put the number of burned villages at more than 300 and the refugees at more than 30,000.

The Emperor had inadvertently chosen a propitious moment to strike. Within five months of the opening of the anti-insurgent campaign, Israel launched the six-day war. By smashing the Arab armies and planting its flag at the Jordan River and the Suez Canal, Israel trivialized Arab interest in events on the periphery of the Middle East.

The only promising development in an otherwise grim year for the ELF was the triumph in Aden of the National Liberation Front. With guerrilla entrepots in the Sudan largely closed thanks to the Emperor's diplomacy, Aden would become a valuable staging base for the movement of arms and munitions.

Not unnaturally, by the end of 1967 Ethiopian officials believed they had broken the movement's back. In fact, it was at least a year before the ELF was able to demonstrate that news of its demise was premature. The reorganization and rearmament of its forces began slowly in 1968, then seems to have accelerated the following year when Muammar el-Qaddafi and his fellow officers seized power in Libya. The new Libyan regime, militantly pan-Islamic, soon adopted the Eritrean movement. Arms were transported to Southern Yemen, then whisked across the narrow sea to scattered points on the long Eritrean coast. Another 1969 coup, this one in the Sudan, produced a regime less willing to accommodate Ethiopian imperatives. The Sudanese pipeline and sanctuary were temporarily reopened.

While beginning again to flex their muscles in the bush, the insurgents opened a new front with a series of attacks on Ethiopian Airlines planes. The campaign began in March of 1969 and persisted into 1972, when it culminated in a bloody shootout several thousand feet over Addis. All seven ELF agents, five men and two women (including several university students), were shot to death by government agents within seconds after the hijacking was announced. The ferocity of the scene was described by an American professor who was aboard the plane and was himself wounded by a grenade fragment. "The last thing I saw before the firing stopped," he said, "was a beautiful Ethiopian girl crawling by the row of seats in which I was crouched. She had a grenade in the hand she was using to push her-

self along and she was using her other hand in a futile effort to
staunch the blood flowing out of her side. She died a few feet up the
aisle."

This aborted hijacking was a microcosm of events in Eritrea at the
second peak of the insurgent challenge. Throughout 1969, insurgent
activities multiplied. Roads were mined; small police and army units
were ambushed; the U.S. consul-general in Asmara was kidnapped,
subjected to a lecture on the movement, then released. The imperial
government responded in the spring of 1970 by again unleashing the
Second Division for a bout of destruction. This time, however, the
carnage earned only a brief respite. By late summer, the government's version of security was on a downward spiral. One district
governor was killed in a brush with guerrillas. Bridges were blown
up. The roads were alive with ambushes; the division commander
stumbled into one of them and was killed. The armed forces responded with a rampage through nearby villages, massacring
hundreds. A civilian governor who had generally opposed high-pro-
file military operations was replaced by a general. The imperial authorities slapped martial law on most of the province, and the army
and air force expanded the zone of their destructive operations. A
largely Muslim town was pulverized from the air. Sweeps continued.
There were no official reports of battles lost and won, but that some
were fought was evidenced by a flow of military casualties into the
army hospitals of Asmara.

The immediate and longer term impact of the Ethiopian army's
1970–71 campaign is uncertain. For the short term, it apparently
effected a sharp reduction in insurgent military operations. But in the
process it may, in the traditional way of anti-insurgent forces, have
enhanced popular receptivity to the ELF's program. One local Ethiopian official complained to Bowyer Bell, a student of the insurgency:
"All we're doing is alienating the countryside, making the population
more bitter than it was before."[6] Elsewhere Bell describes the imperial army as "contemptuous of the people in the Eritrean province
and apparently [regarding] the Muslims especially with suspicion and
distaste."[7]

While it therefore appears that the 1970–71 campaign prepared
the ground for yet more determined and comprehensive uprisings,
events conspired to slow its growth. First, the Emperor, quick as ever
to exploit opportunity, reduced the ELF's access to foreign support.
Ironically, it was Gen. Gaafar Mohammed Nimeri's decision to conciliate his southern insurrectionaries by granting them a considerable
degree of autonomy which enabled Haile Selassie to narrow if not
altogether close the Sudanese door for his northern insurgents. When
the Emperor extended his good offices to the Sudanese belligerents
to facilitate their peace negotiations, Nimeri responded by withdrawing semiofficial support from the liberation movement. The length of

the border and pockets of loyal sympathy for the movement kept the frontier permeable, but the Sudan's value as a base area had been reduced.

A second blow was the establishment of full diplomatic ties with the Chinese, who coincidentally declared that it was not their policy to support subversion of governments with whom they enjoyed formal relations. Whatever the generic validity of that declaration, I was assured by one of the best-informed diplomats in Addis that the Chinese had by 1974 terminated all assistance to the ELF, an assurance consistent with the uniformly favorable attention then bestowed on the Chinese by the government-controlled press in Addis.

A third initiative was directed toward the government of the People's Democratic Republic of Yemen (PDRY). It was reminded that the large Yemeni population in Ethiopia and its valuable remittances to relatives in the PDRY existed at the Emperor's sufferance. While this warning did not eliminate Aden as a trans-shipment point for Libyan and other arms, it allegedly produced a lower level of open cooperation in the arms traffic.

While trying through the instrument of diplomacy to isolate the ELF cadres from the outside world, the Emperor moved simultaneously to cut their domestic ties by measures of tactical conciliation. No concessions were made on the basic issue of autonomy or representative government; but the army was again reined in, and some additional funds were provided for reconstruction and development, largely, it appears, in areas where Christians predominated.

While the Emperor was trying to kill it, the ELF on its own initiative took a fling at self-destruction. Divisive tensions wrack every liberation movement. They spring from many sources: abrasions between fighting units and the political directorate ensconced in some friendly foreign capital far from the zone of danger and unsure of its control; the temptations offered by competing, often mutually antagonistic, foreign patrons; disputes over the terms of settlement and the anticipated allocation of victory's benefits; difficulties of communication and supply; and the inevitable defectors and informants who intensify the paranoia native to an underground struggle. The ELF demonstrated all of these generic tensions plus others which vary with time and place. One of the variables which has haunted the Eritrean insurgency is the lack of a pre-existing sense of common identity or purpose in the population base from which the insurgents spring, a characteristic common to most African rebellions. There is, more precisely, neither a profound sense of nationalism nor a shared ideological experience to help activists in overcoming clan, class, linguistic, regional, religious, and personal differences. Nor is there a single charismatic leader.

External forces have aggravated indigenous sources of discord. For instance, initial support from Saudi Arabia allegedly was withdrawn because Christian participation diluted the element of pan-Islamic nationalism in the movement. A comparable desire to pull the ELF into a belligerently Islamic orientation, as well as distaste for its acceptance of aid and training from nominal or actual Marxist countries, may explain fluctuations in the measure of Libyan support.

In the face of its internal tensions and their external irritants, sustained unity within the ELF would have been miraculous. There having been no divine intervention, in 1968–69 the movement splintered. Outside Eritrea, there appeared two organized fragments, the ELF-General Command and the ELF-Popular Forces which may or may not have included all of the fighting bands. The competitors quickly associated themselves, respectively, with Baghdad and Damascus.

At the time of the split, Osman Saleh Sabbe, the leading figure in the Popular Forces, and his General Command rivals indicted each other for associating with reactionary regimes and for being representative of backward, tribal, and exclusively Muslim elements in Eritrea. The Popular Forces specifically accused the General Command of assassinating two Christian members of the ELF while the General Command anathematized Saleh Sabbe and his associates for remaining outside Eritrea during the bitter fighting ignited in 1967–68 by Ethiopia's first big push against the insurgents. Saleh Sabbe, apparently conceding that the split was, at least in part, one between local military commanders and the political leadership, accused the General Command activists of having failed to follow orders during that period.

Reports of bloody shootouts between Muslim and Christian bands as well as of confessional antagonism (for example, a refusal to eat together) within nominally integrated guerrilla units underlined the reality of Muslim-Christian hostility. Religion was not the only axis of animosity. Regional, tribal, and ideological differences supplemented it.

In 1972, a year after another Ethiopian offensive had savagely punished both insurgent groups, the General Command metamorphosed into the "Revolutionary Council" and, according to Osman Saleh Sabbe, decided to liquidate his group. Whoever initiated it, a virtual civil war erupted early in 1972 and continued its fratricidal course until the fall of 1974 when, again according to Saleh Sabbe, popular pressure drove both sides to conciliate their animosities.

Despite the energy wasted in this internecine struggle, the guerrillas gradually succeeded in mounting a new and yet more serious threat to imperial authority. Incidents of violence multiplied, spurring a perceptible migration of Italian capital and driving a Japanese firm to suspend copper-mining activities. By the summer of 1974 the distinguished British journalist, Colin Legum, returned from the Horn and announced, "There can no longer be any serious hope of defeating the rebels by military force. The only practical question is what kind of political settlement is possible." At that point, virtually no one in the country with any claim to objectivity disagreed. The Soviet-Cuban expeditionary force was not yet even a smudge on the horizon.

Notes

For information on the history and ethnology of Eritrea, the author is particularly indebted to G. K. N. Trevaskis, *Eritrea: A Colony in Transition* (London:Oxford University Press, 1960).

1. Trevaskis, p. 75.

2. *Ibid,* p. 96.

3. United Nations, General Assembly, Resolution 390 A (V): Final Report of the United Nations Commission in Eritrea (Seventh Session, Supplement Number Fifteen A/2188), pp. 74–5.

4. *Ibid.*

5. For useful accounts of the insurgency, see *inter alia:* Mordechai Abir, "The Contentious Horn of Africa," *Conflict Studies* 24 (June 1972): J. B. Bell, "Endemic Insurgency and International Order: The Eritrean Experience," *Orbis* 18 (1974): 431; J. F. Campbell, "Background to the Eritrean Conflict." *Africa Report,* May 1971, p. 19; C. Clapham, "Ethiopia and Somalia" in *Conflicts in Africa: Adelphi Papers Number Ninety-three* (London: The International Institute for Strategic Studies, 1972); F. Halliday, "The Fighting in Eritrea," *New Left Review,* May-June 1971, p. 57; P. Robbs, "Battle for the Red Sea," *Africa Report,* March-April 1975, p. 14; and B. Whitaker, ed., *The Fourth World* (New York: Schocken Books, 1972).

6. *Time,* March 10, 1971, p. 35.

7. Bell, "Endemic Insurgency," p. 440.

3 Ethiopia After the Revolution

Eritrea

CONCILIATION CONFOUNDED

For a number of reasons, there was a widespread expectation that Ethiopia's new rulers would seek a political settlement through major concessions. In the first place, the sheer fact that it represented a radical constitutional break with the old order induced the conviction that wherever that order had failed, the Dergue would try out different policies. Second, since the new government seemed committed to a secularized state free of Shoan domination, to the elimination of corruption in provincial as well as national government, and to radical reform generally, it had bases for appealing to the Eritreans that had been utterly unavailable to the Emperor. Secularization would appeal to the Muslim half of the Eritrean population. Radicalization would appeal to that wing of the secessionist movement, allegedly concentrated in the ELF-Popular Forces, which had hitherto equated secession with reform. Diffusion of power beyond the Shoan elite could assuage the large Tigrean element in the Eritrean population. Finally, since the decentralization of governmental functions to representative regional institutions had been an anathema to the Emperor, there was a hope that such decentralization would be included in the program of the new order—if for no better reason than the dialectic of reaction and revolution.

Concrete signs gave weight to these speculations. In the late spring of 1974, the Endalkachew government, necessarily acting with the consent if not at the instance of the Dergue, appointed a Christian and a Muslim Eritrean to serve as deputy governors-general in the province. These appointments were followed at the end of August by the selection of a distinguished jurist, Immanuel Andermichael, a nonpolitical Eritrean Christian, as governor-general. The stage seemed set for a major initiative.

Gen. Aman Michael Andom, being, on the one hand, an Eritrean Christian (but from the small Protestant minority within the Christian community) and, on the other, the hard-nosed commander of the Ethiopian division that had bashed the Somalis in 1964, had ideal credentials for reconciling Eritrean and Ethiopian nationalism. In Eritrea and apparently among liberation movement leaders in Arab capitals, there was a mood of high expectation. Everyone seemed to recognize that this was one of those rare, fleeting moments when it is possible to overcome historical inertia and to break decisively with the past.

Within Eritrea, there was a palpable lull in hostilities. The scent of a settlement, coupled with the Second Division's passivity, drew the guerrillas out of their myriad rural hideouts toward the main towns and cities. With peace seemingly in the offing or, alternatively, with an opportunity for more effective war should the revolution produce the collapse of authority at the center, a rash of talks broke out among the hostile wings of the liberation movement.

General Aman moved quickly to seize the day. Through the good offices of President Nimeri, whose naturally pro-Muslim sentiments were inevitably qualified by ambivalence about secessionist movements, Aman opened negotiations with spokesmen for the insurgents. Although the precise terms of his overture have never been officially announced, it appears that he proposed internal autonomy for all of Eritrea except the port of Assab and possibly a strip of land connecting Assab to the highlands. The port and access route would remain under the direct authority of Addis. Both movements responded with a public reaffirmation of their commitment to full independence. Yet Western sources continued to believe that important elements in the movement, particularly many Christians, would settle for less.

Perhaps they were right. We will never know, because some time on November 23, 1974—"Bloody Saturday" as it is now remembered—an army unit arrived at General Aman's villa and announced that by order of the Dergue he was under arrest. When Aman refused to submit, an intense firefight erupted. The inhabitants of the villa fought desperately and, for a while, successfully. Then tanks, called in by the conspirators, crashed through the thick walls that had protected the defenders.

The subsequent official account declared that the general had died resisting arrest. But some in Addis believed that, in the grand Ethiopian tradition, he had chosen suicide over capture. By whatever means, he perished. And with him perished two young members of the Dergue, close to sixty of the imprisoned paladins of the old regime, and the hope for peace in Eritrea.

The particular event which allegedly galvanized the general's opponents to stage this coup within the revolutionary coup was his refusal to dispatch additional troops to Eritrea, a gambit guaranteed to snap the sprig of conciliation. Apparently, there was a great deal of discord in the government and Aman's refusal represented only a small part of it. Rightly or wrongly—events suggest rightly—General Aman was identified with the "moderate" position on every important conflicted issue. He was thought to oppose summary justice for the elite and to support a flexible and discriminating land reform and a pluralistic government as well as a negotiated settlement in Eritrea. Differences over these fundamental issues, sufficient in themselves to trigger fratricide, were aggravated by the deep insecurity of all the main actors. Together they had overthrown in a historical instant the accumulated institutions of a millennium. In so doing, they had created virtually a political state of nature. The traditional sources of authority were in ruins. No one knew where power lay, who would obey what order. Conceivably, with one daring thrust, any of the factions within the armed forces could eliminate the others. As in the condition of unstable deterrence between nuclear powers, everyone feared a first strike.

Deliberations of the Dergue and the individual views of its members remain a riddle buried in an enigma. It is still impossible to tell whether Maj. Mengistu Haile Mariam and Lt. Col. Atnafu Abate, the apparent leaders of the anti-Aman thrust, opposed any concessions which would create a special status for Eritrea or became discouraged at the initial Eritrean response and concerned about the perceptible accretions of strength to the liberation movement during the de facto stand-down. Perhaps both precipitants were at work. Or perhaps Aman's opponents concluded simply that the liberation movements had to be badly bloodied before they would negotiate on acceptable terms. Bloodying the insurgents had systematically failed in the past. But in the past the alternative to struggle had been capitulation to an intolerable imperial order. The conspirators may have concluded that, as a prelude to compromise negotiated in the context of a revolutionized society, it could work.

And so within hours of Aman's death, trucks crowded with reinforcements for the 10,000 men of the Second Division rumbled through the streets of Addis. The reinforcements may also have been intended to neutralize that division if, following news of Aman's death, it decided to impose order not on Eritrea but on Addis. The Eritreans responded with a coordinated assault in the very heart of Asmara. It was war *à outrance.*

Christians and Muslims, Marxists and conservatives, General Command and Popular Forces—these distinctions no longer mattered. For the first time one could speak without baroque hyperbole of a "people's war." And since it was the "people" who were making war on them, the Ethiopian armed forces began unequivocally making war on the "people." Outside the major cities, the Ethiopian air force in its American planes, flown by American-trained pilots, dropped American bombs on the towns and villages where the insurgents were or might have been or might soon be. Within Asmara, suspected insurgents began to die violently. The only rule of war recognized by either side was efficacy.

With the struggle entering a seemingly apocalyptic phase, the Arab states finally began to show signs of broader and unembarrassed support. A government spokesman in the parliament of impeccably conservative Kuwait assured his listeners that the government would not stand by while fellow Muslims were massacred and hinted broadly of extensive aid. The Saudis also claimed that they were assisting the insurgents. When a delegation sent by the Dergue to major Arab capitals failed to secure assurances of nonintervention, Addis began to complain openly and with increasing bitterness of Arab intervention.

Each side seemed to exaggerate. Although apparently well-equipped with mines, small arms, and machine guns, the liberation forces still failed to display very much in the way of an effective riposte to armor and air power. The really sophisticated instruments of modern insurgency, hand-carried anti-tank and anti-aircraft weapons, were not deployed in substantial quantities. On the Arab side, support was still a good deal more rhetorical than real. At least there remained plenty of room for escalation.

After the assault on Asmara itself had been blunted, liberation movement forces continued to operate nearby and to threaten the thin supply routes to the highlands and the coast. For a short time, it even seemed possible that the insurgents might succeed in strangling the Ethiopian forces based in the city. But in the end, their inability to hold off armor and to reduce their vulnerability to air power assured continued Ethiopian control of the major cities and most of the towns. Those that could not be controlled could at least be devastated by bombardment and temporary occupation whenever the insurgents attempted to make a stand. Without a major qualitative step-up in external assistance, the insurgents seemed unable to enter the phase of sustained frontal combat with large units of the imperial armed forces.

By the spring of 1975, stalemate prevailed. Addis could neither occupy the countryside nor decimate the insurgents. The insurgents could not take any of the principal cities nor hold the towns nor indefinitely block the supply routes.

After the terrible slaughter of the prior few months, the avenue of conciliation seemed hopelessly blocked. For the insurgents, the only ways out seemed to be a massive escalation of external support, another outbreak of fratricide in the Dergue, a mutiny against the Dergue by one or more of the divisions in the field, or a U.S. decision to close its military pipeline to the Dergue. For the Dergue, on the other hand, the only perceived through-route was the familiar one murderously pioneered by predecessors in the counterinsurgency game: drain the rural sea, and the guerrilla fish will die.

Hitherto, divisions of opinion, particularly in the Christian community, on the virtues of independence had been a source of constraint on Ethiopian strategy. More highly educated than any other element in the Ethiopian mosaic, enjoying the commercial sophistication common among peoples of trading coasts, drawn painfully into the modern world through the medium of the colonial experience, Eritreans were disproportionately represented in public administration and commerce throughout the empire. Even in the armed forces, particularly the navy, they were not unrepresented, though their number had dwindled as the civil war intensified. Addis alone was thought to have an Eritrean population in excess of 100,000.

Before Aman's death, a large proportion of the Eritrean Christian elite seemed antagonistic to the demand for complete independence, although many apparently preferred some degree of home rule. But after the fall of Aman, reports of an anti-Eritrean pogrom in Addis, and the insurgent offensive, these moderates began tumbling toward the secessionist pole. In Eritrea, whole detachments of the locally recruited and officered police deserted to the countryside after assisting in the release of movement prisoners. Elsewhere in the empire, Eritreans, particularly students, began drifting back to their homes where their only possible occupation would be insurgency.

Having at last converted the great mass of Eritreans into the enemy, the masters of Addis could now pursue the logic of counterinsurgency to its murderous end. The loss of constraint coincided felicitously with the arrival of opportunity. The drought which had devastated Wallo and Tigre now tightened its grip on Eritrea. To be sure, the government by this time had a functioning relief agency. And there was food for it to distribute. But this little impediment to conscripting famine as an ally was overcome by fiat: the agency would not function in rural Eritrea. The Dergue also ordered foreign and international relief agencies to close their feeding stations in the countryside. Food in excess of the needs of the garrisons and, barely, the population of the occupied urban areas was barred from the province.

In this instance, nature helped to thwart the vicious purposes of men. According to reports, the 1975–76 harvests were relatively bountiful. The fact remains, however, that the government of Ethiopia tried, with careful premeditation, to orchestrate the starvation of Eritrea's rural population. This did not deter then-Secretary of State Henry Kissinger from vetoing proposals to terminate military assistance for Ethiopia. Indeed he approved a $4.3 million increase over the 1975 assistance program plus the prospective licensing of commercial arms sales valued at over $53 million. Meanwhile, most congressmen normally sensitive to the human rights dimensions of foreign policy seemed indifferent to the plight of the Eritreans. The political and human rights organs of the United Nations were equally mute. And there was not even a formal peep from the Organization of African Unity.

THE LIBERATION THAT ALMOST WAS

The Dergue's murderous tactics failed to halt the rot in its position. Insurgent forces, strengthened by new recruits and still broader popular support, tightened the noose around Asmara, Massawa, and the three or four other cities to which Ethiopian troops still clung, and for the first time demonstrated their ability to seize and hold large towns. Victory—the complete, decisive extrusion from Eritrea of Ethiopian power—was at last within reach.

But division within the rebellion remained a formidable obstacle to final success. In 1977, a united liberation movement might have established a provisional government and secured recognition from at least several Arab states. Recognition would in turn have facilitated access to economic and military aid. Even without recognition, as the government of a sovereign state, a unified guerrilla administration was liable to obtain more aid and to administer it more efficiently.

Arab patrons, sensitive to the costs of disunity and no doubt seeking relief from the movements' competitive solicitations, pressed them to integrate. The new adherents of both movements, primarily urbanized Christians who probably joined whichever group they first managed to contact, were less responsive than the old-timers to regional and tribal differences. Moreover, their recruitment diluted the traditional religious division already thinned out by the growing secularism and political radicalization of the movements but particularly of the ELF-Popular Forces or, as it was by then generally known, the Eritrean Popular Liberation Forces (EPLF) elite. Collectively these factors inspired an effort to go beyond the informal and limited coordination achieved in 1974—effected largely through a de facto division of territory—and to attempt the real unification of all insurgent forces. Under the aegis of Sudan's President Nimeri, Saleh Sabbe organized a meeting in Khartoum, which culminated in the Unity Agreement of September 1975.

Shadowed by bad auguries, part of Saleh Sabbe's group having from the start opposed full integration, the essay in unity was abruptly halted when a majority of the EPLF leadership voted to reject it. The rejectionists proposed instead a "united front of independent parties" and close coordination of military operations.

What began as an exercise in unification concluded in further fragmentation. First Saleh Sabbe and his supporters seceded or were expelled from the EPLF. Then the ELF declared that it was not prepared to implement the unity agreement with the Saleh Sabbe faction alone, which had adopted the name ELF-PLF or simply PLF (Popular Liberation Forces). Shortly thereafter, a small segment of the ELF split off from the main body and linked up with Saleh Sabbe. Thus, one year after Khartoum there were three liberation movements deploying armed forces, conducting a civil administration, maintaining separate infrastructures in the Sudan and missions abroad, and soliciting economic and military aid throughout the Arab world.

At least the movements did not regress to mutual decimation. De facto coordination, sometimes close, continued. In September, 1977, for instance, at the floodtide of Eritrean strength, a combined ELF-PLF force liberated Agordat, Eritrea's fifth largest city, and set up a joint administration.

Cooperation survived, but real unity continued to be frustrated by differences beyond the normal obstacles of personality, ego, ambition, and paranoia. Western intelligence sources had from the beginning credited the EPLF with leftist tendencies. The radicalizing experience of fighting a people's war, the assistance rendered by Marxist states, the adhesion of students who had been driven left by the experience of living under a neo-feudal autocracy enjoying lavish American patronage, and the withdrawal of Saleh Sabbe, who is a sophisticated, ideologically undogmatic nationalist, by all accounts left the EPLF with an avowedly Marxist leadership, though one apparently uncommitted to any particular one of the competing communist dogmas. Its abstractions were, like Mao's early thought, anchored in the experienced reality of grass-roots egalitarianism imposed by the terrible discipline of guerrilla warfare.[1]

The candor and clarity of its Marxist commitment is only one of the EPLF's identifying characteristics. In addition, it is believed to incorporate the largest number of Christians and to draw its Muslim activists primarily from Eastern Eritrea, particularly from the town dwellers of Massawa and members of the Samhar and Saho tribes.

Until the mid-1970s the ELF was seen as essentially a Muslim group, drawing the bulk of its recruits from Western Eritrea and led by Muslim notables with roots in the post-war political struggles preceding federation with Ethiopia. Its character appears to have been altered more than that of the EPLF by the recent influx of young Christians. They, as well as the radicalizing dynamic of guerrilla struggle, have now given the ELF a leftist tilt sufficient to mellow its ideological differences with the EPLF.

Adherents of the Muslim faith are plainly dominant today only in the PLF. But since Saleh Sabbe, its leader, has consistently struggled against religious chauvinism, it is doubtful that the group's confessional balance evidences a narrow religious interest.

The allocation of Arab-state support among the three movements seems to correlate almost as much with personal contacts as with ideological or religious sympathies. Because Saleh Sabbe has been the best known and apparently most effective spokesman for the Eritrean struggle for over a decade, this highly intelligent man remains the favored recipient of Arab support, although he commands the group generally conceded to have the fewest fighters and the least influence within Eritrea.

Western appraisals of each group's strength and of the total forces in the field vary considerably. The International Institute for Strategic Studies' 1977 *Strategic Survey* credits the ELF with 22,000 fighters, the EPLF with 12,000, and the PLF with 2,000. Other accounts, relying on Eritrean information or Western intelligence sources, suggested that the PLF figure should be doubled and the ELF-EPLF adjusted to show virtual equivalence in military manpower. But the most recent estimate by a normally well-informed source claims major accretion of strength for the EPLF to a level of approximately 20,000 military cadres, with the ELF shrinking below 10,000. While all specific figures are highly uncertain, particularly after the 1978 Ethiopian counteroffensive, most official and unofficial sources now agree that the EPLF has become the preeminent movement, a position earned by the elan of its cadres and the humane and efficient character of its civil administration.

When the Soviet Union and Cuba—in former days Eritrean sympathizers (it is believed that some EPLF officers were trained in Cuba)—committed themselves to consolidating the Ethiopian revolution, Libya, once the first or second largest armorer of Eritrean liberation, closed its arms pipeline. The People's Democratic Republic of Yemen, for years complicit in the rebellion as an arms transfer center, ended its support. In addition, it allowed pilots, lent to the Dergue primarily for the Ogaden campaign, to fly missions against the Eritreans. But, according to Eritrean sources, in the late spring of 1978 the Yemenis shifted to a more neutral footing.

Iraq and Syria are long-time supporters of the rebellion and reportedly continue to funnel arms through the Sudan, as does Saudi Arabia. Conservative Kuwait has given financial aid mostly to the EPLF, which had developed personal ties with Kuwaiti leaders by setting up an office there.

The Sudan has tried to maintain amicable relations with each of the three factions while urging them towards unity. In an effort to seem impartial and avoid strife, President Nimeri distributed arms for a time to all the groups even if the original Arab source had earmarked them for only one. In 1977 the Saudis tried but failed to arrange a merger of the movements—employing the carrot of additional aid to the EPLF, the group with which they had the least sympathetic ties. After this failure, the Saudis reportedly required Nimeri to forward their aid exclusively to the PLF.

Until the spring of 1978 the three factions hung on to their autonomy while inching achingly close to final victory. They were suffocating Asmara, fighting practically in Masawa's streets, and effectively administering upwards of 90 percent of Eritrea's territory. In large areas they operated underground hospitals and factories, managed collective farms, and even ran buses between liberated towns.

But throughout April and most of May the Dergue accumulated large new increments of force, transferring thousands of veterans that had just been fighting the Somalis in the Ogaden to beleaguered strongpoints within Eritrea and to bases on its periphery. At least several thousand Cubans moved north from the Ogaden with them. U.S.- and Soviet-supplied planes, flown by Cuban-, Soviet- and U.S.-trained Ethiopian pilots—and probably by Cubans as well—ranged over Eritrea profligately dispensing napalm and cluster bombs and death as if the whole place were a vast free-fire zone.

Finally, in late May the Dergue threw 20,000 troops into a violent offensive. In the Ogaden campaign, Cuban forces spearheaded the offensive. Here there was no Cuban spearhead, but Cubans helped run the logistical system which provided the fuel and spares and ordnance and repairs necessary to sustain the assault. The Dergue's offensive coincided with—as its imminence may have inspired—an agreement between the ELF and the EPLF to establish a joint military command and to merge their respective civilian administrations. According to a report to the *Times* of London from a journalist in Eritrea, as their first post-merger decision, the movements' leaders ordered the PLF to join them or face suppression.

Throughout June the battle raged across Eritrea, killing and mutilating, while propelling thousands, perhaps tens of thousands of noncombatants over the Sudanese border into packed, miserable refugee camps. Without air support, lightly armed against Ethiopian tanks, artillery, and multiple rocket launchers, the guerrillas yielded ground, but slowly and only after desperate resistance.

Before the Dergue's counteroffensive, President Nimeri confirmed to a Western journalist his fear that the weight of Ethiopian weaponry and its indiscriminate employment would depopulate Eritrea and force the liberation movements out of rubble-strewn towns back to their old guerrilla redoubts. The Sudan would be left with a vast refugee population while Eritrea was consigned to endless war. The weight and ferocity of the Ethiopian assault may gradually have driven ELF and EPLF leaders to the same pessimistic reassessment of their prospects.

Mengistu Haile Mariam, emergent as the Dergue's apparently undisputed master, had several times endorsed a vaguely-defined regional autonomy for all of the empire's peripheral regions. His generalities offered a basis for negotiation if the movements could contemplate something less than full independence as the result of their eighteen-year struggle. Whatever influence actually drove them, the fact is that on June 20, 1978, ten days after the secretary general of the ELF, Ahmed Nasser, returned from a visit to Moscow, ELF and EPLF leaders met in Aden and signed an agreement to seek a peaceful settlement of the conflict.

They proposed negotiations without conditions. And for the first time they did not coincidentally reaffirm an immutable commitment to independence. Saleh Sabbe immediately denounced them for selling out Eritrean nationhood. Publicly the Dergue said nothing while it pursued a relentless counteroffensive which by the beginning of 1979 had driven the Eritreans back to their rural redoubts and coincidentally driven tens, perhaps hundreds, of thousands of additional refugees into the Sudan. The Dergue had made a desert and called it "victory." But not peace. Seemingly the struggle will go on until Mengistu offers a tolerable settlement. At this point he seems interested only in unconditional surrender or perpetual war.

Consolidation and Reform

The torrents of revolution poured through the gap created by Aman's death and engulfed almost sixty leaders of the old order. With a few exceptions—notably the last two prime ministers, Aklilu Habte-Wold and Endalkachew Makonnen—they seemed to have been drawn almost at random from the collection of dignitaries marooned in the Fourth Division's barracks. In groups of ten, they were hustled through the quiet campsite to hear a sentence of death pronounced by the staccato chatter of machine guns.

Although the primary reason for this freshet of executions probably was to distract attention from the blow against Aman, it also effectively signaled a decisive turn in the revolution. The hasty men of iron had won. Social transformation would be conducted from the top and, like the war in Eritrea, through the medium of bayonets. There would be no compromise, no equivocation.

RURAL LAND REFORM

If, following the massacre, any doubt remained on this score, it was soon dissipated by the land reform decree. Announcement of the reform had been awaited with breathless expectancy. In Ethiopa, land is pretty close to everything: it is the margin of existence for the peasant masses who comprise over eighty percent of the population; it is the state's primary source of foreign exchange; it is the symbol of social hierarchy and the reward for loyal servants of the regime.[2] For decades, the land question had haunted Ethiopian political life. Foreign advisers of every political and ideological stripe had proclaimed it the key to the country's putative potential as the breadbasket of the Middle East.* It was enthroned in imperial and parliamentary rheto-

---

*This euphoric prophesy has been lowered, as the overcrowded highland's topsoil has washed away. But with its underdeveloped lands in the south and southwest, Ethiopia still has the potential to feed its twenty-eight million people adequately while substantially increasing its exports of agricultural commodities which, together with the price of coffee, have given it comfortable hard currency reserves (an import cover of from nine to twelve months).

ric. There was even a Ministry of Land Reform. But, like a child's toy car resting on its back while its wheels spin, reform was noise without movement.

No mystery had attended the Emperor's studied failure to act. Significant change in land tenure meant trouble, personal loss, or both. Who, after all, were the leading landowners? The imperial family, the church, the nobility, a host of provincial gentry, and senior figures on both the civilian and military sides of the regime—in short, most of the politically sentient elements of the realm. Remarkable were those among them who yearned for a reduction either in the rents they were entitled to extract or in the size of their holdings. The imperial holdings not only yielded rents to supplement funds that, though nominally public, were equally at the Emperor's disposal but, in addition, provided a reservoir of land available to reward useful functionaries, to satiate the ambitious, and to corrupt incipient reformers.

In the decade preceding the Emperor's fall, agricultural modernization, encouraged by the World Bank and the U.S. Agency for International Development, had, if anything, stiffened resistance to egalitarian reform. Modernization meant consolidation of holdings (often by the removal of tenants), mechanization, and production for export. The result was vastly increased land values and a major increment in foreign exchange earnings. Coffee and leguminous crops were favored. The high prices generally prevailing in the early seventies, particularly for pulses, together with the sharp increase in production were largely responsible for the comfortable foreign exchange surplus that was the Emperor's unintended bequest to his militant young heirs.

Reform was not only threatening to the whole, seemingly stable structure of power; in addition, it was hellishly complicated. Landholding patterns were at least as diverse as the ethnic mosaic. In many cases, they were also obscure both physically and juridically. There were no formal surveys, no land registration, few records of any kind. No William the Conqueror had ever appeared to sort things out. And if one had tried, he might soon have expired from frustration.

At best, one could speak of general tendencies in different regions. In the northern plateau, including Tigre and the Christian highlands of Eritrea, much land was held communally, though farmed individually; there were areas where plots were exchanged at regular intervals to promote a more even distribution of the land's bounty. In several of the southern, predominantly Galla provinces, the pattern was at the other end of the continuum of equity. These were the territories taken by conquest rather than elite assimilation. Most of the conquering had been accomplished within the past century by Menelik II. The tenants, groaning under rents trampolining as high as two-thirds of each crop, were the descendants of the former owners, the subjugated Gallas. The owners, sometimes absentee, were in many cases the descendants of the very soldiers who had done the subjugating. Between landlord and tenant, divided by class interest, culture, and history, tension always ran high. Here was the classic terrain for equitable reform. Between these two extremes, tenure displayed stunning variations. There were, in effect, individual landowners who might or might not pay some fee in kind to another person or an institution with residual claims. In the case of a clear tenancy, such matters as the size of the rent, the landlord's services (seed, animals, credit, etc.), and stability of tenure varied extensively.

These intimidating complexities seemed almost to defy generally applicable legislation. Not surprisingly, the men who had dealt so summarily with General Aman's defiance showed no less capacity for decision in this instance. Some four months after his death, in the early spring of 1975 just before the planting season, they proclaimed the nationalization of all rural land. Henceforth it was to be "the collective property of the Ethiopian people."* By itself, the rhetorical act of nationalization was not so much revolutionary as a logical corollary of the Emperor's disestablishment. Typical of feudal systems, in theory land in Ethiopia belonged ultimately to the monarch who was the surrogate of God. The monarch having been replaced by a government ruling in the name of the people, it followed that the people and their surrogates succeeded to all his entitlements.

What lent revolutionary meaning to the shift in nominal title were the changes in real rights and interests concurrently announced. In one stroke, the Dergue eliminated absentee ownership, established a ten-hectare limit on all holdings, granted tenants and hired laborers possessory rights over the land they presently tilled, and abolished rent and other obligations owed to the erstwhile landowners. Moreover, by henceforth prohibiting private persons from hiring farm labor—except in the case of widows dependent for their livelihood on inherited land or landholders too sick to farm and with minor children—the Dergue sought to bar the reappearance of tenant farming. As a further step towards transforming the local structure of power and the distribution of rural income, the proclamation abolished all obligations and dues owed "the numerous informal officials and notables who under the imperial system had constituted the grass roots level of political administration" rather in the fashion of England's Tory squirearchy.[3]

In the years preceding the proclamation, a commercial sector characterized by large farms, professional management, and a differ-

---

*The discussion which follows rests largely on the work of John M. Cohen, Arthur A. Goldsmith, Peter H. Koehn and John W. Mellor, (see works cited in the bibliography), supplemented or confirmed by information obtained from U.S. and European government experts.

entiated labor force equipped with relatively modern technology had begun to account for a very considerable proportion of agricultural exports and a significant proportion of locally-marketed food stuffs. These farms, numbering perhaps 5,000 and covering generally superior land estimated at roughly 70,000 hectares, were dealt with separately in the new law. The farms had been operated as a single economic unit; their immediate division into small plots for distribution to farm workers, many of whom might be unfamiliar with aspects of farming other than the ones to which they had been assigned, was plainly impractical. As an interim measure, the law provided for continued operation of the farms by their present managers, subject to government supervision. Ultimate disposition of each commercial farm was left to future decisions, the indicated alternatives being, on the one hand, fragmentation and disposal of the fragments to peasant associations for distribution as individual farms subject to the ten-hectare limit or, on the other hand, transformation of existing units into collective farms to be run by their former laborers and resettled persons drawn from the swollen ranks of landless peasants and unemployed urban dwellers.

Like the creeping coup that had preceded it, the land-reform proclamation evidenced in its various parts a sophisticated prudence about the means for prosecuting revolutionary ends. The effort to keep the commercial farms intact and functioning in order both to maintain essential production and to keep options open for subsequent rural reforms was one example of a subtlety at odds with the massacres of General Andom and the old elite. Another was the ten-hectare limit. Two surveys conducted for the pre-revolutionary government had found in areas outside the north with its peculiar communal tenures an average farm size of under three hectares. The ten-hectare limit thus made a place in the new order for the wealthier small farmers rather than driving them into the arms of the great landowners, the natural enemies of the revolution. It also offered peasants scratching a subsistence income on smaller plots the prospect of larger and potentially more efficient holdings, once the process of redistribution got under way.

Yet another sign at least of an effort to make prudent discriminations was the proclamation's special provision for the northern tenures. In all other regions the proclamation confirmed the tiller's existing possessory rights, whether those of ownership or tenancy. But in the north, the norm is a patchwork of rights in different bits of land, the rights varying from those tantamount to ownership to those indistinguishable from a simple tenancy. In the north, but rarely anywhere else, a man might work one piece of land as a tenant while owning and leasing out another. One expert on northern land tenure claims that tenants "are almost invariably landowners themselves and often the more prosperous of the parties. . . . [T]hey own plow oxen and farm . . . . the land of poorer households which lack this asset."[4] In the north application of the otherwise general grant of possessory rights to tillers would have grossly disturbed expectations among persons of the same social and economic class, capriciously enriching some at the expense of others, penalizing a rational, mutually advantageous rather than exploitative distribution of ownership and tenancy. Imposed on a peasantry noted for its belligerent opposition to externally-imposed change, this would have been an invitation to war.

At the same time, the Dergue was not prepared to leave the northern tenure untouched. To deal with the problem of the tenant who was elsewhere a landlord, the proclamation limited its grant of possessory rights to those tenants without comparable rights in other land. A second provision uniquely applicable to the north was concerned not with equity but with production. The north had for centuries labored under a plague of land litigation, the result of its immensely complicated tenure system which spewed out claims deriving from tenuous skeins of kinship, uncertain boundaries, poorly recorded, not necessarily consistent decisions, and the inevitable play of discretion by elders and official judges subject to a great number of influences including their own caprice. Litigation, a wasteful dispersion of energy in itself, also made tenures insecure and thus discouraged investment and innovation. The Dergue's answer was to freeze the existing, hitherto transitory pattern of land holdings by precluding the extension of new claims. According to one set of U.S. experts on Ethiopian land tenure, the freeze was likely to mobilize peasants behind elite resistance to the Dergue because the successful prosecution of land claims had been a principal means of upward mobility for the clever and enterprising as well as an accepted, comfortably familiar feature of agrarian life.

Though not without inflammatory ingredients, the land-reform proclamation did seem an attempt to avoid aggravations that were not inevitable incidents of measures necessary for the furtherance of basic Dergue objectives: gutting the old elite, galvanizing a popular base, and eliminating both gross inequities and major obstacles to the growth of productivity. The smaller landlords could find a limited solace in provisions which authorized compensation for physical assets (though not the underlying land), required a distribution of land to landlords who, having leased all their farms, were nowhere in possession on the date of the law, and obligated past tenants to repay within a three-year period the value of oxen provided by the farmer and retained after the reform.

The Dergue's tax policies complemented the reform's popularity among groups who unarguably benefited, while tending to allay the anger of those farmers on whom reform had a more uncertain impact. Coincident with the new law's promulgation, the Dergue suspended the land tax. Subsequently, in January, 1976, it adopted a highly progressive income tax so structured as to impose rates of only fifteen percent on the overwhelming majority of Ethiopian farmers.

Neither the suspension of the land tax nor much of anything else could conciliate the small group of really large land owners. But as a class they were already poorly positioned to organize dangerous opposition. Many of the greatest among them—the natural leaders—were already dead, detained, or exiled. Their fate no doubt intimidated lesser figures. Equally intimidating where it existed was the unharnessed animosity of a once passive tenantry. Particularly in areas where rents were high and landlords and tenants ethnically distinct, preeminently the Galla Provinces in the south, peasants had anticipated the proclamation by making a revolution on their own. Rents were withheld, landowners beaten, manor houses put to the torch. For those areas, the reform meant a regularization of the revolutionary process, the confirmation of a new order. Opposition among the large provincial landlords may also have been eased by allowing time before the proclamation for some liquidation of assets and their reinvestment in urban land, an established alternative source of income for the wealthy. These assets enjoyed a brief respite from revolutionary appropriations before being swept up in the less generally anticipated urban land nationalization.

ORGANIZING THE RURAL MASSES

It took only an act of will to declare a new order for the countryside where about ninety percent of Ethiopians pass their generally brief lives. Bringing it into being was another matter altogether. Enforcement was only part of the problem, in the longer run probably a decidedly smaller part. The proclamation established a structure leaving much to be filled in. How, for instance, was land from farms exceeding the ten-hectare limit to be distributed? Listing broad priorities among potential recipients—for example, evicted tenants residing in the area, the landless, those with insufficient land—as the law does, left space for an almost infinite number of additional and inevitable choices. Identical quantities of land, after all, vary enormously in present and potential value. Land could not simply be distributed like sacks of rice to persons in each category until the supply was exhausted. Only persons familiar with local conditions could make an equitable and sensible allocation. Local officials might have the requisite knowledge; but, since they were on the whole beneficiaries of the preexisting system, the Dergue could not trust them. That left the peasants themselves.

The need to localize centers of decision was one reason for the law's requirement that peasant associations be formed throughout the country. A second reason was enforcement. Eritrea and the Somali threat committed most of the regime's troops. The rest were required to police Addis and a few other major cities and as a mobile reserve for use against the mini-insurrections that continually boiled up around the country. In large measure, then, the peasants had to expedite their own revolutionary destiny. Organization would give them power. It would at the same time impose some discipline on a necessarily untidy process, provide links between the individual peasant and the public authorities, and lay the basis for communally organized activities such as marketing, the purchase and maintenance of machines, and so on. Finally, the units that would be established might some day define the limits of collectives and state farms, if the regime ultimately chose to move in that direction.

To these notional peasant associations, one for every 800 hectares, the Dergue, through its initial and subsequent proclamations, awarded an intimidating number of tasks: expropriation and distribution of land; administration and conservation of public property, including forests and bodies of water (reservoirs, lakes, etc.); establishment of judicial tribunals which would have exclusive authority to hear land disputes arising within the area of the association; establishment of marketing and credit cooperatives; construction of schools, clinics and other welfare institutions; and organization of peasant defense squads and other groups needed for productive activities or to support government programs.

If these peasant associations—averaging one for each 800 hectares—were formed throughout Ethiopia, they would number around 50,000. To oversee this vast assemblage, the government decreed the establishment of two higher levels of peasant self-administration. Under the law, the executive committees of the local associations, clustered into groups of about 100 each, would constitute the second or *woreda* level which would in turn elect delegates to form the apex of the system, the *awraja* level. The *woreda*-level associations were empowered to alter the geographic boundaries of local associations in order to promote equality among them, to request a local association to distribute land to particular landless persons, and to establish a tribunal to hear appeals from first-level tribunals. Tribunals would also function at the *awraja* level but only to resolve disputes between associations. The *awraja*-level associations were apparently intended as the main point of contact with the government ministries, communicating grassroots requests to the relevant ministries and promoting local compliance with government directives. In addition, they might serve as a kind of planning unit for projects affecting a large piece of the countryside.

All of this was theory. The human resources available at the center for translating the law into fact were not exactly luxurious. Local officials tended to be corrupt, incompetent, and complicit in the traditional order. Never a singular beneficiary of imperial or parliamentary favor (the parliament having been dominated by landowners), the Ministry of Land Reform had only a handful of officials (most of them ill trained) available for work in the field. By cannibalizing other ministries, the Dergue could have enlarged the number of Land Reform Ministry officials by a factor of five or ten; even then the resulting cadres were grossly insufficient in relation to Ethiopia's size and population, as well as to the immensity of the proposed reforms. Moreover, young and able civil servants were needed to replace unsympathetic, politically-suspect, or uneducated officials at every level of government, but particularly in Addis and the main provincial centers. Peasants were already implementing one essential feature of the reform in some parts of the country, acting for the first time as masters of their land. But in other areas they were still harnessed by landlord power or by a reflex of obedience; or possibly some were even uninformed about revolutionary developments in Addis.

Transferring the land to its tillers was only one of the reform's objectives. The Dergue also wanted to create a great reservoir of supporters that could be mobilized to help provide services needed to increase production and enhance welfare and to establish a framework for effective control of the countryside. In short, the Dergue needed cadres who would attempt to organize as well as galvanize the peasant masses. In 1974, only the students, heavily concentrated in the university and the secondary schools of Addis, could provide them.

Consequently, shortly after promulgating the basic reform law, the government announced that the entire student population of the university in Addis and of the senior secondary schools would be dispatched to the countryside to assist in implementing the decreed reforms and to promote modernization. Not all students embraced this sudden, heroic opportunity with unqualified zeal. Student opposition flowed in part from the absence of prior consultation and the anticipation of rude conditions of life in the Bronze Age countryside, in part from the dark suspicion that the Dergue's overriding motive was to remove a rumbling source of opposition from the center of power.

Throughout the sixties and on into the seventies, as the student population had multiplied, relations between students and the various elements of the security forces had been decidedly on the ragged side. As a group, the former were the one consistent center of root-and-branch opposition to the established order of things, although by virtue of receiving a higher education they were assured a comparatively comfortable place in it. Over the years they had at intervals been clubbed, gassed, imprisoned, expelled, and, on occasion, shot down by security forces sent to pacify demonstrations or terminate subversive meetings.

When the armed forces had at last moved against the Emperor, the students had rallied in support. But although it is probable that at least a few of the younger officers had attended the university and virtually all shared the students' desire for the modernization of Ethiopia, during the turbulent months preceding the Emperor's fall, the Dergue, swathed in secrecy, remained aloof.

The sense of being as much outside the ambit of decision-making as passive time-servers in the civil service must have galled the young men and women who, after years of student protests, undoubtedly saw themselves as the true vanguard of the revolution. Gall was succeeded by deep concern once the character of the new order became manifest following Aman's death. An open system in which students, workers, and soldiers would together remake Ethiopia through collective decisions held no apparent allure for the Dergue.

So some students resisted only to have the Dergue once again demonstrate both its effective control of the means of coercion and its willingness to employ them. Almost a thousand students soon found themselves under detention. The remainder, whether enthusiasts or skeptics, were trucked out into the immense countryside for a rendezvous with the rural masses many miles and in some respects a psychological millennium away.

As far as one can tell from the slender news brought back by a few adventurous scholars and diplomats, supplemented by trustworthy Ethiopian sources and between-the-lines reading of official declarations, things went much better than one might have suspected. Perhaps three-quarters of the 57,000 students reportedly trucked out to the countryside remained there for appreciable periods actively bearing the glad tidings and proposing and goading action.

Sometimes they were too successful in marshalling peasant discontent and focusing hostility on local officials whose natural antagonism for these young firebrands the firebrands cordially reciprocated. The Dergue soon made clear that, whatever its ultimate ends, it had no immediate intention of dismantling local administration—still, of course, appointed in and ruled from Addis—in favor of the incipient peasant associations, the probable prevalence and efficacy of which were merely speculative. In a number of cases where students attempted to gut the authority of the local administration, the Dergue intervened on the latter's behalf. Students probably had a good deal of trouble of a more lethal kind with alliances of local landowners in areas where the peasants were inert and the Dergue's grasp not yet felt. But despite the immense difficulties faced by these young revolutionaries, they clearly played an impressive part in giving shape and substance to the great reform.

Reform has made the greatest progress in areas (mostly in the central, southern, and western provinces) previously characterized by absentee landlords with large holdings worked by numerous tenants often under very onerous terms. Although it effectively stripped the Ethiopian elite of its economic base in the countryside, the reform did not and plainly was not intended to produce instant equality. A farmer with ten hectares of fertile land and oxen to pull his plow lives within the dreams but far beyond the reach of the numerous former tenants now blessed with the right to occupy the hectare or two from which they had been scratching a living. According to reports, the gaps among farmers are actually a good deal wider than the ten-hectare limit would imply because holdings of twenty and thirty hectares have thus far generally escaped expropriation.

So if the great landowners are gone and the gentry gone as well or reduced to the level of farmers, a relatively wealthy kulak class remains, probably strengthened by the removal of their social and economic betters. Unless and until the Dergue or whatever other group controls the state brings credit, marketing facilities, extension services, and other forms of assistance to the countryside, wealthy peasants with animals for rent and surplus cash to lend, and equipped with the greater education and know-how normally coincident with relative wealth, will tend to exercise political as well as economic power within whatever legal and administrative structures Addis may establish. This tendency may be overcome, however, by the militant young cadres multiplying out of the Dergue's training programs.

Below the poorest farmers—now at least confirmed in possession and liberated from the burden of crop-sharing (if they had been tenants) and various fees extracted by the local elite—are the great number of landless peasants: life-long laborers or tenants expelled before the revolution by landholders moving, often with the guidance or assistance of aid donors like the World Bank, into more capital-intensive commercial farming. Since tenancy and private wage labor have been abolished, this desperate rural subproletariat must be resettled or its members will be carried by the current of their despair into the hungry cities and will be doomed to drift there hopelessly until the countryside is wealthy enough to provide a market for Ethiopian industry. To millions of Ethiopians reform is only a promise of relief from absolute poverty, a promise requiring great political will, large additional resources, and certainly peace for its fulfillment.

But peace is a dream. The reality is a Groszian nightmare of hatred and betrayal, of lust for power and freedom, and of death. Perhaps this reality is the sign of a real revolution in any large, old, and complicated society filled with a million accumulated animosities and aspirations for so long held tensely at bay by power ringed with an enormous, because hardly questioned, authority.

URBAN REFORMS

Though determined to monopolize real power, the Dergue was sensitive to the need for mass support. Land to the tillers was one means to that end. The urban land and extra-house nationalization proclaimed in July, 1975, was another.

It's value inflated by virtue of its attractions to an upper class with surplus wealth and few other local investment opportunities, urban land was owned by a very small number of people. A 1966 survey, for instance, indicated that five percent of the population of Addis owned ninety-five percent of all privately-held land. Although ownership of houses was less concentrated, surveys made in the late 1960s showed tenancy to be the norm: sixty percent of the housing units in Addis and seventy percent in Asmara were rented.

As the government-controlled press noted with increasing vehemence in the months preceding the decree, rent income sustained or aggravated the vast discrepancies in the distribution of wealth that the Dergue proposed to eliminate. The fact that rural landholders fearing nationalization of their estates had preemptively shifted resources into urban land speculation only intensified demands for urban land reform. It soon came, essentially in the form previously adopted for the countryside.

For the purposes of this discussion the law's sophisticated complexities* are largely irrelevant. Basically, it nationalized all urban land, shops, multifamily dwellings, and single-family homes that were not occupied by their owners. Tenants were confirmed in their possession of a house and up to 500 square meters of associated land and were relieved of rent, debt, and other obligations owed to the landlords. In effect they became tenants of the state; in fact, however, tenancies seem to have been transformed into cooperatives, explained below. As an interim measure pending adoption of a new rent schedule, the law cut rents from fifteen percent on the most substantial homes to a maximum of fifty percent on the poorest.

The new law also paralleled its rural predecessor in establishing a hierarchy of associations designed both to facilitate grass-roots cooperation and to extend the nerves of government. A neighborhood or *kebele,* defined for this purpose as 300 to 500 contiguous households, is the basic unit to be organized into a cooperative society of urban dwellers. Each society must establish an executive committee, a public welfare committee, and a judicial tribunal (to hear land and housing disputes) and presumably is free to create other mechanisms which its members deem necessary to carry out the society's multiple functions which include: maintaining nationalized units, collecting land and house rents up to $E100 (the few rents above that threshold would be collected by the Ministry of Public Works and Housing), setting up schools and clinics in cooperation with government agencies, constructing roads and low-rent housing units, and protecting life and property within its jurisdiction.

After 1,200 to 1,400 students commissioned to organize the associations were summarily detained for alleged dissidence, the Dergue

---

* For an excellent description and analysis on which I have heavily relied, see John M. Cohen and Peter H. Koehn, "Rural and Urban Land Reform in Ethiopia," *African Law Studies* 14 (1977), pp. 26-40.

conscripted and rapidly trained 900 civil service and military personnel. Particularly in Addis, organization proceeded very rapidly, despite the fact that the *kebele* boundaries were purposely defined to cut
across those of the well established self-help associations whose leaders were generally wealthy and persons of status under the old regime. Dergue organizers attempted to find a new leadership more in
tune with revolutionary ideals. By September, 1975, most of Addis's
300 *kebeles* had elected provisional committees instructed to carry on
the organizational task.

As the *kebeles* developed into functioning units, the rest of the organizational pyramid could easily be constructed. In the larger con-
urbations the pyramid had three levels, the highest one being the
Central Cooperative Society empowered to coordinate the lower
units. In Addis itself, the pyramid rose through five levels. Whatever
the highest level—in smaller towns there were only two—a later proclamation endowed it with many of the functions and attributes of the
preexisting municipal governments.

When the underground opposition in the cities, above all the
EPRP, launched its campaign of urban terrorism, the Dergue turned
to the *kebeles* for the raw material of counterterror. Within each *kebele*
it organized squads to support regular troops in carrying out the work
of maintaining order. Aside from helping to manufacture corpses,
the *kebeles* must have proved an invaluable source of intelligence to an
army that without them might easily have been isolated in a sea of
hidden enemies.

After reaching an initial peak in a 1977 May-Day weekend massacre, the killing dropped off modestly before it reached an unparal-
leled crescendo in November when Mengistu arranged the execution
of his vice-chairman, Atnafu Abate, the one Dergue member who
seemed almost Mengistu's equal in power and authority. In April
Abate had warned that "a thousand reactionaries [would] die for
every revolutionary murdered." Through no choice of his own, he
joined the swelling thousands.

Calling unabashedly for a "red terror" to overwhelm the "white
terror," Mengistu directed the Dergue's security forces, *kebele* vigi-
lantes, worker's defense squads, and elements of the newly trained
peasant's militia into a new orgy of killing. One diplomatic source
estimated the slaughter of 10,000 mostly young Ethiopians between
November, 1977, and March, 1978.

Struggles for Power and Autonomy

To an outsider, possibly to many of those inside as well, the political
struggles in Ethiopia of the past four years approximate that hyper-
bolic Churchillian image—the riddle buried in an enigma. Organizations of a political sort clutter the Ethiopian urban landscape. Some

seem to have died at birth; others flare suddenly into life, pursue a meteoric career, then abruptly subside into senescence or are even extinguished altogether. One struggles to make sense out of this shifting set of players, to sort out ideological, regional, ethnic, personal, and other conceivable motives.

Some things are clear. To begin with, the Dergue has contended with two essentially different kinds of foes: those, like the Somalis and Eritreans and Afars, who are struggling either to detach themselves wholly from the febrile body of the old Empire or at least to win local autonomy; and those, like the Ethiopian Democratic Union (EDU) and the Ethiopian Peoples Revolutionary Party (EPRP), intent on wresting control of the state machinery from the Dergue.

THE RIVALS OF THE DERGUE

It is also clear that for at least two years, 1976 and 1977, the EPRP succeeded in mounting a powerful, well-organized conspiratorial challenge in Addis and the main provincial cities. Its militants and sympathizers numbered in the thousands and were drawn principally from the ranks of students, the urban middle class (especially civil servants and school teachers), and the working-class aristocracy—people who at the time of the revolution were securely employed in the private sector at wages well above minimum subsistence levels and were for the most part unionized. These middle-class Ethiopians were disillusioned for the same reasons as many of the students had been: They were locked outside the engine room of the revolution they had sought and to some extent helped to make. The unions, after lending strong support to the coup, thus emboldening the military while unnerving the Emperor's men, quickly became restless under the new dispensation. Prices remained high, wages far below the aspirations of these worker aristocrats who, with their regular wages drawn from the tiny modern industrial and commercial sectors of the economy, stood far above the great mass of the population.

The new government did not court popularity. It encouraged no pretense. The function of workers was to work. Strikes were forbidden. When the economy improved, they would be rewarded. In the meantime—but this was implicit—the first claims on the bulging national reserves were drought relief, rural reform, and military refurbishment, not necessarily in that order of precedence. When the workers threatened to manifest their disillusion by meetings, pamphleteering, and parades, they discovered that the new rulers were, if anything, less charitable toward dissidence than the Emperor had been.

In September, 1975, a year after the Emperor's fall, the Dergue, faced with a general strike-threat from the 125,000-member Ethiopian Labour Confederation, sent its security forces raging through the streets of Addis. Their orders: to arrest anyone distributing the confederation's manifesto condemning the Dergue and demanding the establishment of democratic liberties. When unarmed Ethiopian Airlines employees attempted to prevent the arrest of a coworker engaged in distributing the manifesto, the security forces opened fire, killing four and wounding twenty-nine. A false peace settled briefly over the capital.

In Begemdir and adjacent west Tigre, the EDU—a makeshift amalgam of liberals and conservatives including some real luminaries of the old order—harassed the Dergue's lines of communication and occasionally beseiged and once or twice actually occupied larger towns only to be driven out by government reenforcements. Although the EDU has sanctuary in the Sudan* and can operate in rugged terrain suited to guerrilla tactics—terrain that has the added advantage of being occupied by a conservative peasantry attached to the national church and with a long history of antagonism to central authority—it does not seem to have acquired momentum in spite of some early success. Internal divisions—between Shoans and Tigres, conservatives and leftists—have not helped. Although its announced program of democratic reform along lines drawn by European social democratic parties has an obvious ideological appeal to the United States and other Western nations, the EDU's proposals do not seem to impress Western diplomats, normally given to wishful thinking.

The EDU shares the field in Tigre with the Tigrean Popular Liberation Front (TPLF), a reputedly Marxist group recruited from the province's small urban intelligentsia. Orginally espousing Tigrean secession, possibly as a prelude to federation with an independent Eritrea, by 1978 its declarations began to emphasize class rather than ethnic struggle. With its modest numbers, estimated at no more than 2,000, and its geographic isolation, if the TPLF has any future at all it would seem to be as an auxiliary of the neighboring EPLF.

The extent of active and passive opposition to the Dergue in the principal cities has been unclear. For a time it may have been general among students in Addis, extending down even into the primary schools. We know, at least, that squads operating under the Dergue's aegis massacred children who were no more than eleven or twelve for distributing anti-regime leaflets and other "subversive" acts.

The fact that during the day most people go about their work, that the wheels of government, commerce, and industry keep turning reveals little beyond the central but obvious fact that the Dergue enjoys an overwhelming preponderance of naked force. Open opposition is suicidal. And people have to eat. All one can finally say is that the actions carried out by the EPRP (including bold assassinations of regime luminaries and the clandestine publication of two newspapers), the vehemence of the Dergue's propaganda, the ferocity and

* The prevailing situation is obscure.

dimensions of its countersubversive or "red terror" campaign, and the number of urban dissidents reportedly killed (diplomatic sources estimate at least 10,000 in a country where not many more than a couple of million people, including the subproletariat, live in the larger cities) together evidence a broadly-based opposition movement.

Civilian opposition plainly has not been uniform. In fact, one apparent cause of the holocaust that engulfed Addis in late 1976 and continued throughout the following year was the EPRP's struggle not only with the Dergue itself but also with a civilian group, Mei'son, allied with the Dergue and competing at least rhetorically with the EPRP in protestations of revolutionary purity. Led by Haile Fida, a Sorbonne-educated Marxist who returned to Ethiopia in 1975 to become ideological advisor to Mengistu Haile Mariam, Mei'son was for a time the most important of several groups—led, like the EPRP, by former members of the students' movement—who chose collaboration with the military as a means for advancing the revolution and, one might cynically suppose, themselves. Its leaders, aside from Haile Fida, held a number of government ministries. But Mei'son's main role and opportunity lay in a mandate winkled out of the Dergue to indoctrinate and mobilize both the peasant and the urban neighborhood associations. The Dergue now accuses Mei'son militants of being agents of the 1977 pre-May Day massacres which reportedly took the lives of 300 to 500 students, many not yet in their teens, although there seems little doubt that regular troops also were involved.

While persons suspected of EPRP membership were being stacked up like so many cords of wood in the morgue and along the streets of Addis, Mei'son flared brightly and then died to an ember. Without warning, Haile Fida, Daniel Tadesse (Minister of Urban Development and Housing), and other leaders simply disappeared. Some reports had them dead. According to others, they were imprisoned. A third rumor, which had them making their way surreptitiously back to their home province of Wollega, raises the question, mooted before and after Mei'son's demise, whether ideology or provincial loyalty fueled its bid for power. The question and the lack of any consensus answer underscores the inability to fix the dominant character of political competition among groups with a common class or professional base. At the same time, Mei'son's eclipse does reenforce a more substantive and important conclusion—that the Dergue, or at least the faction led by Mengistu Haile Mariam, has no intention at present of sharing power with civilian groups of any kind.

ETHNIC DISSIDENCE

Except as a program for shifting the country's center of gravity away from Shoa, a separatist nationalism seems incongruous in a province like Tigre that has always been part of the country's cultural and political heartland. The recrudescence of Oromo nationalism in the southern provinces, where Amhara masters had for generations exploited the native peasantry, was an altogether different matter. The tenants might be grateful for liberation from their landlords without necessarily developing a sudden attachment to an Addis-based government. Moreover, having at last become de facto masters of their own land, the Oromos may resent pressure for collectivization coming from the Dergue's student legionnaires.

We know that there is insurgency among Oromos. Beyond that we know very little, except that the insurgency does not now seem to be regarded by the Dergue as a major threat. One suspects that most farmers will stick to farming as long as the Dergue refrains from forced collectivization and high taxation. History nevertheless suggests the dangers of underrating the potency of a long-suppressed nationalism.

The Afar nomads of the eastern lowlands have represented another center of ethnic dissidence. Numbering less than 200,000, this very traditional and distinctive people, adherents of Islam, inhabit the forbidding terrain between southern Eritrea and the port of Djibouti.

With the possible exception of the small number of Afars who have entered the modern economy, Afar tribesmen on both sides of the border owed at least nominal allegiance to Sultan Ali Mireh Hanfare who, like his predecessors, headquartered until June, 1975, in the small oasis town of Asieta, located 340 miles east of Addis near the border of the French territory. He had initially given his backing to the Dergue on the understanding that it would generally follow the Emperor's policy of treating the sultan's domain as a de facto semi-autonomous fiefdom. It appears that relations began to curdle when, in the course of its desperate offensive in the fall of 1974, the ELF extended its operations into Afar country in the extreme south of Eritrea near the port of Assab. Since it is widely assumed in Ethiopia that, as one diplomat put it, "nothing goes on in Afar territory for very long without the sultan's knowledge or expressed consent,"[5] the Dergue undoubtedly concluded that the sultan was an undependable associate. Perhaps that is one reason it began, as part of the land reform program, to move highlanders down into the Afar grazing lands.

It was a risk and arguably not a very well-calculated one. Nothing short of a direct attack on the sultan was more likely to incite rebellion. And rebellion by the reportedly 5,000 well-armed men subject to the sultan's direction would threaten Ethiopia's two southern lifelines to the Red Sea—the road linking Addis Ababa to Assab and the Franco-Ethiopian railway with its coastal terminus in Djibouti. Periodic interdiction of the route to Massawa, along with its perpetual hazards, had aggravated Addis's dependence on these other two ports. In addition, practically all of the country's petroleum supplies are carried inland by tank trucks from the aging refinery at Assab.

Perhaps it was the vulnerability of the Assab and Djibouti routes, together with the perceived unreliability of the sultan, which led first to the introduction of alien highlanders and then to a build-up of troops. And these considerations may have been compounded by the regime's manifest intolerance of alternative sources of power or authority as well as of every vestige of traditional society. Whatever its motives, the regime's actions had one probable outcome.

It is unclear just what ignited the kindling. One spark would have sufficed. What we do know is that in June, 1975, the Dergue attacked Asieta, reportedly with jet aircraft and tanks, driving the sultan and many of his followers across the border into French territory. At about the same time, Afar warriors damaged a key bridge on the Assab road, producing a run on gasoline supplies in the capital. The interruption of traffic was, however, temporary. Since then, the Dergue's overwhelming military superiority seems to have reduced guerrilla activities to the level of a dangerous nuisance.

The Afars revolt confounded the Dergue with enemies along its entire eastern flank: in the north, there were the Eritreans; below them, the Afars; and finally, for over a thousand miles from Djibouti to the Kenya border, the great hereditary foe—the Somalis.

Notes

1. For a sympathetic account of the EPLF's achievements, see Gerard Chaliand, "The Horn of Africa's Dilemma," *Foreign Policy* 30 (Spring 1978): 116-131. Chaliand, a French political scientist, spent two months in Eritrea with the EPLF in 1977.

2. John M. Cohen, "Ethiopia After Haile Selassie: The Government Land Factor," *African Affairs* 72 (October 1973) and R.K. Pankhurst, *State and Land in Ethiopian History* (Addis Ababa: Institute of Ethiopian Studies, 1966).

3. John M. Cohen, Arthur A. Goldsmith, and John W. Mellor, "Rural Development Issues Following Ethiopian Land Reform," *Africa Today* 23 (April-June 1976), p. 11.

4. John M. Cohen and Peter H. Koehn, "Rural and Urban Land Reform in Ethiopia," *African Law Studies* 14 (1977), p. 7.

5. *Financial Times,* June 20, 1975, p. 7.

Part Two

Ethiopia and the Somalis

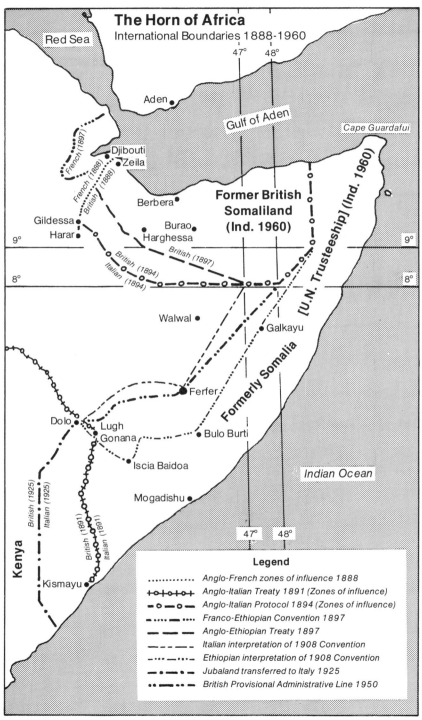

The Horn of Africa
International Boundaries 1888-1960

Red Sea

47° 48°

Aden

Gulf of Aden

Cape Guardafui

French (1897)

French (1888)
British (1888)

Djibouti
Zeila

Berbera

Former British Somaliland (Ind. 1960)

Gildessa
Harar

Burao
Harghessa

British (1897)

9°   9°

British (1894)
Italian (1894)

8°   8°

Walwal

Galkayu

[U.N. Trusteeship] (Ind. 1960)

Formerly Somalia

Ferfer

Dolo
Lugh
Gonana

Bulo Burti

Iscia Baidoa

Indian Ocean

Mogadishu

Kenya

British (1925)
Italian (1925)

British (1891)
Italian (1891)

47° 48°

Kismayu

Legend

·············	Anglo-French zones of influence 1888
+0+0+0+	Anglo-Italian Treaty 1891 (Zones of influence)
—0—0—	Anglo-Italian Protocol 1894 (Zones of influence)
—·····—·····—	Franco-Ethiopian Convention 1897
— — —	Anglo-Ethiopian Treaty 1897
– – – –	Italian interpretation of 1908 Convention
—···—···—	Ethiopian interpretation of 1908 Convention
—·—·—·—	Jubaland transferred to Italy 1925
··—··—··—	British Provisional Administrative Line 1950

© John Drysdale. *The Somali Dispute* (New York: Praeger, 1964). Reprinted by permission of the publisher.

The Roots of Conflict 4

The Land and People

Peripheral threats to the Ethiopian empire assume a common geometric form. Like the Eritreans, the Somalis occupy a triangular slice of East Africa. Its base is the African littoral of the Gulf of Aden stretching from Djibouti to the easternmost tip of the continent at Cape Guardafui roughly parallel to the southeastern coast of the Arabian Peninsula. Its peak thrusts deeply into northeast Kenya. The Indian Ocean bounds it on one long side, the great East African Rift on the other. The result is an area of some 370,000 square miles, nearly as large as Ethiopia.*

Except in the narrow belt between the two southern rivers, the Juba and the Shebelle, and in the far northwest of the plateau overlapping the political frontier with Ethiopia, the land is an arid savannah, an endless vista of coarse grass punctuated by thorn trees, giant anthills, and the thick-trunked baobabs.

This severe land supports a population variously estimated at three and a half to five million people, about three-quarters of whom are nomadic pastoralists. Though most nomads have sheep, goats, and cattle as well, the camel is king. John Drysdale, a former member of the British colonial administration, explains why:

> The Somali camel, a one-humped beast, can go longer without water than any other breed of camel. In the very driest weather it need not be watered more than once every three weeks. It can thus browse a hundred miles or so from the nearest wells. Herdsmen will drive their camels in the dry season to pastures seven days distant from the wells, graze them for a week and march

---

* This is the area occupied by the Somali people; the Democratic Republic of Somalia occupies an area of 246,000 square miles.

them back again for water; and repeat this performance for three
or four months between [rainy] seasons. . . . The nomad subsists
during this period entirely on camel's milk. Not even the morn-
ing dew passes between his lips; that he collects to wash himself.[1]

The Somalis are as culturally uniform as the Ethiopians are mixed.
From Djibouti in the north to Kenya's Tana River in the south, they
speak a common language, enjoy a rich oral literature centered on
poetic forms, organize communal life around similar, egalitarian social institutions, distinguish themselves from their Bantu and Nilotic
neighbors by emphasizing a geneology stretching back to an original
Arab ancestor, and manifest a powerful devotion to Islam. These cultural factors as well as the millennial occupation of contiguous territory and at least 500 years of intermittent conflict with the Christian
occupants of the Ethiopian plateau make for an indisputable shared
sense of nationhood. That sense has survived long association with
Hamitic kinsmen who border them on three sides: the Afars (or Dan-
akils) in the north and the various branches of the Galla in the west
and south. Surviving as well the political divisions imposed initially
during the colonial scramble and partially sustained—in some ways
aggravated—through the era of decolonization, that sense now constitutes the root of the Somali problem.

Ethnologists agree that the Somalis made an unambiguous appearance on the historical stage about A.D. 1000 along the coast of
the Gulf of Aden. During the next 900 years, they gradually elbowed
their way south until, at the turn of the twentieth century, they
reached the Tana River.

The word *they* is deceptive if taken to mean a well-organized collective thrust. Despite their cultural bonds, the Somalis did not move,
think, or act as a political unit. They were divided into a few great
clan-families, subdivided into clans, and then divided once again into
patrilineal kinship groups. Each individual Somali had some sense of
attachment to each of these progressively smaller hereditary groupings; but as Ian Lewis, a leading British authority on the Somalis, has
noted,

> . . . his most binding and most frequently mobilized loyalty is to
> his *diya*-paying group. This unit with a fighting strength of from
> a few hundred to a few thousand men, consists of close kinsmen
> united by a specific contractual alliance whose terms stipulate that
> they should pay and receive blood-compensation (Arabic, *diya*) in
> concert. An injury done by or to any member of the group impli-
> cates all those who are a party to its treaty. Thus if a man of one
> group is killed by a man of another, the first group will collec-
> tively claim the damages due from the second. At the same time
> within any group a high degree of co-operation and mutual col-
> laboration prevails.[2]

Originating in the harshest area of the Horn except for the Danakil Depression, the Somalis moved south—and to a limited degree west—in search of pasture and water. There is no sign that they moved as a horde, pouring down the northeast flank of Africa in one irresistible flow. Rather, there must have been an irregular progression of salient and then consolidation effected by the periodic mobilization of *diya* and larger kin groupings as required by the nature of the opposition.

The main opposition came from the Galla, who had preceded the Somalis as wanderers through the reaches of the Horn. Some historians believe that one reason for the sustained Galla surge from the southwest into the Ethiopian highlands during the late sixteenth and seventeenth centuries was intensification of the Somali push south. In an ironic sequence of cause and effect, according to this theory, Galla triumphs followed by Amhara recovery and partial assimilation of the Galla elite finally closed off Somali expansion westward and thus fixed the ultimate dimensions of Somali occupation.

Gallas were not the only opponents. Parochial allegiances and, above all, the exigencies of survival in a harsh environment produced conflict among Somalis themselves, generally organized around *diya*-paying groups.

The story of Somali expansion is not only a tale of conflict. There were also some elements of cooperation and integration with prior inhabitants of the Horn and to some extent with Persian merchants who founded trading colonies at scattered locations along the coast.

But these are mere footnotes to the main tale of Somali expansion largely through the violent expulsion of predecessor peoples and the consequent establishment of a single cultural nation in continuous occupation of a vast though impoverished territory, spreading westward from the sea to the long interface with Ethiopian power.

The interface passes through three more or less distinct areas. Beginning in the north, there is the high, relatively well-watered, and regrettably small region of sorghum cultivation running between the Somali provincial center of Harghessa and Harar, an ancient Muslim city annexed by Menelik in 1887. While part of the region is cultivated by Somali farmers, because of its abundant water during the winter dry season it is also an important gathering place for the pastoral northern clans.

South of this region is a broad sweep of dry grassland, now entirely under Ethiopian administration, called the Haud. Lacking any permanent source of water, it is habitable only during and shortly following the rainy seasons. The fact that it is used transiently makes its pasturage superior to the heavily grazed areas farther north. In the south, the Haud merges with the still larger plains of the Ogaden which, in turn, roll south across the Kenya border. On the west, the plains sweep up to the Ethiopian highlands. On the east, they slip imperceptibly into the southern lowlands of Somalia.

The economic links among these areas and between them and the remainder of Somali-occupied territory are as intimate as the cultural ones. Spring and autumn see several hundred thousand herdsmen from both northern and central Somalia flooding into every part of the Haud. Somalis from the Ogaden move their herds and flocks into the Haud's periphery. After the rains, some northern clansmen, rather than returning home, go down to the wells of Ogaden clans who welcome them in reciprocity for assistance rendered by the northerners in connection with the export of livestock through the port of Berbera. Ogaden Somalis, some of whom move back and forth across the political border in their restless search for better pasture, also export livestock through the southern ports of Mogadishu and Kismayu. This, at least, was the timeless order of life before the devastation wrought by drought and the Ogaden war.

Cultural homogeneity, a tradition of conflict with the Amharas and Gallas, and economic dependence on an open border would be sufficient in themselves to generate a powerful irredentist sentiment. Dispersal of clan families and smaller lineage groups across the surrounding international frontiers intensifies that sentiment. It is rather as if during the sixteenth century the Scottish highlands had been divided into an English-controlled shire and an independent kingdom and that the resulting border had passed right through the middle of Campbell, Macgregor, and other clan lands. If, in addition, English troops had engaged in periodic "tax-collecting" expeditions against the segments of the clan-families over whom they were nominally sovereign, what highland government could have afforded to ignore the issue of "lost lands," at least while there was any real hope for their recovery?

The Colonial Partitions

The origin of existing frontiers on the Horn of Africa can easily be traced as far back as the last European scramble for African territories, which erupted on the continent like a plague in the last quarter of the nineteenth century. British, French, and Italian interests mingled competitively in and around the Horn.

The British were concerned about insuring the continuity of meat supplies from Somalia for their naval base across the gulf in Aden, a splendid port set down in the middle of rocky desolation. A modest degree of order on the Somali coast and unhindered movement along the caravan routes from the interior were essential to stable exports.

During the 1870s, these conditions were maintained by an Egyptian force that occupied the main northern ports and the interior of the Somali plateau as far west as Harar. Although initially hostile to the Egyptian presence, the British gradually recognized that occupation of the Somali coast by the army of a government over which it exercised considerable and growing influence was not inimical to their ancillary interests in the territory. In 1877, they formally recognized Egyptian jurisdiction and pressured the Italians, then ensconced around Assab, to recognize Egyptian sovereignty to the north and south.

The subsequent British occupation of Egypt in 1882 would only have enhanced the charms of an Egyptian proxy opposite Aden if the Mahdists had not, in the meantime, set about expelling the Egyptians and their British patrons from the Sudan. London concluded on behalf of Cairo that the Mahdist threat required the recall of Egyptian forces from peripheral assignments.

Gloomy intelligence from the English consul on the Somali coast followed the decision to withdraw. He predicted an outbreak of fighting between the Somalis and Gallas in the interior and an assault by the northern clans on the retiring Egyptian columns. There was, moreover, news of Mahdist stirrings among the Somalis and, to complicate matters still further, the prospect of incursions from the increasingly powerful emperor of the Abyssinians. So despite their reluctance to assume the costs of a direct presence, the British resolved to fill the imminent vacuum.

The way to a low-profile British occupation was prepared by the negotiation of treaties of protection with the elders of the Somali clans. There are two related explanations for Somali receptivity to British overtures. On the one hand, the Somalis probably were already sensitive to the growing Abyssinian power along their western flank. On the other, the agreements urged on them by the British appeared similar in character to the contractual alliances used so extensively in Somali clan politics. In the preamble of each treaty, the Somali party declared its purpose to be "the maintenance of our independence, the preservation of order, and other good and sufficient reasons." No land was ceded. Each clan simply pledged "never to cede, sell, mortgage, or otherwise give for occupation, save to the British Government, any portion of the territory presently inhabited by them or being under their control." The British, on their part, undertook to extend to the clansmen concerned and to their territories "the gracious favour and protection of Her Majesty the Queen-Empress."

By the end of 1884, as the Egyptians were beginning their pullout from the interior, three British vice-consuls were established on the Somali coast, prepared—with the aid of forty members of the Aden police, one hundred Somali coast police who were quickly recruited and armed, and an irregular force of armed caravan guards paid by the concerned merchants—to protect the slender national interest which had deposited them on that very unpacific littoral.

They were given explicit directions that their duties were those of British agents in a native state: they were to keep the peace, but not to assume powers beyond this. No grandiose schemes were to be entertained; expenditure was to be limited to a minimum, and was to be provided by the local port revenues.[3]

Almost immediately this plan for a wafer-thin, low-cost presence was threatened by a Gallic encroachment from the north. The French, having negotiated a protectorate agreement with that part of the Issa clan dominant in the Djibouti area, claimed jurisdiction over the port of Djibouti in the face of British insistence that the port fell within the sphere of its own protectorate. After much public gnashing of teeth and flexing of muscles, the two powers were suddenly seized by a taste for conciliation. Under the Anglo-French agreement of 1888, they recognized a line between Djibouti and Zeila as the frontier of French Somaliland and the British Somaliland Protectorate. It was a tidy little arrangement marred only by a dubious consistency with the protective obligations assumed by both parties in their respective agreements with the Issas.

For the French, as for the British, the Horn's importance stemmed from its location astride the short route to Europe. The Italians, late-comers to the Game of Nations, found the Horn arresting in its own right, there being few other places left where one could act out tardy dreams of empire. Their occupation of the Eritrean coast was facilitated by the British who, while preferring an exclusive hegemony along the Red Sea, were prepared during the early 1880s to favor a relatively weak Italy there over a considerably more puissant France.

With the coast in hand, the Italians began vigorously laying the foundations for military disaster. At first, however, everything seemed to be proceeding smoothly. They established cordial relations with King Menelik of Shoa and administered a defeat, albeit an ambiguous one, to the forces of the Tigrean emperor, Yohannes. Following the death of Yohannes in 1889, Menelik, having succeeded to the imperial throne, concluded the Treaty of Ucciali with the Italians. It recognized their sovereignty over Eritrea and, as construed by the Italians, committed Menelik to conduct his foreign relations through them, an interpretation which reduced Ethiopia to the status of a protectorate. Menelik would later claim that the Amharic version of the treaty did not contain any such commitment.

For the time being, however, he humored his Italian allies. They responded generously with loans, arms, and ammunition. Moreover, in 1890 they sponsored Ethiopian participation in the Brussels General Act, which empowered Ethiopia as a Christian state to import munitions legally, thus legitimizing the active arms trade it had been carrying on for some years with French merchants. The influx of modern weapons completely destabilized the relationship between indigenous forces. They enabled Menelik first to consolidate his hold over the plateau and then to launch his own imperial mission as well as to decimate the armies of his erstwhile superior. Fanning out in a long arc from southeast to southwest, in ten years Menelik's troops doubled the size of his kingdom. By the early 1890s, they were encroaching on the Somali lands along virtually their entire western margin. Meanwhile, the Italians, naively secure in their northern salient, were establishing, with British blessings, a second East African presence, this one on the Indian Ocean along the Benadir coast between the Juba River and the British Somaliland Protectorate.

The defeat at Adowa effectively blunted Italian encroachment on Ethiopia from the north. In the south, however, far from the center of Menelik's power, the Italians pushed steadily inward toward another rendezvous with the Ethiopians.

If the position of the Italians along the Indian Ocean coast of Somalia was largely unaffected by Adowa, the same could not be said of their British allies to the north who had until then blithely assumed that French and Italian recognition of their protectorate guaranteed its security. Reluctance to treat the Ethiopians as an important if not the leading actor in the historical drama on the Horn (occasioned no doubt by a coalition of contempt for native dynasties and wishful thinking) had survived increasing Ethiopian pressure on the northern clans who were periodically savaged by well-armed military expeditions dispatched from Harar. Nor was there any reason to believe that these were simply plundering expeditions rather than firm heralds of Ethiopian ambition to extend the empire's frontiers. As early as 1891, Menelik dispatched a letter to the British government outlining vast territorial claims. "Whilst tracing today the actual boundaries of my Empire," wrote Menelik, "I shall endeavor, if God gives me life and strength, to re-establish the ancient frontiers of Ethiopia up to Khartoum, and as far as Lake Nyanza* with all the Gallas." He included in these aspirational frontiers more than half of the British Protectorate. Assured by the Italians that Menelik was safely ensconced under their thumb, the British ignored what must have seemed to them the ravings of another deranged Abyssinian potentate. The emperor Tewodros had displayed a similar verbal audacity, but when it came to the test of arms, his boasts had proved as empty as his armory. So why worry?

Adowa provided an abrupt answer. It was accompanied by the multiplication of Ethiopian belligerents along the protectorate's borders. Ras Makonnen, Menelik's representative in Harar and the father of Haile Selassie, threatened to assert by force Ethiopian jurisdiction over the land well east of the line acknowledged in an 1894

* Lake Victoria.

Anglo-Italian protocol as defining the frontier between their respective domains.

With events moving rapidly toward a violent climax, the British decided to subordinate racial pride to a crassly economic calculus of the national interest. If, as appeared likely, the emperor could himself maintain the requisite degree of order within his possessions, there was no need for a costly armed struggle over who owned exactly which piece of land in which the British had such marginal interests.

Less than twelve months after Adowa, the British government dispatched a special envoy, Rennell Rodd, to settle all outstanding issues between Britain and the now clearly formidable Menelik. Rodd knew that, with respect to the matter of the protectorate's border, he would be negotiating from a position of pathetic weakness, for not only was his government extremely reluctant to pursue its claims by military means; in addition, it was anxious for Ethiopian support of Britain's campaign against the Sudanese Mahdists. Furthermore, Rodd was preceded by a French envoy who had gracefully sustained the traditional cordiality of Franco-Ethiopian relations by agreeing to redraw the frontier of the French enclave to a point no greater than one hundred kilometers inland, a very considerable retrenchment of French claims.

Within the limitations of his hand, Rodd played his cards effectively. He convinced Menelik to drop an initial claim to the entire British Protectorate; the precise boundary limitation was left to subsequent negotiations between Rodd and Ras Makonnen. But an annexed stipulation that such Somali clansmen who, as a result of any adjustment of boundaries, might eventually become Ethiopian subjects were to be well treated and assured of "orderly government" foreshadowed some measure of territorial concession by the British. After prolonged negotiations in Harar, Rodd and Makonnen managed the following compromise: Britain abandoned its claims to some 67,000 square miles of land in and immediately north of the Haud; Ethiopia, for its part, recognized British suzerainty to a line 50 miles west of the main interior Somali town, Harghessa.

In what appears to have been a display of syntactical wiliness, Rodd secured Ethiopian *recognition* of British authority while describing Britain's concession as a mere withdrawal of claims to act on behalf of peoples occupying the westernmost part of the Somali Plateau. Under the agreement, Britain neither formally ceded the land in question nor recognized Ethiopia as the new governing authority. Hence, there was no formal conflict with the Anglo-Italian protocol of 1894. The treaties of protection fared less well. Britain had implicitly promised to protect the independence of the clans. Independence was meaningless if it could be exercised only by relinquishing control of land essential to the clan's economy. From Lord Salisbury's Olympian perspective, this was a matter of little consequence. "[He] was

not much preoccupied about Abyssinian encroachments in Somaliland," Rodd wrote following an interview with that distinguished
personage.

The handful of colonial servants responsible for the administration of the protectorate were rather more agitated. But they drew
solace from the treaty's provision that Somalis would be free to use
wells and graze their cattle on both sides of the frontier without
hindrance and also from two assumptions: that there would be a very
low order of permanent Somali settlement in the relinquished land
and, second, that the Ethiopians would not attempt to establish themselves in the area as the effective administering authority. The former
assumption was gradually dispelled, on the one hand, by a rapid increase in the settlement of Somali nomads for purposes of sorghum
cultivation and, on the other, by a continuing growth in the use of the
Haud by clans unable to maintain their herds in the eroded, overgrazed north. The second assumption subsided at a rate which varied
for different parts of the relinquished area largely as a function of
soil fertility. As far as merely pastoral land was concerned, for several
decades "administration" continued to be indistinguishable from
sporadic extortionate intrusions by Ethiopian raiding parties. The
thinness of their administrative presence postponed until 1934 a felt
need on the Ethiopians' part for on-the-ground demarcation of the
border. And it was only then that the Somali nomads discovered the
contents of the agreement which, whatever its formal terms, remitted
the Somali clans to the de facto authority of a hostile Christian empire, a consequence clearly envisioned by both parties to the treaty.

Cultivated or cultivable land drew earlier and more-sustained attention from the Ethiopian authorities. Frustrated by Somali resistance to exactions of grain and meat designed for the support of Ethiopian officials and occupying troops, beginning around 1918 they
began to settle Galla and Amhara farmers in areas of Somali cultivation and pasturage.

Rodd, astride his mule on the road to Harar for the second phase
of his negotiations, passed his Italian counterpart, Major Nerazzini,
bound for Addis in pursuit of a southern border agreement. By all
accounts, Nerazzini's negotiations with Menelik were concluded am-
icably, but with exceeding informality. Apparently, they simply drew
an agreed line on two copies of a map. Nothing was put in writing.
The maps were eventually lost. And the only surviving direct evidence of their agreement is Nerazzini's report to his government in
which he claimed Ethiopian recognition of an Italian zone of absolute
possession "from the intersection of our frontier with that of British
Somaliland, . . . parallel to the coast extending about 180 miles inland," a distance considerably short of Italian claims before Adowa.
Since Rodd was engaged with Makonnen in fixing the boundaries of
British Somaliland at the very time Nerazzini was negotiating with

Menelik, one could have anticipated discordant interpretations of their agreement.

The expectation was quickly fulfilled. In 1908, coincident with the payment of three million Italian lira to Menelik, the parties agreed on a clarification which at least the Italians believed confirmed Nerazzini's version of his agreement with Menelik. Thereafter, as Italian power grew alongside its imperial interests in southern Somalia, the incentive to further clarification correspondingly receded, to vanish altogether with the rise of a fascist dictator determined to erect an Italian empire on the Horn of Africa.

All in all, 1897 was a banner year for Ethiopia. Each of its European colonial neighbors had sharply contracted its territorial claims and manifested a pressing desire for Ethiopian friendship. It was now evident that friendship would be given only on terms of absolute equality. There would be no more nonsense about protectorates. A great year for Ethiopians; a black one for Somalis, although, since they were neither consulted before nor informed after the agreements, it was years before they would appreciate what had happened.

From 1897 to 1935, the only significant change in the political frontiers dividing the Somali people occurred in the south. Under the terms of an 1891 agreement, the Italians recognized a zone of British influence from the southern border of Kenya all the way north to the Juba River which flows through the Ogaden and southern Somalia to the sea. During the first four years after the conclusion of that accord, the port of Kismayu and the surrounding territory was left in the hands of the Imperial British East Africa Company. The company might as well have assumed responsibility for the domestication of a spitting cobra. Relations with the fractious local clans came to a pustulant head in 1895 with a savage battle in and around the town followed by the withdrawal of the Somali population to the countryside. Before the year's end, the company gave its concession up as a thoroughly bad show. The British government, assuming control, proclaimed a protectorate over "Jubaland."

The change in the administration did not alter the belligerent temper of the Jubaland clans. A costly punitive expedition quickly dispatched to the interior to confirm British authority, though unable to force a battle, was repeatedly harassed and finally returned to the coast with little if any accomplishment to its credit. It seemed likely that more such expeditions would be required. And they were.

Jubaland, embracing what is today southern Somalia and the northeast district of Kenya, had as little material value to the British as their possessions in the northern Horn. But administration has its own logic, which is order. Order meant action to reduce three kinds of conflicts: between Somali clans, between Somalis and Gallas, and between Somalis and the plundering expeditions which sallied periodically out of the Ethiopian highlands. To that end, the British gradually extended their effective authority farther and farther into the interior. They exercised their extended reach to terminate the 900-year march of the Somali nation down the coast of East Africa. Confronted by British power, the Somalis were forced to accept the Tana River as their southern frontier. There it has remained.

The Anglo-Italian alliance in the First World War created a respectable rationale for Britain to reduce its unrewarding obligations north of the Tana River. Among the inducements for Italian participation in the war was a British commitment in 1915, under the secret Treaty of London, that if Great Britain increased its colonial territory in Africa at the expense of Germany, the British government would agree in principle that Italy might claim some equitable compensation. Having through the acquisition of the German colony of Tanganyika satisfied the condition precedent, Britain concluded a convention ceding 33,000 square miles of Jubaland to Italy. Implementation of the convention was postponed by five years of wrangling over unrelated conditions of the postwar settlement. During the interregnum, several members of Parliament thought to question the compatibility of the transfer with "the principle of self-determination" and, more generally, with the welfare of Jubaland's inhabitants. The foreign secretary disposed of such cavils by noting that "no condition as to the consent of the inhabitants was made in the Treaty of London." On June 29, 1925, the transfer to Italy was completed.

Although L. S. Amery, a government spokesman in the House of Commons, had insisted that "the reason for the cession of the territory as a whole is to keep these tribes together as a single unit, and give them the full use of their natural grazing ground" and the Earl of Onslow had assured such lords as were present, *compos mentis*, and awake that "the line has been drawn as closely as possible in accordance with racial divisions," in fact, thousands of square miles inhabited by tens of thousands of Somalis—the current population approaches a quarter of a million—were sliced off the main body of Somali territory, thus planting additional seeds of conflict.

No account of Somali modern history would be complete without some reference to the unsuccessful war of independence organized and led by Sheikh Mohammed Abdille Hassan. To the British, held at bay for twenty years by his tactical brilliance and political virtuosity, he was the "Mad Mullah," as if no sane Somali could object to such a benevolent protector. Sheikh Mohammed, after traveling to Mecca and joining an ascetic, reforming religious order, returned to the northern Somali coast around 1897 to teach, preach, and with messianic zeal exhort his countrymen to return to the strict path of Muslim devotion. Whether they emerged in Roman Palestine, British Somaliland, or any other place under alien domination, messianic figures of this type posed threats to law and order. The sheikh was no exception. He would have been a troublemaker under any circumstances. Under the actual circumstances of his emergence, including the inspirational example of the Mahdists' holy struggle for freedom in the Sudan, the activities of Christian missionaries operating along the coast under the protection of colonial governments, and, above all, British supineness in the face of Ethiopian encroachment on Somali lands, the trouble he would make was bound to be large.

At the turn of the century, this extraordinary man set about liberating his people from "infidel" domination. He soon announced his intention with the sure eloquence which helped make him a myth in his own lifetime. In a letter addressed to the English people, he wrote:

> If the country (Somaliland) was cultivated, or contained houses or property it would be worth your while to fight. . . . If you want wood or stone you can get them in plenty. There are also many ant heaps. The sun is very hot. All you can get from me is war, nothing else.[4]

Such gorgeous arrogance is reminiscent of a neighboring reformer, Tewodros, who announced defiantly:

> I know the tactics of European governments when they desire to acquire an eastern state. First they send out missionaries, then consuls to support the missionaries, then battalions to support the consuls. I am not a Rajah of Hindustan to be made a mock of in that way. I prefer to have to deal with the battalions straight away![5]

Sheikh Mohammed had to deal not only with British battalions but with Ethiopian ones as well. His aim was liberation of all Somalis from every alien power. He appealed for support not merely to the Darods, his patrilineal clan, and the Dublahantes, his mother's people, but to all Somalis. He was, in short, the first truly nationalist leader.

Ancient divisions branded on Somali society by the ruthless conditions of survival could not be erased overnight. Nor for that matter in twenty years. Nor by any single man. The determined divisiveness of his people, perhaps as much as the Ethiopian-British alliance, the coastal blockade on arms, and the troops and even planes thrown into the struggle by the British, finally defeated him. But not before he awakened and nourished the idea that beyond the ties of lineage and blood-contract there were bonds among all Somalis which in the modern world must take precedence, for narrower loyalties lead only to submission. His call to the nation, his appeal to moral regeneration, and his vision of liberation, captured in the lines of his abundant poetry, quickly passed into the vital oral tradition which linked a trader in Djibouti to a nomad in the Ogaden. So though he was defeated, he did not entirely fail.

The defeat and death of Sheikh Mohammed, coming as it did at the end of an exhausting European war in which the three European powers on the Horn had been allied, seemed to promise an extended period of tranquility. There was no figure of comparable appeal and ability to marshal internal dissidents; the state actors were nominally satisfied with existing boundaries. And though there remained some uncertainty about the precise location of the frontier between Italian Somaliland and Ethiopia, uncertainty seemed to function within a rather narrow order of magnitude. The whole place seemed nothing short of a political Elysium but for one small difficulty: the Italian Right had neither forgotten Adowa nor surrendered its dreams of empire, dreams that may easily have been sharpened by the niggardly compensation awarded to Italy for its dreadful losses incurred during the World War.

By the late 1920s, the colonial authorities in Mogadishu, following up earlier political and economic infiltration, were conducting covert military probes of parts of the Ogaden farther inland than any interpretation of the 1897 and 1908 agreements could justify.

> Several prominent religious leaders across the border had now been won to the Italian cause by generous gifts. Irregular Somali groups, who could be disclaimed conveniently as bandits, were also recruited and provided with arms to stir up trouble in the area. Thus in the Mustahil region, Ololdin, the forceful Ajuran sultan, was paid and armed by the Italians to attack the Ethiopian tribute-gathering expeditions whose arbitrary activities constituted virtually all that there was at this time in the way of Ethiopian administration.[6]

The Emperor, at the center of his Byzantine web in Addis, took note of the Italian encroachments and, although he made no official protests, maneuvered to resist them. He cultivated the support of Ogaden Somalis by offering guns and ammunition to those who expressed hostility to the Italians. And lest the Italians think that Ethiopia had lost its sting, he sent out still larger and better-armed tribute-gathering parties to points farther and farther east.

But he was playing a losing game. In currying favor with the clans, as with armaments and great-power diplomacy, the Italians had irremediable advantages. They were not historic enemies of the Somalis. They could offer far more in the way of money and guns. And, although as Christian as the Amharas, they seemed a good deal more respectful of Muslim sentiment. Tribute was not their game. The focus for exploitation and Italian settlement was the inter-river area

nearer the Indian Ocean coast. From the Ogaden tribes and other
Somali nomads they sought military support. And for the most part
they got it. There were 40,000 Somali troops in the Italian army
which in 1935, after a carefully orchestrated "border incident" deep
inside the Ogaden, marched into the highlands and occupied Addis,
thus launching the Italian East African empire.

Il Duce's forces went from victory to victory. British Somaliland
was next on the agenda. On August 4, 1940, Italy threw in entire
divisions supported by tanks and artillery against a mixed handful of
lightly armed defenders. After seven days of bitter combat, British
survivors were evacuated to Aden through the port of Berbera. For
the first time, the great majority of Somalis were united within a single political enterprise. Only Djibouti and the Northern Frontier District of Kenya were excluded. And the latter was added seven months
later when the British blasted their way back into Somalia and rolled
up the Italian army all the way to the farthest extremities of Ethiopia.
French Somaliland remained, as ever, aloof. Its Vichy master successfully endured a British blockade until late 1942 when, with the prospect of German victory annulled, one of his unit commanders withdrew across the border, received DeGaulle's imprimatur, and marched
back in for the glory of Free France. *Plus ça change, plus c'est la même
chose.*

Occupation by a single power coincided with a quickening of the
nationalist ideal illuminated by Sheikh Mohammed. He had fought
his war in the countryside. But in Somalia after his death, as in most
other parts of Africa, the city became the focus of nationalist activity.
There, thrown together with men and women unrelated by ties of
blood, freed of the economic and martial imperatives which in the
country compelled parochial attachments, and confronted by a people alien in color and culture, Somalis discovered the possibility and
potential efficacy of new and larger alliances based on the common
denominators of language, religion, and a shared oppression. The
southern towns and cities, their economies stimulated by preparations
for war, grew throughout the 1930s, Italian defeat brought economic
depression. Demobilized Somali troops further swelled the urban
population. In Eritrea, unemployment and the deflation of Italian
prestige had released a subterranean current of hostility. Somalia was
no different. With the approval of the British administration, a group
of young activists founded the first Somali political movement, the
Somali Youth Club. It pledged opposition to any renewal of Italian
hegemony.

Set against the favorable omens of a unified administration and
incipient political organization was the triumphant return from exile
of Haile Selassie. The ageless perfection of imperial dignity, so trim,
graceful, and supremely cool that physically larger men seemed gross
by comparison, he began a relentless campaign for the consolidation

of personal power and the expansion of the Ethiopian state. The anointed martyr of fascist aggression, as wily as ever, cloaked his own ambitions in the rhetoric of liberation and restoration. Shortly before his return, he announced these themes in leaflets showered over Eritrea by the Royal Air Force. "I have come," he proclaimed, "to restore the independence of my country, including Eritrea and the Benadir [the old name for the coast of southern Somalia] whose people will henceforth dwell under the shade of the Ethiopian flag." In a later memorandum to the United Nations, his government would claim that "prior to the race of the European powers to divide up the continent of Africa, Ethiopia included an extensive coastline along the Red Sea and Indian Ocean." A thrilling piece of mendacity, of course, yet thoroughly consistent with universal canons of diplomatic propriety. What matters to most governments almost all the time is results. Haile Selassie had few rivals in the ability to obtain them.

The British, having betrayed the Somalis for reasons of state in 1897, had a solid precedent for doing it again. And England is, after all, a common-law country where precedent really counts. John Drysdale, distinguished chronicler of the Somali-Ethiopian dispute, believed that Anthony Eden foreshadowed the renewed fragmentation of the Somali nation in a major policy statement to the House of Commons in early February, 1941:

> His Majesty's Government would welcome the reappearance of an Ethiopian State and recognize the claim of the Emperor Haile Selassie to the throne. . . . [His Majesty's Government] reaffirm that they have themselves no territorial ambitions in Abyssinia.

Recognition of Selassie's claim to the throne was consistent with the overall policy of restoring the status quo wherever it had enhanced British power, wealth, and influence: a king in Greece, an emperor in Ethiopia, His Majesty's government in Burma, Malaya, Hong Kong, and every other corner of the empire on which the sun would nevertheless soon set. That was to be expected. The denial of territorial ambitions was a nice gesture, calculated to heighten the distinction between Nazi aggression and Allied response. Moreover, the British had never reallyhworked up a consistent interest in Ethiopia, even at the highwater mark of European frenzy over colonial opportunities in Africa. There were enough other places for the provision of outdoor relief to the younger sons of the gentry.

Surrender of Somali-occupied land was not the logical converse either of this self-denying ordinance or of the "reappearance" of an independent Ethiopian state. That state had existed in one form or another for 2,000 years. From the High Middle Ages until Menelik's Western-armed essays in black imperialism, its writ had not run in any Somali-occupied territory, although from time to time it might have succeeded in exacting a payment of tribute from one or another nomadic group. What Menelik had taken by force or the threat thereof, the Italians had taken back in kind. Britain had recognized each successive act of conquest. Since Britain and most other Western states had extended de jure recognition to Italian absorption of Ethiopia before the outbreak of World War II, no principle of prewar legitimacy required re-establishment of the Ethiopian state *within the particular boundaries hacked out by Menelik*. And if the Somalis or the Eritreans were not deemed ready to manage their own affairs and the British were unwilling to acquire title to the border territories wrenched by Italy from Ethiopian hands, there was the alternative of a trusteeship, whether administered by the United Kingdom, a group of United Nations members, or the United Nations itself.

This was logically possible. It just was not what His Britannic Majesty's government had in mind. In 1942, Whitehall responded to the Emperor's tireless exhortations by concluding an agreement with him restoring full sovereignty to Ethiopia and confirming the prewar boundary between Ethiopia and the British Protectorate; the agreement was, however, qualified by an associated military convention granting Britain temporary administrative authority in the Ogaden and the Reserved Area. The former was defined as stretching from the northeast corner of Kenya to the southern boundary of British Somaliland; for the sake of administrative convenience, it would continue to be administered as part of Italian Somaliland. The Reserved Area included the Haud and the grain-producing areas to the west of the protectorate, in short, most of the territory subject to the 1897 agreement.

Following the convention's renewal in 1944, the Emperor began to press hard for the rapid withdrawal of British authority. In the meantime, sympathy for the Somalis was percolating up from British officers on the Horn to rarified levels of political decision. Drysdale writes that, as early as 1943, the men in the field had come to appreciate the humanitarian case for a unified administration responsive to the problems of a people

> who live precarious lives from one long drought to another; people who must follow the rains in one season and orbit around wells in the next; people who have their own unique system of social security and administration of justice. Thzse people also need, from time to time, the intervention and assistance of a modern centralised government to regulate and control water and pasture; to extract underground water intelligently so that it does not upset the delicate balance between migrations, pasture and waters; to bolster their judicial system which artificial boundaries destroy; and to restore equilibrium between clans by a policy of disarmament.[7]

Their arguments finally had consequential impact in Whitehall. When, in 1946, the Big Four took up the question of Italian Somaliland, the British foreign secretary, Ernest Bevin, proposed that

> British Somaliland, Italian Somaliland, and the adjacent part of Ethiopia, if Ethiopia agreed, should be lumped together as a trust territory, so that the nomads should lead their frugal existence with the least possible hindrance and there might be a real chance of a decent economic life, as understood in that territory.

The proposal, however well intentioned, was intrinsically flawed by the provisions requiring Ethiopian agreement and proposing a British trustee. The former could not be satisfied. The latter, although it was not put forward as an essential condition, nevertheless encouraged perception of the plan as a stratagem for British imperial expansion.

Unable to satisfy the conditions for its omnibus plan, Britain then attempted a bilateral deal with the Ethiopians, who were offered the port of Zeila in the extreme north of the protectorate in return for cession to Britain of the Ogaden and the Haud. Had the British succeeded, the broader Somali unity they had urged on their allies would have been consummated in 1960 when the protectorate and Italian Somaliland achieved independence and then immediately merged.

But like Britain's earlier initiative, it was no sooner launched than it sank. The French, exercising rights under a 1906 agreement with the United Kingdom, vetoed the proposal for construction of a rail link from Ethiopia to Zeila which would, of course, have reduced the commerce of Djibouti. That, however, was a mere footnote to the inevitable disinterest of the Ethiopians once it became evident that they would acquire direct access to the sea through hegemony in Eritrea.

After withdrawing from the Ogaden in 1948 but retaining certain residual rights of supervision over Somali clans pasturing transiently in the Haud, the British government made a last futile effort to fulfill its original protective obligation by offering to purchase the southern and western grazing areas of the protectorate clans. Haile Selassie rejected the idea out of hand.

Somali nationalism raced unsuccessfully to catch up with the irretrievable flow of events. Its leading institutional expression, the Somali Youth Club, opened at Mogadishu in May, 1943, with thirteen members, including several prominent religious leaders, representing all of the main clan groups. They were united by a desire to transcend clan rivalries and to forge a political nation which would be both the embodiment of Islamic values and a vehicle of secular progress. This marriage of tradition and modernity, consummated in the tolerant political atmosphere maintained by the British administration, appealed strongly to younger, educated Somalis then beginning to multiply in the civil service and also in the gendarmerie whose British senior officers employed a conscious policy of clan-mixing at every level and promoted a code of translineage loyalty. Within three years, the original club had acquired what British officials estimated to be no less than 25,000 affiliates scattered throughout British-occupied territory. Already a de facto political institution, in 1947 it adopted the corresponding forms by changing its name to the Somali Youth League (SYL) and announcing a program emphasizing promotion of Somali unity, repudiation of clan distinctions, the spread of modern education, and development of a written script for the Somali language. As a prelude to full independence, it urged a ten-year trusteeship under Big Four administration.

Despite compelling evidence of widespread public support for the SYL and equally extensive hostility to the Italians, Britain joined the United States and France in supporting an Italian trusteeship, the result urged by Italy's newly elected Christian Democratic government. Russia, having witnessed the defeat of its favorite party in the 1948 Italian elections, found categorical merit in the idea of a trusteeship by the Big Four. And so, under the rule of unanimity, the Somali issue was shuffled over to the United Nations General Assembly, where a majority, as ever in search of the golden mean, decided in favor of Italian administration but only for ten years and under close United Nations supervision. That stout champion of Somali self-determination, Emperor Haile Selassie, responded with a condemnatory cable to the United Nations Secretary-General: "In overriding the principles of self-determination of peoples so clearly expressed by the Somali people . . . the fourth General Assembly failed in its responsibility for reaching decisions urgently required in the interests of peace and justice. . . ."

Particularly in light of the fact that in reaching this result the General Assembly had modified a Bevin-Sforza "compromise" calling for an Italian trusteeship to last an unspecified period, SYL demonstrations at home and diplomacy abroad could be credited with a partial victory. The sense of achievement in the case of Italian Somalia could only be heightened by the string of disasters on the Ethiopian front. They were epitomized by the 1948 massacre of SYL supporters in Jijiga following Britain's agreement to withdraw from the Ogaden. As described by John Drysdale with that legal punctilio so characteristic of British colonial officials:

> . . . Major Demeka, the governor-designate of the Ogaden Province, requested the British military administration, which was still in charge, to remove the SYL flag flying from party headquarters. It had been run up to give offense to the Ethiopians and was in fact illegal. As the leaders refused to pull down their flag, the

police brought it down with a machine gun mounted on an armoured car. Disturbances followed, during which a policeman was killed and another wounded by the explosion of a hand grenade thrown from the roof of the SYL headquarters. The police opened fire on the crowd, killing twenty-five of them and that was the end of the final act of defiance by the SYL before it was proscribed, as are all political parties in Ethiopia. Thus, after thirteen years, Ethiopian administration of Jijiga and Dagabur was resumed. Ethiopian district governors were then dispatched to [the main district towns], and the eastern part of the Ogaden was administered by Ethiopian officials on September 23, 1948, for the first time in its history.[8]

In the words of Ian Lewis's epitaph for the Ogaden Somalis, "The tribute-gathering sorties which Ras Makonnen had sent out from Harar and Jijiga at the turn of the century, which had created a basis for Ethiopia's pretensions to sovereignty over the Ogaden, had at last borne fruit."[9]

The turbulence of the late 1940s was followed in the south by ten relatively pacific years. They began somewhat inauspiciously with the establishment of an Italian trusteeship administration inclined neither to forgive nor to forget its opponents. Symptomatic was the allocation of pains and indulgences within the former gendarmerie. Somalis suspected of infection by Anglophilia or nationalism—primarily SYL members—were weeded out of promotion courses and either sacked or banished to remote bush posts. Fortunately for the trust territory's tranquility, an evident desire to satisfy the obligations of a trustee quickly dispelled the initial spirit of revanche.

Even while applying the *lex talionis*, Italian officials had initiated programs for the repair and enlargement of the territory's physical infrastructure, for the development of agriculture, and for the promotion of basic education and technical training. Progress accelerated as Italian officials lost either the arrogance or paranoia which had prompted their initial repression.

As early as 1956, the Italian administration replaced all expatriate district and provincial commissioners with Somalis. Two years later, Col. Mohammed Abshir assumed command of the Somali police force.

The administration managed a parallel transfer of political authority. Municipal elections in 1954 were followed two years later by elections to form a parliamentary government with power over domestic legislation, subject to veto by the head of the administration. Of sixty available seats, the SYL won forty-three; the next largest party won only thirteen. Four years later, the league enlarged its already huge majority and was then authorized to form the first government of an independent Somali state.

Events moved more erratically in the British Somaliland Protectorate. Prior to 1955, the festering situation in the transborder grazing lands absorbed indigenous concern. Ethiopian officials worked ceaselessly to undermine the continued British presence. Conflict revolved around the issue of who should be regarded as an Ethiopian subject. While the Emperor had reaffirmed the provisions of the 1897 agreement concerning free movement, he was clearly determined to enhance the charms of at least nominal identification with Ethiopia. To that end, his officials violated the nomads' democratic tradition by appointing some of their number as, in effect, chiefs to serve as intermediaries with Ethiopian authorities. These appointed officials were paid by the Ethiopian government. Perhaps because British officials in the field struggled to preserve Somali rights, political activity within the protectorate seemed narcotized until suddenly, at the end of 1954, quite without warning to the Somalis, the British government concluded a new agreement with the Emperor ceding the last vestige of its authority in the Reserved Area. In return, the Ethiopian government reaffirmed once again the right of British-protected clans to graze and water in the traditional manner.

Somalis in the protectorate had apparently clung to the hope of ultimate diplomatic action by the British to re-create a unified administration or at least to strengthen the safeguards for cross-border migration. Now, obviously feeling the victims of an ultimate betrayal (when, in fact, the British had one more stiletto to plant in the Somali back), they staged mass demonstrations throughout the protectorate demanding recovery of the lost territories and, for the first time, independence. As a step toward the former objective, they asked the British authorities to sponsor resolutions in the United Nations General Assembly calling for an advisory opinion of the International Court of Justice on the status of the ceded territories, in effect on the power of the United Kingdom to cede them.

Apparently fearing the precedential consequence of any external appreciation of agreements with or concerning its colonies and protectorates, the British government refused. A Colonial Office publication defended the decision on the grounds that "the Protectorate having been established in 1887, HMG [Her Majesty's Government] had been fully entitled to conclude the Treaty of 1897." This was, of course, one of the issues which the Somalis wished to submit for adjudication.

The only British concession to Somali feeling concerning the lost grazing areas was the foredoomed offer mentioned above to purchase the land. In addition to failing on that score, the British were unable to moderate Ethiopian efforts to extract acknowledgment of Ethiopian nationality and deference to Ethiopian authority from the nomadic Somali clans.

Failure in Addis coincided with British announcement of a program looking toward rapid achievement of internal self-government in the protectorate and of sympathy for the aspiration to union with Italian Somalia. Final cession of British authority in the transborder grazing lands undoubtedly shredded British prestige and hence the authority of the protectorate administration. As in many other colonial settings, its rule had rested on the acquiescence of the governed induced by their political fragmentation, their absorption in parochial matters left untouched by the administration, and undoubtedly their assumption that behind all the bumptious self-confidence of the handful of administrators there lay real power which could be mobilized against the Somalis and which could also protect their interests from more-dangerous predators. The unequivocal loss of the grazing lands destroyed the three pillars of colonial bluff: it created an issue transcending clan lines, it directly affected the lives of individual Somalis, and it revealed the emptiness of the protector's promises. Either the protector was weak or it had betrayed its clients. In either event, it was useless. With the basis for acquiescence destroyed, the British could either leave or fight.

In Kenya they had fought for a while. It had 40,000 white settlers, British investments worth millions of pounds, a first-class port, and a rich agriculture. Yet even Kenya proved too expensive once the native population achieved a modest degree of political mobilization. The protectorate had no settlers, no investment, no wealth, and a port incomparably inferior to Aden and Mombasa. It was as poor as the day the British had arrived. Clearly it was time to leave.

The administration set about frantically creating the apparatus of a parliamentary government and indigenous administration. Scholarships and training courses rained down on the population. There was a little flurry of public works activity. It must have been like a manic exercise in spring cleaning after years of winter.

Notes

For information on Somali history and society the author is particularly indebted to books by John Drysdale and Ian Lewis: Drysdale, *The Somali Dispute* (New York: Praeger, 1964); Lewis, *The Modern History of Somaliland* (New York: Praeger, 1965). Two other valuable sources are Irving Kaplan *et al*, *Area Handbook for Somalia* (Washington, D.C.: American University Foreign Area Studies, 1970) and S. Touval, *Somali Nationalism* (Cambridge: Harvard University Press, 1963).

1. Drysdale, p. 10.

2. Lewis, p. 11.

3. *Ibid.*

4. Quoted in Drysdale, p. 32.

5. Quoted in Greenfield, p. 70.

6. Lewis, p. 108.

7. Drysdale, p. 62.

8. *Ibid*, pp. 70–1.

9. Lewis, p. 130.

5 Independence: A Partial Victory

On June 26, 1960, the British Somaliland Protectorate achieved full independence. Five days later, when the Italian Trust Territory of Somalia emerged from its cocoon as an independent state, the two entities united pursuant to accords negotiated during the preceding months. The accords established a unitary republic with northern and southern regions. On the flag of the new state there was a five-pointed star. Those points, a government spokesman announced and the constitution affirmed, represented the five fragments of the Somali nation created by the colonial impact on the Horn. Fusion of the protectorate and the trust territory was the first step toward the consummation of national unity. The Somalis were determined that it would not be the last.

Freedom and its Discontents

The Somali Democratic Republic launched its pursuit of national unity from a miserably weak economic base. Bananas and cattle were the only two exports of any substantial value. The foreign exchange they earned was insufficient to permit infrastructure maintenance and to satisfy existing consumer demand, much less to support any program of military and economic development. Government revenues, essentially import and export duties, were equally inadequate despite the extremely narrow range of public service activities. Mogadishu, for instance, had no potable water until the end of the decade.

The new government was therefore compelled to live off foreign aid. Britain promised £1.5 million during the first year of independence with further grants to be negotiated. Italy offered an annual grant of £3 million. Both sums represented a mélange of budgetary support, technical assistance, and development projects. In the sphere of development, Britain and Italy were quickly joined by a host of other donors, including the United States, West Germany, the USSR,

Czechoslovakia, the People's Republic of China, the United Arab Republic, the United Nations Development Programme, and other specialized agencies of the United Nations.

The donors piled proposals and to a lesser extent money on a structure of government characterized by political sophistication at the highest levels and managerial incompetence nearly everywhere. Flaunting the most atrocious characteristics of the Italian bureaucracy from which southern-born officials drew their inspiration, the civil service wallowed in a morass of indolence and red tape. Northerners who migrated to Mogadishu often complained bitterly about deviations from the starchy efficiency they imputed to British colonial officials. But either because they were too few or the atmosphere too seductive, the northerners seemed unable to affect the overall tone of public life in this miniature Rome on the Indian Ocean. The single, clear exception to the general standard of public service was the 5,000-man police force, which combined ordinary police functions with intelligence and paramilitary operations designed to prevent interclan violence and to safeguard the border. Foreign observers were pretty much uniform in the belief that its efficiency, vigor, and honesty compared favorably with similar units in other parts of the globe.

It is uncertain whether the bureaucratic slough of inefficiency had a great deal of economic consequence. There was, of course, no effective planning mechanism, no basis for project selection and integration. And most of the various donors were far too busy ignoring each other and scratching for an edge in the local influence game to attempt any coordination themselves. Still, the country needed so much of everything that there was little risk of wasteful duplication. There were, however, disastrous failures of coordination: a milk-bottling plant without milk; a magnificent hospital without technicians, maintenance crews, or doctors; and so on.

Even if every failure of conception, coordination, and execution in the first few years of independence had been averted—something that happens in no country whatever its stage of development or form of government—the economic and social consequences would, I think, have been marginal to the country's extreme poverty, a poverty of natural resources, technology, basic education, health, nutrition, infrastructure, plant, and equipment. Not different or better projects but rather a totally different model of development emphasizing austere administrative expenditure, severe restrictions on private affluence, and the mobilization of all local and donated resources to raise the subsistence levels among the eighty percent of the population struggling to survive from one season of rains to another conceivably might have altered the face of poverty in Somalia. It would have taken that model plus a government with the prestige, power, competence, and commitment required to make that model work.

The government which assumed office in 1960 had none of these qualities. To some degree it serviced, to some degree it simply fed on the laissez faire economy inherited from the colonial era. It interfered hardly at all with the pre-existing pattern of rural and urban life. It acted, in short, like most postcolonial governments. Because it started from a very low economic base, the country was far poorer after half a decade of independence than countries like Kenya or Ghana which had launched themselves from a much higher plateau. Because its government effectively represented the tense balance of forces in an unusually egalitarian social system, Somalia seemed freer, less coercive than most of its counterparts. And this was what many Westerners who lived in Somalia during the early 1960s found so engaging, this and the system of private generosity—part Islamic, in large part the triumph of clan over class—which seemed to dull the sharper edges of privation. At the same time, there was a sense both among foreign observers and the narrow wedge of modernizers—students, a few professionals, recent graduates in the civil service, the police, and the army—that economically the society was having difficulty moving off dead center, that it was stagnant, falling further behind the wealthier countries of Africa. And some, certainly some of the students, began to wonder whether a political system organized like this one could ever effect the necessary changes. It is, of course, hard to accept, even to contemplate the possibility that the inherent obstacles to full-scale modernization may be insuperable.

If an outsider had concluded—on the basis of the casual flow of petitioners to the government compound, the vigorous debates in the National Assembly, the spirited political rallies, the incessant political chatter on the streets and in the coffee-houses, and the total absence of that telltale guarded sibilance of speech familiar to travelers through any police state—that Somalia was a real democracy, he would have been right. But it was, nevertheless, a rather special kind of democracy.

Despite the growth of nationalist sentiment, for the average Somali, when it came to domestic politics, kinship remained the basis of selection. The relevant kinship group might be defined more broadly than it had been in the past when there was rarely a means for marshaling entire clans or clan-families, which, in the case of the largest ones, might have hundreds of thousands of members. Electoral competition and the related struggle for jobs and development funds now lent significance to these more extended relationships. There were enough cabinet posts to assure balanced representation only among the larger lineage groups.

Americans can attest that there is nothing very special about ethnic politics. It is all a matter of degree. In Somalia, the degree was on the extreme side.

Ethnic politics of any kind tends to subordinate the electoral significance of a candidate's program and personal qualities. Somali ethnic politics heightened this tendency because it mirrored the traditional hierarchies of prestige within the clans: older men in general, elders from particularly distinguished families, men with a reputation for religiosity (which could be fostered by a pilgrimage to Mecca), and wealthy men—both of the last two more likely to be older than younger. The importance of these qualities further limited the pool of potentially successful candidates and thus effected the further subordination of program and personal qualities relevant to the formulation and implementation of a development program. Ethnic politics also introduced an element of gerontocracy into the political system, again a question of degree but one which is fairly consequential in an impoverished, ancient society experiencing the traumas of modernization.

All of these sociological dimensions of the political process reinforced the natural tendency of democratic politics to prevent the articulation and implementation of a coherent policy of social transformation and to encourage an emphasis on the division of spoils within the existing societal parameters. As long as there are enough goods to satisfy the expectations of all major groups, this kind of arrangement is likely to be stable. In developing, and particularly in recently decolonized, countries, that essential condition of stability is difficult to find. Where there is no large industrial-commercial sector, government employment is the primary source of affluence, power, and status. There are never enough desirable jobs for the accumulating layers of university graduates.

Aggravating these tensions is the inevitable disillusion which follows the consummation of independence. The oppressor leaves, yet so many of those problems of poverty and inequality, of personal and group animosity, once attributed (in many cases justly) to him, hang on. The celebrants wake up with a coppery taste in their mouths. The streets are still dusty and potholed. The same twisted-limbed beggars haunt the corners. There is too little work and too little money. Independence has come, but the texture of life feels the same. That was the postindependence story of Somalia.

Mutilation of the Pan-Somali Dream

In its pursuit of Somali unification, as in its nominal quest for economic development, the civilian government failed. But in the former case, the responsibility for failure lay not in itself but in its stars: forces beyond the reach of any Somali diplomacy were completing their disintegrating work.

KENYA'S SOMALIS

Following the independence and the unification of the north and south, the principal focus of pan-Somali concern shifted to the Northern Frontier District (NFD) of Kenya and to the Ogaden. The NFD—

comprising over a third of Kenya's territory but including less than ten, perhaps no more than five, percent of its population and an even more negligible proportion of its wealth—had a long history of separate administration under the umbrella of Kenya's colonial government. Over sixty percent of its 400,000-odd inhabitants were ethnic Somalis; cultural and religious ties bound a substantial percentage of the remainder to the Somali majority. Since the early part of the century, movement into and out of the region had been carefully controlled, primarily to prevent any further Somali migration southward.

By 1960, the independence of Kenya had become an issue not of whether but of when. While there was as yet no firm date, everyone saw the accelerated political pace.

Representatives of the NFD's population had stood aloof from the nationalist movements in the rest of the colony. Now, with independence close, they began to assert a distinct nationalist animus. Warmly supported from Mogadishu, a demonstrable majority demanded the right to choose association with their kin or cultural cousins in the Somali Republic and optimistically anticipated an affirmative response.

Somali optimism was reinforced when Reginald Maudling, the British secretary of state for colonial affairs, admitted an official NFD delegation to the 1962 constitutional conference and, at its conclusion, announced in a press conference that "an investigation would be undertaken in order to ascertain public opinion in the area [the NFD] regarding its future and that, for this purpose, an independent commission would be appointed as soon as possible so that its report could be available before the new constitution for Kenya was brought into operation."

Whether, in light of what followed, these gestures should be imputed to a thoroughgoing mendacity or a genuine conflict of opinion within the British government is to this day unclear. The linchpin of British policy in Kenya was the maintenance of an atmosphere conducive to warm relations with the postindependence government. Consequently, once British officials concluded that self-determination for the NFD threatened future entente with Kenya's political elite, their choice was predetermined. There is uncertainty only over the question of when they finally decided that self-determination and paramount British interests were incompatible.

A British decision in the 1950s to offer the NFD Somalis the option of joining their kinsmen might well have seemed a matter of secondary concern to Kenyan nationalists, then busily engaged in constructing effective parties, competing among themselves, and pushing the United Kingdom toward a formal commitment to majority rule within a stated and not-too-distant time. The British could, moreover, have sweetened the pot by combining an independence referendum in the NFD with one in the rest of the colony, thus offering the nationalists an opportunity to demonstrate the force of independence sentiment. Even as late as the constitutional conference, when there still was no specific date for independence, British recognition of the peculiar status of the NFD and of a consequent right to decouple from the rest of the colony might not have irreparably damaged relations with the nationalists, particularly if it had coincided with the announcement of a firm independence date for the remainder of the colony. True, Jomo Kenyatta and the other nationalist leaders were already on record as opposing any cession of Kenyan territory. But their internal struggles, the varieties of British leverage, their willingness to remain at the constitutional conference despite the presence of a separate NFD delegation, and their mild response to Maudling's postconference declaration all support the belief that it was not too late for Britain to remove this source of future conflict.

The opportunity was lost. Months passed without the appointment of a commission. The British government deflected a steady stream of inquiries and remonstrances from Mogadishu. In Kenya, the march toward independence became a stampede. Its imminence hardened nationalist opinion about any diminution of "their" territory. Every inch was sacred. The nationalists feared, moreover, the consequence for their delicately poised tribal politics of a separatist movement anywhere in the colony. If the Somalis, then why not the coastal people, united in their fear of Kikuyu domination?

At last, the promised commission arrived. Publicly, it had the mandate promised by Maudling. Surreptitiously, it was instructed that there could be no question of secession before Kenya received independence, a restriction which appeared to be in direct conflict with the colonial secretary's announcement at the conclusion of the constitutional conference.

In their report, the commissioners found that the Somalis, who they estimated made up sixty-two percent of the NFD's population, "almost unanimously" favored secession from Kenya with the object of "ultimately" joining the Somali Republic. Their preference was shared by a majority of the smaller Muslim communities. The population of two of the area's six districts was virtually unanimous in favoring secession. In three others, large majorities were so inclined.

The report deterred the march of events not at all. A series of unpromising communications from London began to erode the determined optimism hitherto prevailing in Mogadishu. The climax came in March, 1963, some three months after publication of the report, when the new colonial secretary, Duncan Sandys, announced that the NFD would be brought within the framework of Kenya's new constitution, which emphasized the decentralization of power on a regional basis. Somali sentiment was to be accommodated by treating the predominantly Somali sections of the NFD as a distinct region.

The announcement, transmitted to Somalia by the Kenya Broadcasting Corporation, provoked angry and in some cases violent demonstrations throughout the republic. Within six days the Somali National Assembly voted 70 to 14 for a break in diplomatic relations with Britain. After consulting Satow's classic guide to diplomatic etiquette—which rumor has it had to be borrowed from the British embassy—the formalities were rapidly concluded, the ambassador packed his bags, and, in departing, complimented the Somali government for "a most civilized rupture." Along with his personal effects, he took the £ 5 million of British foreign assistance.

Nine months later, independence came to Kenya. Celebrants danced in the streets of Nairobi. But in the NFD, revolt flowered like the bush after the rains.

It was all very brave and in the end very futile. Of the suppression there is no really authoritative account. It still took a pass to get into the area from Kenya, and passes were rarely issued to people not on official business. The terrain was difficult, roads few, movement without escort dangerous. Anyway, as long as the situation promised not to get out of hand, no one other than Somalis cared very much about what was going on. The official word from Nairobi described the violence as the work of *shifta*, the Horn's generic term for raiders of every kind. Songs and poems on Radio Mogadishu praised the "freedom fighters." The Somali government indicted the cruel repression of its kinsmen, being careful, however, to place the main onus on Britain.

Although this attribution of responsibility functioned in part as a euphemism preserving the forms of pan-African brotherhood, it also contained a large dose of truth. Having created the conditions which made revolt inevitable, the British now provided the military means for its suppression: not only the logistics, the weapons, the ammunition, the spares, and the strategy but also officers to supplement the handful of trained Kenyans. They adapted to the conditions of the NFD techniques of counterinsurgency already tested in places like Malaya. They exploited the Somali's dependence on his animals, on the exiguous sources of water, and on his communal ties—in short, the whole fabric of his existence. Military units controlled access to the few important watering places. The authorities seized cattle and camels as collective punishment of the clans for acts attributed to any member. And they restricted the normal movement of the nomads, forcing them to bunch up near well-guarded population centers. "Rather rough, but damned effective!" was the way one knowledgeable British diplomat later summarized the campaign.

The Somali press and radio across the border blared defiance, but there was little the government could offer in terms of concrete assistance other than sanctuary and perhaps a very modest amount of ordnance. Its army was powerless: no armor, primitive logistics, little fuel, an armory of antiquated weapons, a handful of trained officers, and a few thousand lightly armed and poorly organized troops.

And so the revolt died. Not all at once, just a progressive though jagged decline of incidents to the level of a police problem. Within a year, it was clear that as long as power in Nairobi escaped fragmentation through conflict among the main Kenyan tribes, the Somalis of the NFD could never by themselves manage to detach their land from Kenya. Unification of the Somali nation would have to await accretions of strength to the Somali state, a fact lost neither on Jomo Kenyatta nor on his neighbor and generational peer, Haile Selassie. In late 1964, they signed a mutual defense agreement.

ETHIOPIA'S SOMALIS

The old empire and the new Somali Republic had difficulty preserving even the forms of pan-African amity. Achievement of a sovereign political structure in part of their cultural domain had not altered the rancid quality of the Somali's relationship with their Amhara neighbors. Exchanges along their entire interface had progressed from bad to worse through the 1950s as the government in Addis displayed a firm intention and increasing capacity to control all the Somalis on its side of the frontiers.

The precise location of those frontiers was one point of contention left to fester into the next decade. In the course of negotiating the 1948 protocol which governed British evacuation of the Ogaden, the parties had decided to fix a provisional boundary "without prejudice to the international frontiers between Ethiopia and former Italian Somaliland." The line was projected south from a point on the British Somaliland border at the cross section of the forty-seventh parallel and the eighth meridian, the point designated by a 1931 Anglo-Italian boundary commission as the trijunction point between Ethiopia and British and Italian Somalilands. The boundary then proceeded south at such an angle as to leave on the Ethiopian side one hundred kilometers of Ogaden territory effectively occupied and openly administered by Italy without official protest from Ethiopia or any other state for years before the outbreak of the Italo-Ethiopian war. The line actually chosen corresponded generally with Italy's interpretation of its 1908 clarifying agreement.

Before handing over the administration of Somalia to Italy in 1950, the British unilaterally altered the line by choosing a new, more-easterly trijunction point on the northern frontier, thus further enlarging the territory open to Ethiopian administration. Although the British reaffirmed the provisional and nonprejudicial character of the line, Italy expressed its strongest reservations. Not to be outdone, the Emperor laid claim to over 40,000 additional square miles of Somali-occupied territory.

When approving the trusteeship agreement for Somalia, the United Nations General Assembly had recommended that the Ethiopian and Italian governments pursue a settlement of their border dispute through direct negotiation and, if that failed, through mediation and finally, if necessary, arbitration. In each of the five succeeding years, the General Assembly urged speedy resolution of the controversy. Negotiations, after finally commencing in 1955, quickly stumbled to a halt when the Ethiopians objected categorically to the inclusion of Somalis in the Italian delegation. Eventually the Emperor relented, but it soon became evident that negotiation was not a possible route to settlement. The Ethiopian government insisted that the location of the frontier was a narrow, strictly legal issue: interpretation of the 1908 convention. It rejected the Italian claim that subsequent de facto Italian jurisdiction in the Ogaden and subsequent agreements between Italy and the United Kingdom concerning the location of the frontier (basically the 1931 commission report) and "the needs of the local population" were equally relevant considerations.

When, in 1957, the two parties reported the failure of their negotiations to the General Assembly, the assembly approved an Ethiopian proposal for immediate recourse to arbitration. A distinguished arbitral panel was formed the following year; it could not, however, act until the parties reached agreement on its terms of reference. And since the two parties continued to disagree hopelessly about the original meaning of the 1908 convention and about the relevance of other factors—paramount among them being the interests and preferences of the local population—their attempt to negotiate terms of reference simply completed the circle of futility. When, two years after the panel's creation, Somalia achieved independence, the dispute was still unresolved, the borders still in name "provisional."

The new republic challenged its northern as well as its southern border with Ethiopia. Just prior to independence, Somali officials in the British Protectorate had announced that they would not feel bound by the 1897 agreement between Ethiopia and Britain or the more recent confirmation thereof. The unified government of Somalia clung to that position after independence, despite threats from the Emperor to suspend free movement into traditional grazing areas. After independence, the annual migrations continued with little more than the normal level of Ethiopian molestation, molestation which lent a poignant urgency to this controversy over ownership of a seemingly valueless *tranche* of burnt bush. A staff correspondent from the London *Times*, who visited the Haud accompanied by Ethiopian officials, wrote in 1956:

> Individual tribesmen have been brutally treated (it is not possible to describe the intensely painful and humiliating torture) and Ethiopian police have attacked the tribal women. British liaison officers have been threatened by armed police, and attempts have been made to overwhelm and disarm the British tribal policemen. The most recent and serious development has been a blatant attempt to suborn the British tribes. In the case of the Habr Awal, the Ethiopian authorities tried to foist upon it

some settled and partly detribalised members as Sultan and elders, a plan that strikes at the roots of the tribal organisation and loyalty. At the same time, an intertribal meeting was called without notifying the British liaison officers, and Ethiopian officials, alternating between threats and promises, tried to persuade the tribesmen to accept Ethiopian nationality . . . .[1]

The behavior described here appears to have remained fairly typical wherever Amhara troops and police have operated in culturally distinct, primarily Muslim areas, though, to be fair, one must concede the inevitably anecdotal and circumstantial character of the evidence.

The treatment of Muslims by local officials, police, and troops was in step with the Emperor's evident distaste for cultural pluralism. During a 1956 swing through the Ogaden, the Emperor had expressed dissatisfaction with the necessity of employing a Somali interpreter, and he urged his auditors to learn Amharic. In the same year, his government dispatched a UNESCO expert to visit schools in the Somali area in order to study Somali folk music with a view to "integrating" it with the music of the Amhara highlands.

The Emperor's views were not idiosyncratic. Assimilation, particularly of elites, has been a consistent tool of Ethiopian policy. Assimilation has meant mastery of one of the two elite languages—Amharic and Tigrinya (since Menelik and the shift of power to Shoa, only the former really counts)—and at least nominal induction into the Coptic church. Assimilation, understood as the promotion of Amhara cultural integrity, seems to have been an end in itself and also a valued means for preserving the political integrity and the social structure of the highland state. It had diffused the Galla threat. The Emperor clearly hoped that the Somalis too could become good Ethiopians, although he may and certainly he should have suspected that their commitment to Islam would make them far more difficult objects of an assimilationist policy than the largely pagan Gallas. But that must have seemed a minor obstacle compared to an independent Somali state on the border of Ethiopia, certain by virtue of its very existence to excite the nationalist sentiment of all Somalis and equally certain to encourage the political expression of that sentiment.

As generally anticipated, from the inception of Somali independence the border crackled with tension while violence flared across the Ogaden. Events duplicated those in the NFD. Somali clansmen harassed and were harassed by Ethiopian troops. Armed clashes proliferated. Ogaden guerrilla leaders found sanctuary and support across the border. The Somali radio roared encouragement to the "freedom fighters." Addis condemned Somali instigaion of violence. Mogadishu condemned Ethiopian suppression of self-determination.

Aside from the more open character of the rhetorical antagonism between the two African capitals, the principal difference between the

Ogaden and NFD conflicts was the direct involvement of the Somali Republic's armed forces in the former. In 1961 and again in 1964, Somalia and Ethiopia seemed to tremble on the edge of full-scale war. Military units met in bloody combat on the border. Naturally, in each case both sides traced the violence to an aggressive intrusion by the other. The fact that the 1961 collision occurred during an attempted coup in Addis lends credence to Ethiopian allegations of a Somali effort to exploit the confused situation in Ethiopia through probes designed to test the cohesion of the Ethiopian army. More obscure is the immediate cause of the savage exchange of blows in 1964 which included strikes inside Somali territory by the Ethiopian air force.

While there probably were distinct precipitating factors for each of these battles, it is equally probable that with a partially undemarcated border which in any case one party rejected, with troops or paramilitary forces parked on both sides of the disputed frontier engaging in periodic skirmishes, with nomads who could also be guerrillas wandering back and forth on their immemorial rounds carrying reports and sometimes the signs of Ethiopian atrocities, with an Emperor determined to consolidate his grip on this unruly territory and operating through a political apparatus which sucked revenues up to the center from the periphery and in return sent more rapacious administrators, inevitably there would be periodic outbursts of hot war. And given the disequilibrium of forces, it was not merely probable but inevitable that the Somali Republic's forces, however bravely they fought, would be thrashed. It was inevitable, that is, until the Somalis could find a donor willing to alter Ethiopian preponderance.

FRANCE'S SOMALIS

Aside from the port of Djibouti, the Republic of Djibouti or the Territory of the Afars and the Issas,[2] as it was officially called during the ten years before it achieved independence in June, 1977, has languished in an obscurity adequately justified by its size and resources.* The entire territory covers an area of some 8,500 square miles, of which ninety percent is lava-strewn desert and most of the remainder suitable only for grazing. Members of the Somali-speaking Issa clan, who preponderate in the southern part of the territory around the coastal city of Djibouti, are thought to constitute between fifty and sixty percent of a total population** most recently estimated at from 220,000 to 250,000. Their ethnic cousins and Muslim coreligionists, the Afar (or, as they are often called, the Danakil), cluster in the north and west, where they straddle the borders with Ethiopia and Eritrea.

---

* As one wit put it, when the French arrived, the territory's "sole inhabitant was a jackal dying of hunger under a thorn tree."

They number altogether about 200,000; a minority live on the Djibouti side of the frontier. In addition, there is a European population of 8,000 to 10,000, perhaps 5,000 members of the French armed forces, and 8,000 Arabs, in addition to smaller numbers of the usual Mediterranean mélange—Greeks, Lebanese, etc.—that has for centuries carried on commercial ventures along the East and West African coasts.

When the French arrived in the middle of the nineteenth century, they found a series of small independent chiefdoms and sultanates which maintained trading relations with the Ethiopian interior. Beginning a little below the port of Assab, the French extended their authority south through a series of treaties, first with the local Afar potentates and then with the elders of the Somali Issa clan, until they confronted the British. Then, as noted earlier, the two powers divided their spheres with Djibouti going to France. And shortly thereafter, in 1897, a Franco-Ethiopian treaty narrowed and coincidentally confirmed the territory's western frontier.

Ethiopian claims to the exercise of a historical suzerainty over the coast terminated only by French intrusion are mendacious. While it does appear that prior to the nineteenth century some of the northern Afar tribes in the area now called Eritrea conceded a nominal subjection to the rulers of Tigre, those farther south remained independent for centuries prior to French occupation of the coast and Shoan expansion from the interior. In 1895, Menelik conquered the sultan of Aussa, traditionally the most influential Afar leader, and forced him thereafter to pay tribute.

The Franco-Ethiopian entente assumed a powerfully symbiotic economic dimension in 1916 with the completion of the Djibouti-Addis rail link, which established the French port as the principal outlet for Ethiopian trade. The nearby Somali port of Zeila, once a major terminus for caravans from the interior, sank into desuetude. Because of the rail link, now supplemented by an adjacent road, over a third of Ethiopia's external trade was passing through Djibouti—even before the Eritrean war began seriously to limit Ethiopian access to Massawa and Assab. By May, 1977, when Afar or Somali guerrillas cut the rail line, Djibouti's share had risen to about sixty percent. Aside from Ethiopia's transit trade, the territory's economy, such as it is, has relied for decades on bunkering, the military garrison's requirements for goods and services, and a large subsidy from the French government.

Buffered against external forces physically by its interior desert and politically by its size, poverty, passivity, and perpetually amiable relations with Ethiopia, until recently the territory was unaffected by the political turbulence swirling around it. Internal forces also tended toward a seemingly endless stability. Most of the Afars maintained their politically fragmented, tradition-bound pastoral existence far from the capital and the political currents of the modern world. Well over half of the Somalis, on the other hand, lived in the capital where they filled the lower echelons of commerce and administration. Although economically deprived relative to the French and the Levantine trading community, they nevertheless enjoyed a standard of living manifestly superior to that of their fellow Somalis across the border.

Djibouti's subsidized economy was a magnet for Somalis from the British Protectorate, some of whom worked in the port for years while remitting part of their incomes and maintaining second homes across the border. The degree to which comparative prosperity seemed a function of both army expenditure and metropolitan subsidy probably dampened Somali enthusiasm for a fundamental change in political status and thus may have helped DeGaulle's government to extract a *"oui"* from the territory's electorate in the 1958 referendum held throughout France's African possessions on the question of continued association with the motherland.

The referendum followed within a year the establishment of an elected legislature responsible for internal affairs. Both of the main parties in the first legislative election were led by Somalis and represented a cross-communal coalition of Somalis, Afars, and Arabs. After the election, the new assembly elected eight of its members—four Somalis (including the leader of the most successful party), two Afars, one Arab, and one European—to the new executive organ, the Council of Ministers, which was formed under the presidency of the colonial governor. Mohammed Harbi, the party leader, became vice president.

An apparent quickening of Somali nationalist sentiment, stimulated by the pell-mell rush to independence in the protectorate, led within twelve months to a complete reshuffling of the political elements.

The chance occurrence of a referendum inspired by forces entirely exogamous to the territory's affairs gave focus to the new current of Somali nationalist feeling. Mohammed Harbi campaigned for a *"non"* vote by stressing the connection between loosened ties with France and eventual union with Somalia. His main opponent in the earlier election, Hassan Guled, led the opposition canvass, but this time he enjoyed the determined support of the French administration and the resident European population. With only 15,833 names on the electoral register (including Europeans), a vote of 8,661 was sufficient to carry the day for French Somaliland's continuation as an "Overseas Territory within the French Community." With this victory in hand, the French authorities dissolved the assembly and arranged for new elections under a new system of allocating seats. Harbi's party, operating in an environment where the economic life of most people depended on the good will of the administration and the French community, began quickly to disintegrate, a process only hastened by its defeat in the new elections by Hassan Guled's coalition party, which was now showing a strong tilt toward the Afar community. After serving briefly as vice-president of the council, Guled was elected to the French Assembly and was succeeded by an Afar, although Somalis still had a slight plurality in the assembly.

It was at this juncture that the French began to demonstrate special solicitude for the comparatively more backward Afar community. Among measures designed to promote its interests was the redrawing of electoral boundaries, which produced an emphatic reversal of the Somali plurality and moved a reporter for *Le Monde* to refer to "the semi-official support of the administrative authorities" for the Afar political leaders.

The administration's efforts to promote political developments conducive to an indefinite French presence were clearly consistent with the announced aims of the French government. While visiting the territory in 1959, President DeGaulle had stated flatly that France had no intention of relinquishing control over the place, to which it attached great importance. He had, of course, said pretty much the same thing about Algeria. But while *Algérie française* became just plain Algeria, French Somaliland remained unabashedly French. Reviewing a military parade in Djibouti six years after DeGaulle's visit, Pierre Messmer, then France's minister of defense, declared: "France possesses all the military potentialities to beat off any attack whatever and wherever it comes from and will stay in this country as long as she wants to." He then proceeded to Addis for talks with the Emperor, at the conclusion of which he stated that he had conveyed to the Emperor France's determination to remain in Djibouti: "The Sovereign did not object and our interview went on cordially."

President DeGaulle's visit to the territory in August, 1966, lanced the boil of accumulated Somali grievances. When their spokesmen were denied an opportunity to meet with the president, Somalis turned the popular reception planned by the administration into a hostile mass demonstration which escalated into a violent confrontation with French security forces. After suppressing the outburst, the authorities moved quickly and ruthlessly to reinforce their control. Police and troops roamed the city streets and smashed their way into houses, rounding up Somalis who could not prove their citizenship. A lifetime of residence would not suffice. Anyone who could not produce official documents was deemed an illegal alien, although up to that moment the authorities had been notoriously casual about movement and documentation. Somali Republic officials later alleged that even where documents were produced, they were sometimes confiscated by the French police.

Without benefit of formal procedure, of hearing and appeal—indeed, in many cases without benefit of any procedure other than an on-the-spot determination by arresting officers—hundreds, more likely thousands, of men, women, and children were marched to border crossing points and forcibly expelled, leaving behind family and friends, jobs, homes, and personal property. The Somali government responded by closing the border, whereupon the French authorities set up concentration camps outside Djibouti. After collecting a large catch of "illegal aliens," the French took them to a trackless part of the border and pushed them across at gun point. From there they were forced to wander on foot through a semidesert until the survivors reached cross-border villages.

The Somali government contends that within a few months of DeGaulle's abortive visit, the French expelled between 12,000 and 18,000 Somalis from the territory. While any figure is bound to be a very rough estimate, it seems generally agreed that at an absolute minimum the Somali victims of French revenge numbered in the several thousands.[3]

In addition to reducing the Somali population, the French imprisoned nationalist leaders whose status as legal residents was unimpeachable. It was in this atmosphere of violent intimidation that the French conducted the March, 1967, plebiscite in which the inhabitants of what in December, 1966, had by French ukase suddenly become the "Land of the Afars and Issas" again rejected independence. French residents, members of the French armed forces, and their families were among the eligible voters. Mogadishu screamed, "Foul!" but the Franco-Ethiopian entente and the Francophile clients of the Quai d'Orsay who then governed almost all of the nominally independent former French colonies in West Africa insulated the French government from condemnation in international or regional forums.

Then, after eight years without any sign of even a latent inclination to depart, suddenly, near the end of 1975, came the first sign of a French about-face: Giscard's government announced that it would negotiate a timetable for independence.* Subsequently that venerable spokesman for conservative French sentiment, Pierre Messmer, declared Djibouti no longer essential to French security needs. Messmer's statement carried the implication that France contemplated the possibility of real independence for Djibouti rather than its continued existence as a French poodle albeit by another name.

At about the same time, the colonial administration withdrew its thumb from the Afar side of the local political scale, thus allowing the natural Issa majority to reassert itself. Then suspicion of a radical shift in French policy ripened into conviction when France revised the local citizenship law that had been adopted in 1963 to shrink the

---

* In updating this section on Djibouti, I have relied heavily on materials made available to me by Colin Legum, editor of the distinguished annual, *Africa Contemporary Record*.

Somali electorate. Within months of the law's revision, the electorate more than doubled. Most of the increment were Issas.

Though still the colony's chief minister, Ali Aref Bourhan, so long a successful guardian of Afar interests and faithful instrument of French policy, no longer spoke with the voice of France. Facing defeat, his party disintegrated around him, then reconstituted itself into two new Afar parties under leadership prepared to cooperate with the Issas. Isolated, transformed into a political cypher, Ali Aref was not even invited to decorate the Paris "round table" of February, 1977, organized by France to settle the details of the transition to independence. As a further sign of its decisive swing, the French government also ignored the Ethiopian-backed Djibouti Liberation Movement (MLD), although they found room at the conference table for the MLD's Somali-backed counterpart, the Front for the Liberation of the Somali Coast (FLCS).

Participants in the meeting agreed on an early May, 1977, independence referendum and a single list of candidates for the simultaneous election of deputies to the new parliament. On its part, the French government promised military assistance and the maintenance of budgetary support at preindependence levels of well over $100 million. A subsequent meeting of all Djibouti factions including the MLD and a Marxist Afar group, the MPL, held under the auspices of the Organization for African Unity (OAU) in Accra at the end of March, reaffirmed the formal agreements and sustained the conciliatory mood that had made them possible.

As Djibouti hurtled towards its June 27 rendezvous with the problematics of independence, the Somali and Ethiopian governments maneuvered for political position. Each accused the other of murderous designs on the life of the prenatal state. Despite the surrounding tension, the United Patriotic Front, a coalition stitched together at the Accra meeting, proceeded pacifically through the referendum and election, observed by OAU and Arab League representatives. Out of 105,952 registered voters, seventy-seven percent participated, about ninety-nine percent of whom cast their ballots for independence. Ninety-two percent also voted for the single slate and thereby elected thirty-three Issas, thirty Afars, and two Arabs.

To the surprise of no one, on June 24, 1977, a unanimous Chamber of Deputies selected the old Issa politician, Hassan Gouled, to be the first president of the about-to-be republic. June 27 came and went peacefully. Under the terms of the newly signed military assistance agreement, the French army, 4,500-men strong, stayed. It and membership in the OAU and the Arab League (signifying Djibouti's unquestioned status as an independent state) were Djibouti's principal guarantees of continued existence.

In a miserably poor, resourceless country living off the dole, politics and economics are largely interchangeable: most jobs are either in or controlled by the government and are, therefore, deemed possibly the most valuable spoils of electoral success. The Issas had won, but years of French bias had placed Afars in a disproportionate number of jobs. However passionate his commitment to Issa-Afar unity, Hassan Gouled probably could not have entirely resisted Issa demands for a greater, in their minds doubtless juster, share of positions in the administration, the port, and the railroad, Djibouti's only three significant employers. When the national economy is expanding, new demands can sometimes be satisfied without political turmoil by redistributing incremental shares. Where there is no increment, governments reward loyalists by expelling office holders and filling occasional vacancies from the winners' ranks. Afars had what they had through no merit, other than a kind of allegiance by default to the colonial power. In any event, people who have become habituated to valuable opportunities do not cheerfully yield them in the name of abstract justice. While it is unclear just how much job shifting actually occurred, there was enough to antagonize the Afars.

The struggle for jobs placed one terrible strain on the unity that had been achieved just before independence. The Ogaden war added another. The war resulted in a severed rail line and thereby dealt Djibouti's already pathetic economy a devastating blow. Aside from making most railway labor redundant, the line's severance punished the port, more reliant than ever on Ethiopian transit trade as Suez shipping bunkered with growing frequency in Aden and Jedda. Aside from intensifying the struggle for jobs, the war also polarized the Issas and Afars by inducing both sides to arm themselves: the Issas for purposes of joining their Somali brothers in the Ogaden; the Afars primarily to offset Issa firepower which might be employed at home after the war. Some Djibouti Afars also wanted to help an Ethiopian Afar faction which, having rejected Sultan Ali Mireh's leadership, was assisting Addis on the Ogaden front.

Afar anger with a government which seemed to discriminate, on every important front, erupted into scattered acts of violence, quite possibly encouraged if not actively assisted by the Ethiopian government. Followng a December 15 terrorist incident in Djibouti, President Gouled banned the MPL (to which he attributed responsibility), ordered its leaders arrested, and sent security forces sweeping through Afar neighborhoods in search of militants and contraband. Accusing Gouled of "savage tribal repression," the prime minister and four other Afar cabinet members resigned.

With the security operation completed and allegedly successful, the president moved to conciliate. He induced a number of Afar notables to present a list of grievances which they shortly did, citing in particular inequality in the distribution of government posts. Then, presumably by promising corrective measures, he persuaded his former colleagues to rejoin the government and, probably as an earnest of good faith, reshuffled the cabinet to equalize Issa and Afar representation.

The end of the Ogaden war, which came less than two months later, augured relief for Djibouti's prostrate economy. But it also yielded a flood of desperate Somali refugees, who could only complicate life in a country already experiencing sixty percent unemployment. A number of African countries have bad prospects both for economic development and political serenity. But at this time Djibouti is singular in having no apparent prospects at all.

Democracy's End

In June, 1967, the Somali National Assembly elected a former prime minister, Abdirashid Ali Shermarke, to the presidency of the republic. Having risen again to power in part by indicting the incumbent and his allied prime minister (Shermarke's successor in that position) for insufficient militancy on the issue of Somali unity, the new president and his successful nominee for the prime ministership, Mohammed Ibrahim Egal, set busily about conciliating the main enemies of the pan-Somali dream.

They had little choice. The black African states had repeatedly aligned themselves behind Kenyatta and Selassie. The Arab states, never more than distantly sympathetic, were paralyzed now by the results of the June war. Rhetorical belligerence in Mogadishu and insurgency in the NFD and the Ogaden had produced nothing but grief for the Somalis of Kenya and Ethiopia. The Kenyan government claims that from 1963 to 1967 its security forces killed over 2,000 *shifta*. Casualty figures for the Ogaden are unknown. And given the style of Ethiopian administration and the perpetual hostility between the nomads and the Amhara-officered troops sent to keep them in line, some conflict would have occurred even without Mogadishu's encouragement. All one can say with assurance is that Somali government support had not diminished and may have encouraged Ethiopian determination to push assimilation and to assert its authority in every corner of the Ogaden.

The persistent failure of an active pan-Somali policy and the continuing economic stagnation were reinforced as catalysts of a new foreign policy by the economic stringency resulting from the Suez Canal's closure. Somalia's exports of bananas to Europe declined from 94,000 tons in 1966 to 84,000 in 1967, despite the abolition by the government of export duties on bananas, which in the past had yielded almost a million dollars annually in government revenue. The profitability of that export trade was further reduced by the increased cost of packing material and by increased wastage at sea (from fifteen to thirty-five percent) due to the longer transit time.

Shortly after securing parliamentary approval of his new government, Prime Minister Egal used the occasion of a meeting of the Organization of African Unity (OAU) to initiate discussions with both of

Somalia's adversaries. Under the aegis of Zambia's president, Kenneth Kaunda, there was an initial exchange of views with the Kenyans followed quickly by a meeting in the Tanzanian city of Arusha between Egal and Kenyatta. In a formal memorandum of understanding the parties recognized the need to restore amicable relations by stopping all hostile propaganda, gradually phasing out the state of emergency in the border areas, reopening diplomatic relations, creating a committee to review periodically ways and means of furthering the development of good relations, and encouraging the growth of economic and trade ties.

On arriving back in Mogadishu, Egal was received with rather less acclaim than another peacemaker, Neville Chamberlain, had enjoyed on his return from a south German city promising "peace in our time." But despite bitter opposition from those who saw the Arusha memorandum as a sellout, Egal and the president extracted a vote of confidence from the National Assembly.

Unlike Chamberlain's Munich agreement, the Arusha memorandum was an accurate harbinger of improved relations. The two governments rapidly restored trade ties. Provocative poems and songs disappeared from the Somali radio. Kenya lifted the four-year-old state of emergency in the NFD, where calm now prevailed, and proclaimed an amnesty for all guerrillas. The demarche culminated in a state visit to Nairobi in July, 1968, by President Shermarke and Prime Minister Egal.

On the Ethiopian front, progress was less dramatic but still substantial. Initial talks followed by Mogadishu's cessation of hostile broadcasts cleared the air for an official visit by Egal to Addis two months after his appearance in Nairobi. During his visit, Egal and the Emperor agreed to establish direct telecommunication and commercial air links and to promote trade. The Emperor also agreed to lift the state of emergency in the border region. Egal undoubtedly hoped that this would lead in turn to a reduction in the number of violent encounters between Ethiopian security forces and Somali nomads. But whether because of the Emperor's determination to reduce the nomads' independence or his failure adequately to control local officials, reports of Ethiopian-inflicted casualties still flooded across the border periodically to threaten the political foundations of détente.

In their *Area Handbook for Somalia*, a team of scholars working under the auspices of the American University claim that "the 1969 elections were the most impressive in the country's history."[4] Almost 900,000 voters were able to choose among sixty-four parties, including three or four serious coalitions plus a plethora of splinter groups, many representing no more than the entourage of a single local candidate unable to secure adoption by one of the recognized parties. Led by Prime Minister Egal and President Shermarke, the Somali Youth League (SYL) emerged once again with an overwhelming preponderance of assembly seats. And as had happened following previous elections, unaffiliated parliamentarians flocked to join the majority, so that shortly after the election the SYL parliamentary group of 73 swelled to 109 out of a total of 123 seats. By the eve of the June vote to confirm the new Egal government, the largest opposition party had joined the scramble for majority favor to produce an SYL bloc of 120. Although this figure shrank following announcement of the composition of Egal's cabinet, to an outsider the election and its aftermath must have seemed an unassailable mandate for the policies of Egal and Shermarke.

In fact, however, the election was marred by credible charges of pervasive fraud and intimidation. In response to what he regarded as flagrant efforts by the prime minister and the president to employ the police force for partisan purposes, its widely respected commander, Gen. Mohammed Abshir, submitted his resignation early in the electoral campaign. During the ensuing uproar, supporters of the government accused the general of failing to follow the directives of the minister of the interior. After intensive maneuvering, a wealthy SYL power-broker, Haji Mussa Boghor, negotiated a compromise: Abshir agreed not to demand acceptance of his resignation; instead, he would take a leave of absence as police commander until after the election.

With Abshir temporarily out of the way, Shermarke and Egal shuffled senior police officials, apparently to assure the presence of pliable commanders in key election districts. The commander of the northern region, Col. Jama Mohammed Khalib, a man noted for his integrity, efficiency, and political neutrality, was recalled to administrative tasks in Mogadishu.

Authoritative sources believe that these interventions in police operations created a mood of deep bitterness in the officer cadre. Police morale could hardly have been improved by Shermarke's announcement after the election of his acceptance of Abshir's "resignation." Apparently, the president had retained that resignation letter for future use, despite the compromise. Under Abshir's dedicated leadership, the police had been a pillar of Somali democracy. Now, in their enthusiasm for electoral achievement, Egal and Shermarke had undermined it and tainted an election they might well have won in any event. They would soon reap the whirlwind.

The end of Somali parliamentary democracy came with dramatic suddenness. On October 15, 1969, four months after Egal's confirmation by the new assembly, President Shermarke was assassinated during a visit to a drought-stricken district in the north, the area alleged to have been the major scene of electoral shenanigans. Prime Minister Egal, then visiting the United States, hastened back to join the other SYL leaders anxious to select a new president. Late on the night of October 20, word leaked out that the meeting of party notables had selected Haji Mussa Boghor, paragon of the old order, as Shermarke's successor.

Before dawn, Mogadishu was in the hands of the army. Its tanks clanked up the hill in the rear of the city to surround the national police headquarters and the radio station. Although uninvolved in the organization of the coup, the police were in no mood to resist. The acting police commander, Gen. Jama Korshell, a northerner, joined the Supreme Revolutionary Council under the presidency of the coup leader, Maj. Gen. Mohammed Siad Barre, commander of the Somali armed forces.

The roundup of politicians did not stop with Egal and his supporters. Joining them as coerced guests at the president's summer residence in the nearby town of Afgoi were the two leaders of the anti-Shermarke forces in Somali politics, former President Aden Abdullah Osman and former Prime Minister Abdirazak Haji Hussein. With their incarceration, the old order passed into history.

Notes

1. *The Times*(London), October 27, 1956.

2. For a useful overall view of French Somaliland, see Virginia Thompson and Richard Adloff. *Djibouti and the Horn of Africa* (Stanford, California: Stanford University Press, 1968).

3. See I. M. Lewis, "The Referendum in French Somaliland: Aftermath and Prospects in the Somali Dispute, *World Today 23* (July 1967): 310 and "Prospects in the Horn," *Africa Report,* April 1967, p. 37; Thompson and Adloff, *op. cit.,* pp. 94–5; and Paul Mousset, "Referendum à Djibouti," *Revue des Deux Mondes*, April 15, 1967. p. 488.

4. Irving Kaplan *et al, Area Handbook for Somalia* (Washington, D.C.: American University Foreign Area Studies, 1969). p. 228.

Somalia Under the Junta 6

National Socialism

After securing power, the junta under President Mohammed Siad
Barre's leadership declared its intention to implement policies described as "scientific socialism." Since even a careful search conducted by the late Sherlock Holmes would fail to unearth either a
recognizable proletariat or any economic heights to be dominated in
Somalia, most of the classic Marxist and socialist ideas have little relevance to the country's actual circumstances. In practice, scientific
socialism has meant efforts to mobilize all Somalis for public works
activity and to mobilize students for a campaign against illiteracy. It
has also meant promotion of agricultural cooperatives and increased
cultivation in other forms; nationalization of most of the small commercial sector; and a far-flung program of indoctrination in the virtues of self-help, mutual cooperation, and loyalty to the nation and
the regime.

The regime's apex is the Supreme Revolutionary Council (SRC),
consisting of twenty-one army and police officers. It is the fountain-
head of public policy. Policy is elaborated and implemented by a conventional set of ministries, each headed by a secretary of state. Younger
and better-educated than their predecessors, often with English or
U.S. educational backgrounds, the secretaries are the regime's tech-
nocrats. Through their bureaucracies, they conduct the day-to-day
business of government.

There are, however, two activities that fall outside their domain:
internal security and political indoctrination. The former is the province of the National Security Service, headed by Col. Ahmed Sulei-
man Abdulle (President Barre's son-in-law) and composed of carefully selected men from the police and army. Indoctrination has been
carried out by politically reliable cadres operating in provincial and
district centers and responsible directly to the SRC.

111

Another agent of SRC policy operating outside the civil bureaucracy is a kind of youth militia, the *Gul-wa-dayasha* ("Victory Pi-
oneers"). Its main tasks seem to be mobilizing the population for the
compulsory essays in self-help and monitoring the activities of for-
eigners, particularly their contacts with Somalis. A visitor to Mogadishu in 1975 told me that outside his hotel he was under constant surveillance. On one occasion, having sought directions from a Somali,
he turned around after taking a few steps and saw a Victory Pioneer
in his distinctive green uniform interrogating the informant. Another
visitor from the period preceding the Soviets' expulsion, an Englishman who had once served in Somalia, tells of striking up a conversa-
tion with a storekeeper when the man suddenly stiffened, mumbled
something about not having an item that neither had mentioned, and
then hurried into the rear of the shop. The Englishman turned
around to find a Victory Pioneer lounging near the door.

A marked reluctance to issue entry visas to Westerners, particularly Americans, and restraints on their mobility within Somalia have
functioned together with the close surveillance of social contacts and
the tame press to hamper appraisal of the regime's achievements. It
appears, however, that President Barre's government has generated
an impressive momentum toward amelioration of the harsher edges
of the country's poverty. In part, it is a matter of atmosphere. The
good-natured, aimless languor is gone. One senses a bustling pur-
posefulness, an unwonted hustling toward tangible goals.

There are also concrete achievements, particularly in the capital.
Under the self-help program, the Somali people contribute as much
as seven hours a week of their "leisure" time to government-de-
signed projects. The results are particularly prominent in Mogadishu,
where one sees a new hotel, a new office complex for the Foreign
Ministry, new roads and schools, housing estates, and clean streets.
The government has expanded the acreage under cultivation; its goal
is self-sufficiency in basic food items within three years. The emphasis
on agriculture notable in the new five-year plan is not restricted to
food products. Cotton, already grown on a commercial scale, is sched-
uled for major expansion in production.

In the fields of education and public health, progress is more
striking. During 1970–71 alone, the primary school population increased by one hundred percent. There has also been expansion at
the secondary and university levels. Of at least equal significance is
the war on adult illiteracy. The government mobilized students for an
initial national literacy campaign conducted for the benefit of the settled thirty to thirty-five percent of the population. Now it proposes to
reach beyond the towns and villages to the nomadic majority. On the
public health front, the incidence of malaria, tuberculosis, and other
endemic diseases has been sharply reduced. It was these direct con-
tributions to the quality of Everyman's life, as well as the widely prevailing self-help projects, that led Julius Nyerere to remark during

the 1974 meeting in Mogadishu of the OAU heads of state: "The Somalis are practicing what we in Tanzania preach."

To what extent have these gains been paid for through a reduction in the ordinary Somali's sense of personal freedom? The short answer is: We don't know. Such evidence as we have is largely anecdotal, impressionistic, and conflicting. Some Western observers find the atmosphere coercive; others see enthusiasm, pride, and active support for the junta among the generality of urban Somalis. Those who sense a high degree of coercion may or may not be projecting onto Somalis their own thoroughly accurate perception of close surveillance with its attendant psychological discomforts.

The circumstantial evidence is extremely ambiguous. On the one hand, acts such as the 1972 public execution of two SRC members (accused of plotting against President Barre), the 1975 execution of ten conservative religious figures (who had indicted, as a violation of the Koran, the government for its decision to guarantee equal rights for women), and the execution of army officers implicated in the 1978 coup attempt (easily aborted by troops loyal to the regime) imply a feverish insecurity that in turn suggests subterranean currents of opposition to the junta. This assumes, of course, that where there is insecurity there is usually something to be insecure about. On the other hand, President Barre's 1973 decision to release most of the *ancien régime*'s political notables from their enforced residence in what they wryly labeled the "Afgoi Hilton" and his subsequent appointment of several of their number to responsible administrative and diplomatic positions may reflect a solidly based confidence in widespread public support. But, since insecurity can simply be paranoid and confidence either delusive or a function of ruthless authoritarian control, one hesitates to make very much of this circumstantial evidence.

The 1978 rising of a few units of the armed forces in the Mogadishu area no doubt reflected both the disenchantment normally generated by any losing military venture and a lurking, clan-based resentment towards a leadership that, because of its steep pyramidal shape, simply cannot provide balanced representation at the very top of all the important clans. Outside Somalia there is an articulate opposition that solicits support from the conservative Arab states. And within the government and armed forces there may well be a current of opinion that favors restoring close ties with the Soviet Union, probably more on strategic than on ideological grounds. Continued refusal of the United States to provide military assistance until the Somalis suspend ostentatious assistance to the West Somali Liberation Front obviously strengthens this current. But President Barre, a determined pragmatist, is flexible enough to play this card himself, if it seems necessary for internal political or strategic reasons. He can, in other words, co-opt this source of dissent. For the time being, neither internal nor external opponents seem able to mount effective threats to his continued rule. Fallout from the Ogaden war has not consumed Barre at least in part because the decision to strike for Somali freedom was so obviously desired, perhaps even demanded, by politically-relevant opinion within Somalia and in part because Soviet behavior beyond his control was evidently the source of the Somali defeat. With the war issue largely neutralized by this critical element of force majeure, and with many concrete accomplishments to his credit, the president still appears to enjoy a solid base of support and room for political maneuver. But intelligence on the real attitudes of armed forces, whether in Somalia or practically anywhere else in the Third World, is necessarily so uncertain that any statement about the stability of governments has to be hedged around with caveats.

Had Siad Barre attempted to extend the secular revolution to the mass of fiercely independent traditionalists out in the bush, he probably would have encountered bloody resistance. Perhaps he would nevertheless have tried had fate not delivered the nomads into his hands.

By early 1975, it was apparent that the drought that had decimated the Sahel tribes and emptied villages in the Ethiopian heartland was well on its way to destroying the basis for life on the sere plains of the Ogaden and the adjoining Somali territory. Of the Somali Democratic Republic's approximately three million inhabitants, some 800,000 had lost the larger proportion—in many cases all—of their herds. Deaths from starvation were escalating exponentially.

In vivid contrast to Haile Selassie's precedent, the Somali government went public, pleading for international disaster relief. Simultaneously it deployed its full resources, including the armed forces and the students spread around the country as part of the literacy and consciousness-raising campaign, to rescue and to begin the rehabilitation of the ravaged clans. Within a few months, a quarter of a million of the most desperate cases had been drawn into refugee camps run exclusively by Somali students and officials. The inmates were housed, fed, and incorporated into the literacy program.

The drought's impact was intensified by the progressive overgrazing of the plains. It had for years been apparent that the land could not support indefinitely a growing animal and human population, much less allow a margin for development. The herds had been the basis of nomadic life. Now they were decimated beyond hope of renewal without massive external assistance. And full-scale renewal, if it did occur, would in turn aggravate the deterioration of the overgrazed land.

What opportunity offered, President Barre and his colleagues quickly took. With generous Soviet support, they transported roughly 100,000 nomads into hastily prepared agricultural settlements in the relatively fertile southern region of the country. A much smaller number, reportedly about 20,000, were settled along the coast to take up new lives as fishermen. The remainder were to have their herds restocked so that they could return to the traditional nomadic life.

Whether the transplants will hold and whether the restocked herds will survive are open questions. Indeed, the larger effort to transform Somali life, of which the resettlements are only a part, remains terribly problematic. The regime's accomplishments to date seem a function of unusually liberal Soviet support plus a degree of indigenous vision and energy with few obvious parallels in sub-Sahara Africa. But the country's economic margin remains perilously thin. And the threat of renewed war dissipates both its slender resources and the attention of its small elite.

Defense and Foreign Policy

THE MAKING OF AN ARMY

Somalia's first benefactor in the military field was the United Arab Republic (UAR). Immediately after their independence, the Somalis were supplied with a small quantity of obsolete items from UAR inventories. The paucity and particularly the poor quality of the donated material encouraged the new state to look elsewhere for assistance.

In 1961, it received and promptly rejected a modest offer from the Czechs. An initial canvass of the NATO states produced discouraging results. The United States flatly refused Somali overtures. The United Kingdom and Italy at first seemed equally uninterested in becoming donors of military aid. In 1962, however, they reversed their positions and offered a joint program worth $8.4 million. The Somali government quickly accepted. But toward the end of the year, when the Northern Frontier District crisis was sweeping United Kingdom-Somali relations toward the breakpoint, the NATO allies proposed a revised and somewhat expanded program. Under it, the United States, Italy, and West Germany would provide roughly $10 million worth of equipment and training for a force of 5,000 to 6,000 soldiers with a pronounced orientation toward civic action and internal security. In return, the Somali government would undertake not to accept military assistance from any other source.

The offer remained pending for almost a year until it was rejected coincident with the government's announcement that it had accepted a Soviet-authored alternative valued at about $32 million. Although the specific terms of the Soviet-Somali military aid agreement were not published, its principal dimensions were generally understood to be as follows. The Soviets would train and equip with modern weapons a 10,000-man armed force, including a small air wing using jet planes. Most of the program cost would be treated as a grant with the remainder to be repaid over a twenty-year period.

News of the arms agreement was received in Addis with unconcealed anger. Despite Soviet assurances regarding the projected size of the Somali army, the Emperor accused the Russians of generating an arms race on the Horn and of preparing to underwrite a 20,000-man army capable of initiating offensive operations. Both Somali and Russian officials denied the Ethiopian allegations and reaffirmed the purely defensive character of the proposed program.

By 1969, the Somali armed forces had just about completed the build-up projected at the time of the original military aid agreement. Then, following the accession of President Barre, the Soviet military aid program burst through its originally programmed dimensions. Within five years the Somali armed forces did reach the 20,000 figure angrily predicted a decade earlier by Haile Selassie. Particularly in armor and aircraft, the quality as well as the number of its weapons was markedly enhanced. The 1976 inventory included about fifty MIG fighters (among them twenty-four supersonic MIG-21s) and several Ilyushin bombers—on paper close to the strongest air-strike capacity in black Africa. How many planes were actually serviceable at any given moment was, however, uncertain, since there still were glaring maintenance deficiencies, the bugbear of all armies in technologically underdeveloped countries. Maintenance deficiencies also hurt the armored units, beefed up prior to the Ogaden war with T-54 tanks, among the most modern in Soviet inventories.

By contrast, in 1975 the Ethiopians had only thirty-seven combat planes, and, with the exception of nine F-5As, they were useless as contestants for air superiority against the Somali MIGs. But in 1976 the Dergue acquired at least twenty F-5Es, a sophisticated fighter-bomber that compared favorably with anything the Somalis could deploy. On paper, at least, there was a more dramatic difference in armor. The authoritative survey of the International Institute for Strategic Studies for 1975 listed 250 medium tanks and approximately 300 armored personnel carriers in Somali inventories compared to twelve medium and fifty light tanks plus just over 100 armored personnel carriers and armored cars for the Ethiopians. However, with respect to Somali armor as well as aircraft, the institute's estimates were followed by the caveat, "Spares are short and not all equipment is serviceable."

COMPETITORS FOR INFLUENCE

While unrivaled in the military aid field, the Soviet Union remained just one among several important donors of economic assistance. In 1966 the United States, acting under a congressional directive, had terminated the remnants of its once substantial aid program because Somali-registered ships had carried freight to Hanoi. But Italy continued to provide significant support. And, as an associate member of the European Economic Community, Somalia received substantial aid from the European Development Fund, which—among other things—financed expansion of the national university and, jointly with the World Bank, construction of a deep-water port for Mogadishu.

The Chinese had been around virtually since independence, managing, through a low profile and a steady policy of political neutrality, to cultivate the same engaging image they enjoyed in Addis. Unlike Soviet projects, which, on occasion, antagonized the Somalis with cost overruns or other deficiencies, Chinese efforts seemed well conceived and effectively implemented. By far the most ambitious Chinese project, a 1,045-kilometer road running parallel to the Ethiopian border from the old Italian outpost of Beledwein in the south (already connected to Mogadishu by an all-weather road) to Burao, was proceeding on schedule. Its projected cost of approximately $60 million made it the most substantial Chinese ventire in Africa after the Tanzam Railway.

Somalia's accession to the Arab League in 1974 enhanced its prospects for attracting petrodollar aid. Libya, Iraq, and particularly the United Arab Emirates all made significant commitments; actual disbursements apparently lagged a good deal behind. The Saudi Arabian government flatly conditioned an aid offer of $75 million on the progressive contraction of Russian activities in Somalia. When the Somalis refused to satisfy the stipulated condition, the offer was withdrawn. But as Somalis and Russians began their slide toward a decisive rupture, the Saudi government renewed its campaign of financial inducements.

THE REGIME'S FOREIGN POLICY

Growing military strength, the appearance of impressive domestic achievements, and strengthened ties to a renascent Arab world, catapulted the Somalis from their earlier OAU role as a kind of pitiable but irritating problem child to a position of some importance and prestige. In 1973, when Tanzania and Idi Amin's mercenary regime in Uganda teetered on the brink of full-scale war, it was President Barre who acted to mediate their differences. In 1975, Mogadishu was the setting for the annual gathering of the OAU heads of state; and, following precedent, they elected their colleague from the host country to serve as president of the organization for the succeeding year. Of greater significance than President Barre's essentially automatic selection was the good race run by Somali Foreign Minister Omar Arteh Ghalib, with the support of the Arab members and many of the predominantly Muslim black African states, for the vacant OAU post of secretary-general.

For Somalia, the rapid accretion of military and diplomatic clout coincided with gathering tension along the Ethiopian border. The fresh gust of hostility was partially attributable to those ubiquitous sources of discord, oil and gas.

For almost two decades, corporate exploration teams had probed different parts of the Horn with high hopes and no success. Geological promise remained tantalizingly unfulfilled. Most exploration activity had been strung along the Ogaden border; there had also been

activity in the Northern Frontier District of Kenya. Following a
succession of dry wells east of the provisional Ogaden border, exploration activity ground to a virtual halt in Somalia. On the Ethiopian
side of the border, Tenneco, a U.S. company, began drilling in February, 1972. Just over a year later, gas started pouring into a drill hole
at the 11,000-foot mark. According to one unofficial report, the rate
of flow extrapolated to thirty-five million cubic feet per day. A subsequent well in the area turned out dry. Tenneco officials claim that
they are still evaluating the overall results.

The actual find, at a spot only thirty miles from the Somali border,
threatened to tear off what remained of the scab on relations between
the two neighbors. The spirit of détente, conjured into existence by
Egal and Shermarke, had begun to wither from the moment Tenneco
workers first arrived in the area with a guard of thirty-five Ethiopian
troops, which grew quickly to over one hundred. Some observers believe that Ethiopia was concerned not only about the security of drilling operations but also about the flow of cattle across the open border
to Somalia's Indian Ocean ports, a movement which hampered Ethiopian efforts to create a meat-processing industry. When Somalia
countered the gradual build-up of Ethiopian forces along the border
with troop concentrations of its own, the tension level between the
two states rose proportionately.

An attempt in late December, 1973, and in the succeeding January
to lower the diplomatic temperature through face-to-face discussions
culminated in a vitriolic shouting match between negotiators. Shortly
after the Ethiopian delegates had stormed back to Addis from Mogadishu, convoys of additional Ethiopian troops began to roll east to
thicken border defenses.

Though braced for war, neither side seemed eager to initiate it.
They came closest to open conflict the following year when the Somalis threw a contingent of about one hundred men across the border
in the direction of the drilling operation. The Third Division commander responded by dispatching a larger force to the rear of the
Somalis and cutting off their access to water. After several tense days,
during which the Somalis made no effort to force supplies through
the Ethiopian blockade, the probe was withdrawn without further incident.

As the veneer of détente peeled away to expose the old animosities, the Emperor, with the active encouragement of his officer corps,
hustled about in search of more and more modern arms. The U.S.
program, having settled down to a steady $11 million a year, provided
spares, ammunition, training, and a certain amount of weapon replacement. On an official visit to the United States in 1973, the Emperor pressed his case for additional grant aid to allow modernization
of his inventories. He returned with his fur well stroked and his hand
empty. While Ethiopia, like any old friend, would always be welcome
in the Pentagon's cash-and-carry department, President Nixon is re-

ported to have said, the subbasement soup kitchen could not increase its annual dispensation. Access to the bargain basement with its concessional credit terms was left, at best, uncertain. Had the Emperor known of the already firm decision to reduce operations at Kagnew Station, he would have more readily understood the slippage in the great leverage that he once had. But it was only after he had returned to Addis that the news was conveyed to him through the American embassy.

An urgent appeal to Ethiopia's other staunch ally, Israel—which for more than a decade had cooperated with the U.S. Military Assistance Advisory Group (MAAG) in training the Emperor's army for, among other things, the dubious struggle in Eritrea—evoked an equally unsatisfactory response, though for different reasons. The Israelis simply had nothing they were able to spare. Nor, it is reported, were they receptive to the Emperor's proposal that they activate their influence network in the United States on behalf of Ethiopian arms requests, a response which probably convinced the Emperor that his Israeli connection had lost its utility. When, on Yom Kippur, 1973, the Arab armies sliced into Sinai, Haile Selassie finally—and by all accounts reluctantly—clambered onto the Afro-Arab bandwagon and severed diplomatic relations with Israel.

According to one Western diplomatic source, the Emperor, having been rejected by his old consorts, turned at last to a long-frustrated suitor only to be informed by the object of his sudden affection that, as far as the Horn was concerned, the Russian bear was already engaged. Disappointed but undeterred by his various and unexpected rebuffs, the Emperor and his generals continued to press the United States for additional assistance.

Within both the U.S. embassy and the MAAG, opinion was sharply split. The ambassador and his senior political advisers championed the Ethiopian cause in the name of strategic imperatives. Several younger foreign service officers opposed stepped-up aid. They were impressed neither by the "Somali threat" nor by the case for Ethiopia's continued strategic value. On the Somali issue, they found support among U.S. military men, a number of whom insisted that, despite their new equipment, the Somalis still enjoyed strategic inferiority. According to one experienced officer:

> They could race across the border and seize a strip of the Ogaden. Maybe they could surround and chop up the one division opposite them, although that's doubtful. The Ethiopians would almost surely play it smart, drop back to Harar where they have supplies and prepared positions, and wait for reinforcements. The Somalis simply don't have the logistics to get very far into Ethiopia. They wouldn't get anywhere near the heartland. And I'll wager that once the Ethiopians concentrate their forces in the

south, they'll push the Somalis all the way back across the border
and maybe then some. In fact, once the Ethiopians get going,
they might not stop until they get to the sea.

The Ogaden War

In retrospect, as in prospect, the Ogaden war appeared almost inevitable, a matter of destiny beyond human control. For a century the
Somalis had been collecting scores to settle. The liberation of Somali-
populated Ethiopian territory was no mere abstract ideal or chauvin-
ist caprice dressed up in the rags and scabs of imagined grievances.
Ethiopia's black imperialism had drawn real blood, maimed and exploited real people, and had sustained itself to the very end of the
Emperor's reign.

The revolutionary government promised a new deal for all the
empire's national minorities and for the nation's Muslims as a
group. But the men in the Dergue, none of them ethnic Somalis, were
the same men who, as members of the military, had been the Emperor's principal instrument of repression. And, whatever they might
say about regional autonomy, they had in fact chosen to monopolize
power and to exterminate the various advocates of broadly-based civilian rule.

But even if Somalis on both sides of the border had had confidence in the Dergue's vague proposals and protestations of good
faith, they would probably have taken up the gun. For real grievances
did, of course, mix with emotional nationalism and with dreams of a
big Somali state, gaining in international status. Moreover, with the
Emperor gone and the empire in disarray, the Somalis, for the first
time better armed than their opponents, sensed a riptide of opportunity. They would have to race the historical clock, gambling that the
combined pounding of Eritrean and Somali offensives would shatter
Ethiopia's army, thereby releasing all the empire's centrifugal forces
and allowing the victors to reshape the Horn's political geography.
They would leave Ethiopia truncated, isolated, crowded, poor, and
for all those reasons too weak for revenge.

For the Somalis the setting must have been almost irresistibly enticing: the Americans seemingly unprepared for massive involvement
in the Horn or anywhere else in Africa; the Russians apparently too
committed by their investment and lack of immediate alternatives in
North-East Africa intransigently to oppose a Somali offensive; and
the Dergue, convulsed by internal strains, harrassed by disillusioned
civilian radicals, beset by small rebellions in most of Ethiopia and
bleeding men, materiel, and morale out through its Eritrean wound.
But, as enticing as it was, the Ogaden had to wait.

Who or what made the Somalis wait? From all accounts, the Soviets did their best, consistent with the preservation of their investment,
keeping the Somali armed forces on short rations of ammunition,

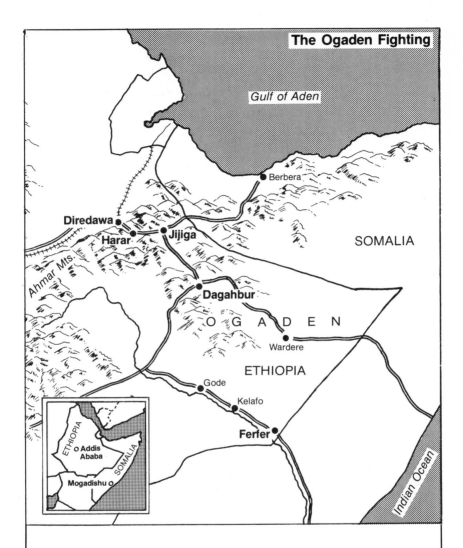

The Ogaden Fighting

Gulf of Aden

Berbera

SOMALIA

Diredawa
Harar · Jijiga
Ahmar Mts.
Dagahbur

O G A D E N

Wardere

ETHIOPIA

Gode
Kelafo

Ferfer

Indian Ocean

ETHIOPIA
o Addis Ababa
SOMALIA
Mogadishu o

1 Somali-backed rebel drive to take Ogaden begins in mid-July 1977 from Ferfer. Somalis are said to commit 10,000 troops. Ethiopian stronghold of Dagahbur falls, and most of Ogaden is quickly overrun.

2 Second stronghold, Jijiga, falls in September, and Somali forces push on toward remaining strong points, Diredawa and Harar.

3 Somalia breaks in November with Soviet Union and Cuba, which subsequently pour aid into Ethiopia. After vast Soviet arms airlift ends in mid-January 1978, Ethiopian counter-offensive begins. Aided by Cuban troops, Ethiopians retake Jijiga on March 5 and Dagahbur three days later.

4 Somalia announces on March 9 that it is withdrawing from the Ogaden.

© 1978 by The New York Times Company. Reprinted by permission.

spare parts, and other essential items. Could that have been enough? A year later the Somalis would go to war faced with the prospect of a total Soviet arms embargo. Almost certainly Somalia's decisive inhibition was the terrible drought-induced famine. Until the end of 1976, the armed forces had to bear a major share of the relief effort.

THE SOVIET COURTSHIP OF ETHIOPIA

At just what point did Siad Barre know beyond hope that his erstwhile Soviet allies would actively oppose him? In January, 1977, when Somali troops apparently made their first probes? By July when Barre openly committed his regular forces? Certainly well before November, when Barre ordered all Soviet advisers out of Somalia, barred access to the supposedly vital air and naval facilities, and severed diplomatic relations with Cuba.

As early as 1975 the Soviet Union had expressed a sympathetic interest in the Ethiopian government's radical rhetoric and revolutionary program; but with the Dergue requesting and receiving increased access to American arms—during 1975–76 Kissinger approved the sale of M-60 tanks and F-5E planes plus Iranian transfer of a squadron of second-hand F-5As—the prerevolutionary patron-client lineup seemed basically undisturbed.

But a year later the Dergue and the Soviet government had begun a serious courtship. Its first tangible result was a Soviet promise of $385 million in military aid, delivered to a delegation from the Dergue visiting Moscow in December, 1976. Through the winter and spring of 1977 the Russians struggled to acquire in Ethiopia the position of influential patron, once held by the United States, without sacrificing their Somali ties. The effort peaked in March at a secret summit meeting held in Aden under the conciliating chairmanship of Fidel Castro. Although the prospects for successful mediation were never bright, changes both in the political character of the Somali and Ethiopian states and in the larger international environment provided a basis for hope if not exactly optimism.

After so many sobering experiences in other parts of the world, the Soviets may not have relied very much on the sudden ideological convergence of the Somali and Ethiopian governments by itself to transform relations between these hereditary enemies. They might reasonably have attached greater weight to the attenuation of Western interests in the Horn, most recently signified by France's *volte-face* in Djibouti and the Carter administration's February, 1977, decision to punish the Ethiopian government for its human rights delinquencies by suspending military assistance. As it seemed to drop out of the competition for influence, the United States necessarily enhanced the appearance of Soviet assets.

Of course, if the Somalis and Ethiopians were interested in aid for no purpose other than securing their respective maximum claims in the Ogaden, there would be little, if anything, on which Soviet leverage could operate. But in fact each of the local parties had other pressing objectives which Soviet aid might help them to realize. Both regimes were attempting, in the face of appalling difficulties, to manage social and economic transformations. So there was a desperate need for large-scale economic and technical assistance.

Both also had uses for military assistance unrelated to the Ogaden. This was particularly true for the Ethiopians, who were losing their war of attrition in Eritrea, while simultaneously hacking away at the Hydra-headed revolts in other parts of the empire, not to mention violent, clandestine opposition in Addis itself. The Somali regime, though fairly secure internally, also had military interests distinct from the Ogaden. There remained the question of self-determination for the Somalis of Kenya, a latent aspiration but one Mogadishu had never waived. There remained, as well, the other, defensive side of Somali ambitions in the Ogaden, namely a fear of Ethiopian claims, occasionally invoked by Haile Selassie, to the Benadir coast, i.e., Somalia.

In short, the Soviets could offer economic support for ambitious domestic programs plus military assistance in furthering ambitions and stilling fears only if the parties would compromise their differences, not simply by pretending they did not exist, but rather through a creative political act that would reduce the political and psychological significance of the existing state boundaries.

Castro's visit was the Soviet bloc's ace. The thrust of Somali nationalism, possibly supplemented by Arab inducements and Ethiopian intransigence (we do not know what, if anything, Mengistu was prepared to yield beyond the abstractions of local self-government), trumped it. By insisting that Somali claims be satisfactorily settled as a precondition to a Marxist Red Sea federation proposed by Castro, Siad Barre placed the burden of choice in front of the Soviet leadership. They would soon pick it up.

GUERRILLA WAR

The origins of the West Somali Liberation Front (WSLF) go back to the founding of the Somali state. In 1961 Ogaden-Somali activists, supported by Mogadishu, first began recruiting their clansmen for guerrilla war. For years thereafter the movement managed only to annoy the Ethiopians, toughening their repression, and to remind the Somali government of its impotence. Conversion of this poorly-armed handful of men into an effective fighting force must have begun some considerable time before January, 1977, when the WSLF began to roll across the Ogaden, shoving the occupants of scattered Ethiopian outposts back towards the key cities of Jijiga, Harar, and Diredawa. Well-armed and coordinated, stiffened, and probably in many cases led by officers with Ogaden clan connections on "leave" from the Somali army, troops of the WSLF seem to have driven ahead without much difficulty.

The front's goals had grown along with its teeth. At a meeting held in mid-January, it announced the formation of two wings representing respectively the Ogaden Somalis and the Abo-speaking people of Bale, Arussi, and Sidamo provinces whom the Ethiopians had previously classified as Oromo. The front claimed both that the Abo-speakers were members of the Somali language group and that they constituted a majority in each of the provinces they inhabited, provinces containing much of Ethiopia's most fertile and least congested land.

Whatever its historical merits, the claim made excellent strategic sense. Loss of the arid, impoverished Ogaden and its three-quarters of a million unruly Somalis could not by itself seriously reduce Ethiopian military potential unless it catalyzed additional territorial losses for Ethiopia or produced a debilitating decentralization of effective power. Without those secondary effects, Somalia would live, like France after World War I, in constant danger of its inherently more powerful neighbor's *revanche.* Somalia's acquisition of Ethiopia's southern provinces promised to alter permanently the Horn's indigenous balance of power. To fulfill that promise all the Somalis had to do was break Ethiopia's will or capacity to resist, an achievement requiring rather more than the conquest of various pinpricks on the map of the Ogaden.

In June and July with the WSLF already controlling at least sixty percent of the Ogaden, Siad Barre threw Somali army units into the battle. Alongside troops of the front they thrust towards Jijiga, as the Soviets moved unequivocally to oppose them.

THE SOVIET SWITCH

Shortly after the failure of Castro's conciliation mission, Mengistu visited Moscow, probably to press for a flat Soviet commitment to support Ethiopia against Somalia in case of war and for accelerated delivery of arms and technical assistance. Although the Soviets passed the word around that they were deeply impressed by Mengistu's personal qualities and revolutionary views, they continued through the spring and, apparently, even into the summer meeting their arms-delivery commitments to the Somalis, probably because they still hoped to manage a compromise settlement.

If Mengistu was disappointed on that score, he must have found some solace in the Soviet arms which began arriving in Assab and Djibouti in early May, even before his trip. As tangible signs of a major Soviet commitment, the arrival of Soviet and, in larger numbers, Cuban advisers sent to assist the changeover from U.S. to Soviet weapons, should have brought a good deal of additional comfort. But nowhere near enough. Neither the weapons nor the technicians nor clandestine Israeli assistance—instructors for the new divisions the Dergue was raising and possibly including spare parts and ammunition for the U.S. equipment still in use—seemed sufficient to halt the Somali tide. By August, Ethiopian sources were conceding loss of the entire Ogaden countryside. And on the margin of their main thrust the Somalis were extending fingers of force into the Abo-inhabited provinces.

The Dergue's anxieties must have edged towards panic in mid-September when, after a brutal struggle, demoralized Ethiopian troops yielded Jijiga and its big tank base. Hardly pausing for breath, Somali units pressed relentlessly westward through the mountains towards the ancient market town of Harar and the rail and industrial center of Diredawa, Ethiopia's third largest city. Other Somali contingents drove up from the South, while still more applied west-to-east pressure. The Dergue responded by mobilizing retired army veterans under the age of sixty and slapped-together peasant militia units, hustling all of them to the front in a melange of military and commandeered civilian vehicles.

On the diplomatic front, Mengistu suddenly made overtures to the U.S. embassy. This followed months of freezing animosity dating back to late April when the Dergue had shut down every U.S. government operation in Ethiopia except the embassy and AID. Out went the MAAG, the USIS, and the U.S. remnant in Kagnew. The United States had quickly retaliated by suspending a $10 million foreign military sales credit and halting delivery of items in the military pipeline. Why did Mengistu begin feeling out the possibility of renewing the arms relationship? Was the overture real or simply calculated to put some fire in the Russian belly? Whatever the case, Mengistu or his representative, which is not clear, made a quick trip to Moscow and Havana and the flirtation with the United States was not soon renewed.

The allegedly inadequate delivery rate for Soviet equipment was not the result of continued fence-straddling. Possibly in mid-summer, certainly no later than the end of August, the Russians had closed the Somali pipeline. Well before then they had ceased direct involvement in maintaining the Somalis' shaky logistic systems. Perhaps the Soviets and Cubans had simply underestimated the speed and force of the Somali drive into Ethiopia. Or perhaps it took some months to organize the logistics necessary for a massive arms transfer.

The transfer began in early November and continued into the new year, the greatest sustained long-distance airlift in Soviet military history. The sea lift, which had begun earlier, also assumed very impressive dimensions. Altogether, between May, 1977, and March, 1978, (primarily in the five months from November to March) the Soviet Union transferred equipment valued by Western intelligence at something in the neighborhood of $1-1.5 billion, roughly four or five times the value of all U.S. military aid delivered to Ethiopia between 1953 and 1977.

Even before the great November airlift could be translated into usable firepower, the Ethiopians had begun to stabilize their positions. The growing length of the Somalis' supply lines helped to slow their momentum. So did Ethiopia's decisive command of the air, achieved by October, perhaps earlier, with the aid of newly arrived Soviet MIGs, Cuban pilots and, on the Somali side, a dearth of spare parts and other logistic deficiencies which stranded a good part of Somalia's air force on the ground.

As the fall went on, the Somali offensive ground to a halt, Soviet arms accompanied by thousands of Cuban combat troops streamed to the front, and President Barre intensified his desperate search for arms. In July he had known a moment of hope when, following consultations with various allied and friendly states—including Britain, France, Egypt, Iran, and Saudi Arabia—the United States had announced that it was ready to join other governments in providing Somalia with an alternative source of military assistance. The official announcement more-or-less coincided with confidential expressions of U.S. interest in putting U.S.-Somali relations on an altogether more intimate footing, conveyed directly to Barre by his personal physician, an American close to Governor Hugh Carey of New York. The precise content of that private message and whatever words passed between Barre and U.S. diplomats in Mogadishu remain obscure. A September, 1977, *Newsweek* story quoted an unnamed State Department official who, noting that the United States had always referred to the possible provision of "defensive weapons," concluded that U.S. offers of aid "were not of such a nature that a prudent man would have mounted an offensive on the basis of them."

In July, 1977, Siad Barre was in no position to be prudent. And so, after the event, he could not reasonably claim that, but for his belief in the availability of U.S. support, he would never have launched the Ogaden campaign. Any suggestion that the WSLF moved without his approval would strain credulity. The Ogaden war was well under way before Barre received any concrete encouragement from the United States. President Barre had been under strong pressure from the army and civilians and WSLF leaders to act. After all, what had all the planning and arming and training been for except to recover the lost lands? And when would there ever again be so good a chance? Reality quickly eclipsed the Somalis' short and happy dream.

In August the United States had announced there would be no arms for Somalia as long as its troops were fighting inside Ethiopian territory. Nor would the United States approve third-party transfers to the Somalis of U.S.-supplied equipment. Britain and France and other West European arms producers also said in effect that they stood behind the no-change-of-borders-by-force rule. Black African opposition to border changing, plus the U.S. stand, inhibited Arab friends as well. Egypt sent some spare parts from its depreciating arsenal of Soviet weapons. Dribs and drabs leaked in from a few other friendly states and the international arms bazaar.

Winter overtook fall. Somali forces, checked around Harar and pounded from the air whenever the sky cleared, watched Ethiopian resources grow while theirs diminished. Acting as if he had been appointed roving ambassador for American right-wing ideologues, Siad Barre, now plainly resigned at least to present defeat, toured friendly capitals delivering Phillipics against the Soviet-Cuban menace to his own country's territorial integrity and, beyond Somalia, to the entire region. Iran and Egypt responded sympathetically with warnings that the Somalis would not fight alone if they were invaded. Backing up Cairo and Tehran, the Carter administration, itself beseiged by demands that it "do something" about the Marxist menace in Africa,* announced that it too viewed Somali security as a matter of major importance. But the Somali army, braced inside Ethiopia awaiting the inevitable blow, would have to fend for itself.

The inevitable was not long in coming. Just after the middle of February, 1978, the Ethiopian counterattack, spearheaded by Cuban armor, smashed into and simultaneously wheeled around the flank of Somali positions. The main Somali force fell back towards Jijiga where, in the first days of March, it was smashed to pieces. On March 9, four days after the fallhof Jijiga, the Somali government radio and President Jimmy Carter practically simultaneously announced a decision by the Central Committee of the Somali Socialist Revolutionary Party to withdraw all Somali units from Ethiopia. The Somali announcement claimed that the Somali government had received assurances from the "big powers . . . that the rights of Western Somalia will be safeguarded." You could call that, plus President Carter's coincident call for the withdrawal of Soviet and Cuban forces from Ethiopia, "putting the best possible face on defeat." You could call it that and you would be right. The Ogaden war was over.

---

* As Japanese in South Africa are deemed "white" so Hawkish circles, which had recently trumpeted the Somali-facilitated threat to Western interests, overlooked the Somali government's own Marxist orientation.

Part Three

A Policy Perspective

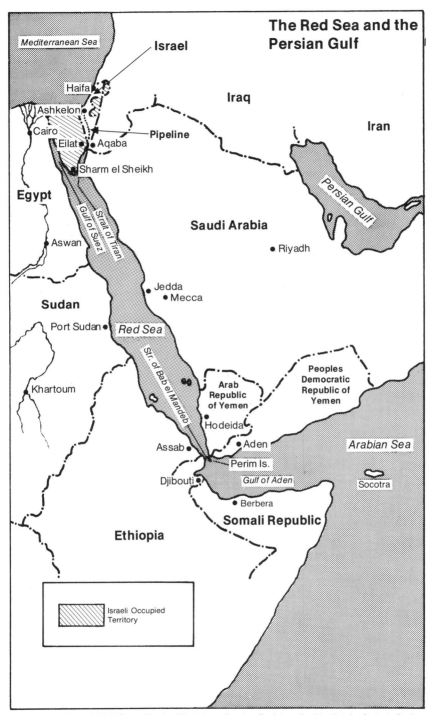

The Red Sea and the Persian Gulf

Mediterranean Sea

Israel

Haifa

Ashkelon

Cairo

Eilat • Aqaba

Sharm el Sheikh

Pipeline

Iraq

Iran

Egypt

Aswan

Persian Gulf

Saudi Arabia

• Riyadh

Sudan

Port Sudan •

Red Sea

Strait of Tiran

Gulf of Suez

Jedda
• Mecca

Khartoum

Str. of Bab el Mandeb

Arab
Republic
of Yemen

Peoples
Democratic
Republic of
Yemen

Arabian Sea

Hodeida

Assab •

Aden

Perim Is.

Djibouti •

Gulf of Aden

Socotra

• Berbera

Somali Republic

Ethiopia

Israeli Occupied
Territory

© *Conflicts in Africa. Adelphi Papers Number Ninety-three.* (London: The International Institute for Strategic Studies, 1972). Reprinted by permission of the publisher.

Detente and the Ogaden War: In Search of a Grand Strategy 7

The Cost of Switching Sides

Events on the Horn, together with the earlier victory of the Soviet-backed and Cuban-aided MPLA (Popular Movement for the Liberation of Angola) in Angola and the subsequent Shaba affair in Zaire, have sharpened the anxieties of Western elites about Soviet intentions and capabilities. While some observers interpret the Soviet-Cuban change of sides on the Horn as little more than the improvised seizure of a target of opportunity with nothing behind it other than the general goal of extending communist influence into areas where it has been thin or altogether excluded, others see in the switch sinister, incontrovertible evidence of a matured strategy, complete with time-tables, to shatter pro-Western governments throughout the region and thereby secure, among other goods, effective control over essential raw materials. How else, they argue, can one reasonably construe Soviet willingness to bear the risks and costs plainly incident to the embrace of Mengistu's regime?

The fact of the matter, however, is that the risks and costs so confidently invoked by these advocates as proof of an extravagant, hugely dangerous Soviet strategy would not have seemed terribly onerous to a prudent Soviet strategist.

Before even considering how the risks and costs probably appeared to Soviet decision-makers, in order to get things into proportion it helps to recall that the Russians and Cubans had already become deeply implicated in the fate of Ethiopia's revolutionary regime before it was made clear to them that their Somali clients would force a choice of sides. With that in mind, let us imagine how the costs of an exclusive alliance with Ethiopia might reasonably have been cal-

131

culated. At least three were salient: the loss of access to air and naval facilities in Somalia; loss of credibility as an ally; and involvement in a military quagmire threatening great cost and little hope of success, the analogue for the Soviet Union of the United States' Vietnam experience.

For reasons developed at length in Chapter 8, the first supposed cost was not very great. Somali facilities were not essential to the Soviet navy's peacetime mission and could be partially duplicated in Aden. Furthermore, their loss was not necessarily irretrievable. As the United States could attract the interest of Arab countries in part because of its influence over a militarily dominant Israel, so a renewed Soviet alliance would necessarily appeal to the Somalis because of Soviet influence over an Ethiopian state restored to its usual position of local hegemony. Moreover, since Somali assets probably have a good deal more positive value to the Soviet Union than the West, the latter was not likely to provide the Somalis with an irresistibly attractive alternative to a renewed Soviet alliance.

Given the circumstances of the alliance switch, considerations of credibility should not have weighed heavily in Soviet strategic accounting. If the Ethiopians had initiated armed conflict, for example, by a preemptive strike against Somali forces or guerrilla-training centers, a Soviet failure to provide logistical support to the Somalis, much less Soviet assistance to the Ethiopians, would have raised serious questions about the reliability of Soviet promises. But once the Somalis violated the post-colonial consensus on the inviolate quality of colonial boundaries, the Russians could invoke respect for regional and international norms against the use of force—as well as a more parochial norm of fraternal obligations among Marxist states—to justify a transfer of allegiance, particularly following what appears to have been a good-faith effort to conciliate the dispute. In any event, the Soviet Union, unlike the United States, does not have to ponder the impact of its acts on nervous alliance partners. There is in the Soviet bloc no analogue to our NATO partners and Japan.

The quagmire problem was more serious but, particularly for a country organized like the Soviet Union, not terribly alarming. To be sure, at the very time the Soviet Union began to tilt perceptibly towards the Ethiopian cause, many observers were beginning to write off the Ethiopian revolutionary junta as a lost cause. How could the body survive, they reasoned, when its trunk bled from a dozen small wounds and its limbs were in so advanced a state of gangrene that they seemed likely soon to fall off? The Dergue itself was rent by conflicting ambitions and paranoid hostilities. Its legitimacy even within the armed forces was suspect both because of its deadly internal strife and its failure to seek a new mandate. And outside the armed forces the Dergue's exclusivity had alienated students, organized workers, and the other groups likely to sympathize with the executioners of the old regime. Many of the most experienced and skilled civil servants, as well as senior officers of the armed forces, were dead, detained, or in exile. Those who remained were believed to be almost paralyzed by fearful uncertainty. The Eritreans were advancing on every front. Aside from a few strongholds, the Ogaden was already in Somali hands. The two lifelines tying Addis to the coast, the railroad and the road to Assab, were in constant danger of severance. All in all, a grim picture.

Arriving on the scene as the saviors of the revolution, the Soviets risked (1) outright failure in case the Dergue simply collapsed or lost all control over its military and civilian instruments outside the capital; or (2) involvement in an endless, exhausting war of attrition not only against all the active opponents of the regime but also against the vast and depressing obstacles to revolutionary development. These risks were evident, but to the Soviets they probably seemed more easily manageable than comparable risks would be for the United States.

If, as is generally assumed, decision-making power in the Soviet Union is very highly concentrated, and if all the leading actors on the Soviet political scene concurred in the decision to intervene, then the domestic political dangers of failure would presumably seem a good deal less than, after the rancorous experience of Korea and Indo-China, they would to an American president contemplating intervention under comparable circumstances. On this assumption, moreover, the Soviets would necessarily be blessed with greater decisional flexibility than would be the government of a democracy; that is to say, the leadership would find it relatively easier either to cut its losses or to increase its involvement.

There is another, more compelling reason why the Soviets should have somewhat greater flexibility, namely their more modest credibility problem in relation to their "allies." Furthermore, the government's relative immunity from general public opinion aids flexibility in a setting where, in order to save the revolution, it might seem necessary at some point to commit Russian troops to combat and thus to sustain casualties. In Vietnam, battle casualties created among U.S. political leaders a feeling that bridges had been burnt and thus propelled us further into the quagmire.

In addition, the military situation may have seemed a good deal more promising than many Western pundits believed. The Somalis were deeply dependent not only on Soviet materiel but also, it is believed, on direct Soviet participation in logistics. The Ethiopian armed forces, on the other hand, were very much more self-sufficient in terms of logistical expertise. By the time of the Emperor's fall, the U.S. MAAG in Ethiopia was down to about fifty men and was not integrated into any sector of the Ethiopian armed forces. Thus, the mere withdrawal of Soviet support was calculated to have an adverse impact on Somali capabilities vis-à-vis their opponents. The more ad-

vanced technical and administrative capacity the Ethiopians were
thought to enjoy also could facilitate comparatively rapid absorption
of Soviet ordnance. Moreover, the Somalis were incapable of striking
at the Ethiopian heartland and were themselves vulnerable to a sustained Ethiopian counterattack, which could ignore the wastes of the
Ogaden and press right into important Somali territory. Furthermore, with all its limitations, the Dergue had already demonstrated
its capacity to mobilize large numbers of peasants for belligerent duty.
As a war machine it was functioning. Finally, it began to be clear that
the Somalis were unlikely to receive substantial support from the
West or even from the Arab states.

If anything, the Somali problem may have seemed a net contribution to the survival of the Dergue in that it allowed the government
in Addis to draw legitimacy from its defense of the empire. At the
core of the empire there is a deep vein of bellicose national feeling.

Eritrea posed the more serious problem. But, if the rest of the
empire could be pacified, and if the Ethiopians could hang on in the
major cities of Eritrea so that the province could not win international
recognition of its independence, then with Soviet support the liberation movements could be gradually reduced. Despite their links to the
Arab world, the Eritreans remained poorly armed. Thus, there was a
good chance that they could be held at bay. They had little response
to air power or heavy armor. With Russo-Cuban support, the Dergue
could maintain the necessary *laagers* within Eritrea to frustrate a bid
for independence before the Dergue could move to the offensive.

Finally, there was the still incalculable question of the competence
and cohesion of the Dergue's dominant group. Soviet officials had
had a chance to observe these men. They may have seen qualities
which made the risks of failure seem smaller than they did to other
observers.

The nub of the matter, then, is that the potential costs were not
extravagant, and so one need not construe the change of partners as
the sign of a master plan that magnified the potential value of a
united Ethiopia under a secure left-wing regime intimately linked to
the Soviet Union. Without such a master plan, victory for the revolutionary government would probably produce rather modest benefits
for the Soviet Union. But only modest benefits were needed to offset
the prospective costs.

One of those benefits was a potentially more stable alliance in
Northeast Africa. As a devoutly Muslim nation and a member of the
Arab League, Somalia could not resist a certain attraction to the conservative Arab bloc led by Saudi Arabia. Thus the Soviets had to compete for Somali loyalty against both the West and the Arabs. At a
minimum, this gave the Somalis added leverage in their dealings with
the Soviets. At worst it threatened an ultimate break. Once the Somalis succeeded in seizing the Ogaden, and if seizure coincided with
the truncation of Ethiopia or its relapse into virtual anarchy, the So-

viet tie would lose much of its allure. Since the Arab states could easily match Soviet largesse on the economic side, with the importance of military assistance diminished, the Arab temptation could prove overwhelming. Ethiopia, on the other hand, its historical memory being one of struggling for survival in a Muslim sea, would be far less susceptible to Arab blandishments.

Despite their radical rhetoric, many of the senior Somali leaders, beginning with President Barre, probably retain the instinctive Western orientation, which is partially a function of being socialized in the British and Italian constabularies and partially a result of the Somali social structure which encourages an independent, individualistic conception of the self in society.

While some Dergue members no doubt had been exposed to Western instructors, in most cases the exposure was a good deal more limited. Noncommissioned officers and private soldiers may have been untouched, particularly because, during the past few years, the number of U.S. instructors had grown so small. Nor can one overlook the intimate association in the Ethiopian mind between the long survival of Haile Selassie and his U.S. aid programs. The United States is an important part of that recent past which the Dergue has attempted utterly to destroy.

Ethiopia, with a population almost ten times larger than Somalia's and far greater international prominence, also seemed a more attractive showcase for Soviet development assistance, provided the revolution succeeded in maintaining the empire's territorial integrity and lifting its people from the abyss of immemorial poverty. On the other hand, the country's great size, diversity, and poverty increased the chance for failure and multiplied the investment required for rapid social and economic transformation. But Ethiopia has sufficient resources to repay part of the Soviet investment, particularly in the long run, if the revolution succeeds. With proper investment and management, Ethiopia can feed its people and still maintain a decent level of agricultural exports. And both in the Ogaden and along the Eritrean coast there are signs of mineral deposits, including oil and gas.

Those gains—in conjunction with the alternative naval and air facilities that the Russians could hope to acquire in a pacified Eritrea and, on the negative side, their desire to avoid complicity in a Somali adventure certain to be labeled "aggression" by most of black Africa—can explain the switch without reference to a satanic Soviet plot.

A Challenge to the Rules of the Game?

Those who argue that the Soviet initiative on the Horn was so risky that it must be part of a strategy for global supremacy also argue—generally without much evidence—that, both on the Horn and elsewhere in Africa, the Soviets have violated hitherto accepted restraints on military intervention, particularly great-power intervention, in the Third World. As in the pre-World War II case of Germany, these violations, they argue, augur a radical assault on the international status quo. But is it clear that the Soviets have in fact broken loose from the rules of the game? In order to assess this charge we must reexamine the state of those rules on the eve of the recent flurry of Soviet initiatives in Africa.

Until the trauma of Vietnam moderated its own interventionary impulse, the United States operated under a cluster of normative restraints that left much to national discretion, but did, nevertheless, shut off certain courses of action. Nominally the United States subscribed to the view that intervention at the request and on behalf of a recognized government was legitimate, while assistance to insurgents was always illicit. From the U.S. perspective the distinction worked nicely in the great generality of cases, first because most governments were fiercely anti-communist. Thus in acting to preserve them, the United States could usually present itself as the champion of international law regardless of the power, capacity, or virtue of its beneficiary, while the Chinese or Russians, as supporters of rebellious factions, were deemed outlaws.

Occasionally, however, where the recognized government appeared indifferent or, worse yet, downright hostile to U.S. interests, this generally satisfactory normative arrangement did not fit American needs. To cope with such cases, while adhering formally to the law, U.S. officials sometimes drew on the expertise of the Central Intelligence Agency. It could channel funds, weapons, and, if need be, men to antigovernment conspirators who met U.S. standards of virtue. It could also channel assurances of open support as soon as the legitimate government was displaced. Thus, the United States eliminated or at least encouraged and facilitated the elimination of democratic and universally recognized governments in Brazil, Chile, Guatemala, and Iran, as well as undemocratic governments in such places as South Vietnam.*

Some flexibility in the norms of nonintervention helped reduce the number of clandestine violations. One was the largely formal distinction between the "legitimate" government and its status-less opponents. A collection of people claiming to embody a given state's sovereignty were deemed the legitimate government if their claim was widely recognized; and the act of recognition, according to many countries including the United States, was highly discretionary. Until the mid-1960s, the United States and its NATO allies could pretty

---

* Ngo-Dinh Diem's government was, of course, replaced by another undemocratic government.

much at will muster a big majority of recognitions for whichever claimant to legitimacy they chose to support. One case in point is the regime the United States and France patched together in Saigon in 1954. Even more blatant was the case of Taiwan. For two decades after the end of the Chinese civil war, a majority of the world's states recognized this rump, which survived as a consequence of U.S. intervention, as the government of all China.

Another phenomenon which helped the United States to live within the rules most of the time was the tendency, still powerful, of diplomats and journalists to ascribe legitimacy to whomever controlled the country's principal cities, especially the capital. Insurgents might dominate the countryside, but, being more lightly armed, they had to remain elusive until the masters of the capital were nearly strangled. So they did not often publish lists of their leaders, and they gave few interviews and no cocktail parties. The recognized government, beneficiary of high-technology weapons and training supplied by the United States, could maintain the illusion of control by temporarily occupying or pulverizing towns and villages which the insurgents actually governed on a day-to-day basis.

In justifying their Angolan and Ethiopian expeditions, the Soviets and their Cuban allies have drawn upon these still widely accepted norms, particularly the right of recognized governments to secure foreign assistance in defending their borders and suppressing insurgents. The Ethiopian government is universally recognized and, at the time it sought Soviet-Cuban aid, was exercising the substance as well as the forms of national independence. Even cold-war fantasts have hesitated to label Mengistu a puppet.

Leonid Brezhnev and Castro can also develop a respectable, if slightly weaker case for their Angolan adventure. While far from universal, recognition of Agostinho Neto's government extended well beyond the Communist bloc. On the other hand, no one at all—not even the United States, South Africa, or Zaire—recognized either of the other factions. Moreover, even if one regards the MPLA as having been only one of three legally equal contenders for power, on the theory that the extent of recognition was insufficient to endow it with exclusive legitimacy, the Soviets and Cubans could invoke U.S. intervention in the Dominican Republic as a precedent for choosing sides in such a case. Far more persuasively they could argue a right of counterintervention, since there is now reason to believe that, prior to Cuba's direct military involvement, the United States encouraged South African intervention and, in concert with the Mobutu Sese Seko regime in Zaire, was facilitating Holden Roberto's bid for power.[1]

Cuba's vigorous denial of involvement in the Shaba invasion, whatever its veracity, itself implicitly confirms the traditional normative structure in that it concedes the impropriety of assisting rebels, even when they are rebelling against a peculiarly shabby regime.*

Intentions and Consequences

Even if it is true that the Soviets have simply improvised in response to an apparently low-cost target of opportunity while remaining within what they might reasonably regard as the rules of the international power game, still one must examine the actual and potential consequences of their actions before concluding that the West should not be particularly concerned about recent events on the Horn.

SHARPENING WESTERN DILEMMAS

The military capacity and political will evidenced by Cuba and the Soviet Union on the Horn have in some degree aggravated the Western dilemma in southern Africa, which to begin with was not enviable. The nature of that dilemma is plain, yet so painful that no part of the establishment—neither political leaders, nor the prestige press, nor the journals of upper-middle brow opinion, nor private opinion molders—seem willing to express it. On the contrary, all the orthodox authors of the Western foreign policy agenda (with a few conservative exceptions) attempt consciously or unconsciously to obscure the dilemma behind a curtain of pathetic cliches.

In essence the dilemma is that we concede the morally-repellent and in varying degrees unstable character of governments in the resource-rich, investment-laden countries of Zaire, Rhodesia, and South Africa. We portray ourselves as the wise and honorable managers of humane and prudent change. But we ourselves are unwilling either to organize the vast military and economic power of the West to induce change or to allow others to impose it by means that offend our sensibilities or that we cannot control or that we lack the necessary consensus to use ourselves. The bare facts are that we have refused to arm those blacks with the courage to resist Ian Smith or Mobutu or the Boers. And when they turn to the Soviet Union as an alternative source of aid, they are immediately condemned and transformed on the Western tongue into communist terrorists.

The London *Economist* typifies both the reflexive Western reaction to change supported by the Soviet Union and the concomitant moral confusion. On May 20, 1978, the lead editorial comment on the armed struggle in Shaba province stated: "A successful breakaway

---

* On the other hand, Soviet support of Vietnam's invasion of Cambodia is pretty clearly a violation of International law, even if the invasion was in fact precipitated by Cambodian incursions on Vietnamese territory. It is, however, consistent with earlier signs that the Soviets feel free to apply a special set of rules to govern relations among communist states.

might be better for Shaba than staying part of Mr. Mobutu's Zaire, or worse, but that is a matter for Zaire and Shaba. The question changes, however, if this week's assault has been organized, *or assisted,* from outside Zaire's borders by countries that want to use a change in Shaba for their own purposes." (Emphasis added)

What neither the *Economist* nor any other shill for respectable opinion bothers to explain is how Shaba can decide to break away without outside support, as long as Mobutu, strutting about in the trappings of legitimacy, can impose his will with guns purchased from revenues paid out to him by Western companies or made available as the result of Western loans or with troops supplied by Morocco with French connivance.

The oozing hypocrisy of this refined form of catch-22 which has dominated Western legal and political thought since the cold war's outset is gussied up by reference to aid from countries "that want to use change in Shaba for their own purposes," as if in the jungle of international politics there were certain noble states that offered military assistance for reasons of high altruism.

The West has the brute military and economic power to impose the kinds of change it purports to support. But in Zaire it props up a government which many Western observers believe to be as vicious as it is corrupt, receiving in return only those concessions needed to assure repayment of Western loans. Meanwhile, in the words of one critic, "Nothing is done to prevent the thief Mobutu from continuing to impoverish the countryside and loot the citizenry."

Western capacity to end the travail of Rhodesia's people and of their neighbors in Zambia and Mozambique is equally apparent. A multi-national occupation of Rhodesia spearheaded by American or European units would probably be welcomed by most sectors of the population if it operated under a mandate to establish the preconditions for democratic government and to guarantee a constitution that did not, like the present one, simply perpetuate white supremacy behind a facade of complaisant black faces.

In the case of South Africa, the West continues to deny aid to the incipient black resistance movements and, more positively, to maintain the economic links which allow the white minority vastly to elaborate the machinery of repression and self-defense, while maintaining one of the world's most luxurious standards of living. To that country's huge suffering majority, we offer a vague evolutionary scenario that has the gauzy substance of a dream and that, at its most optimistic, promises modest change in a generation or two.

The insupportable vice associated with the victories of Soviet-backed forces in Angola and Ethiopia is the provocative contrast they offer to the West's determined failure to achieve the political ends it concedes are desirable—decent government in those southern African states where it exercises enormous influence. This contrast makes the West appear either impotent or hypocritical while giving local advocates of change an alternative to what the West calls "cooperation." "The mere threat of a Cuban-Soviet involvement," the *New York Times* editorialized in mid-May, 1978, "already colors the diplomacy of Rhodesia."[2] The Ogaden war helped that threat become real. And beyond the threat lies the West's African nightmare, a frightening kaleidoscope of destruction, massacre, anti-Western black governments, and superpower confrontation.

The feared train of events could begin around Rhodesia with Soviet-Cuban acceptance of invitations from Zambia and Mozambique to secure their borders from Rhodesian incursions. Soviet-Cuban intervention under that circumstance would receive the support of a clear OAU majority, almost certainly including Nigeria, which is the United States' second largest source of imported oil, a not inconsequential member of OPEC, and the single largest center of Western investment south of the Sahara. Western denunciation of the intervention would implicitly condemn the OAU majority as well. The West's political and moral position would be further undermined in the likely event that the invitation followed a particularly destructive Rhodesian incursion or if a nonaligned state such as Nigeria sent at least token forces to cooperate with the Russo-Cuban contingent.

Within the major Western states these events would intensify conservative demands for recognition of and assistance to whatever facade of mixed-race government Smith would then have in place. From that point one can spin out a dozen different scenarios, each more awful than its predecessor, involving grave damage to the cohesion of Western elites and electorates, a tremendous aggravation of East-West tensions, and, if the West were to align with the white-supremacist regimes, an assault on Western investments and facilities throughout black Africa accompanied by a sharp deterioration in North-South relations.

A BASE TO CHALLENGE THE REGIONAL STATUS QUO?

Apart from its symbolic links to developments in southern Africa, the Horn has gripped Western attention because of a geographic position that makes it appear a convenient base for projecting power into the adjoining seas and the African and Middle Eastern countries which border them.

A strongly-entrenched Ethiopian government in league with the Soviet Union could certainly help to destabilize the Sudan and Kenya and to protect the People's Democratic Republic of Yemen from Saudi pressure. The Sudanese are particularly exposed because political authority in that vast, faction-ridden country is a very fragile thing. By moving, as he recently has, to placate Muslim opponents,[3] President Numeri may alienate the always uneasy, once rebellious, non-Muslim south. In a time of north-south tension in the Sudan, an Ethiopian offer of military assistance and sanctuary to southern dissidents could spark civil war. Or, if Numeri's efforts to conciliate his Muslim opponents fail, the Dergue could, as it did once before, support a renewed effort on their part to seize power in Khartoum. Numeri barely survived the last assault. The next one could be terminal.

Whether political change in neighboring countries achieved with Soviet and Ethiopian aid could much affect Western strategic interests is far from clear, even if one assumes, as I do not, that regimes with programs calling for radical internal change would refuse to cooperate with the West on any acceptable terms. In the foreseeable future will the Sudan, for instance, matter very much in regional— much less in global—power politics? Though the Sudan is geographically intimate with Egypt, a country whose political orientation is of manifest importance, the disproportion between the two states in population, technological sophistication, and raw military power is so great it seems doubtful that events in the Sudan could greatly influence the struggle for power in Cairo.

To be candid, however, Egypt's President Anwar Sadat does not seem to accept that judgment. For him the physical proximity of a potentially unfriendly state—even one, unlike Libya, without the magical power of petrodollars—is a matter of substantial concern. Witness his defense agreement with Numeri and other signs of his determination to help the present Sudanese government retain power.

The Saudi government, while sharing Sadat's interest in the Sudan, where it is making substantial economic investments, is more immediately concerned about the hostile regime in the People's Democratic Republic of Yemen (South Yemen) and the always precarious situation in the Yemen Arab Republic (North Yemen), where pro-Saudi elements now hold power. The disproportions which filter the projection of Sudanese influence into Egypt are not nearly so marked in the case of the Yemens and Saudi Arabia, which underneath its patina of high technology remains a very small, traditional society. Its borders with the Yemens are impossible to close, in part because of their length and the often spectacularly difficult terrain, but primarily because the Saudis are so dependent on Yemeni workers, hundreds of thousands of them. The Saudis will find it more difficult to neutralize the People's Democratic Republic of Yemen if across the throat of the Red Sea it is backed up by a well-armed communist regime.

I do not want to exaggerate this particular source of Saudi anxiety. On any scale of risks to the Saudi status quo, the Yemeni problem would not rank near the top. But it cannot be dismissed. And the recent political and military changes on the Horn may have contributed to its troublesome potential.

Any assessment of the ways in which the Soviet-Cuban expedition to the Horn might impact materially on Western interests as they are currently defined must take account of the fact that by African standards the Ethiopian armed forces have been and remain well-disciplined, able in assimilating increasingly more sophisticated weapons systems, and tough. With Soviet assistance, Ethiopia could develop elite units capable of handling most African opponents, units that could play the kind of interventionary role now played by Moroccans on one side and Cubans on the other. Nor would they be pushovers for small, lightly-armed European spearheads like the French Foreign Legion. One element of U.S. efforts to contain Soviet-Cuban moves in Africa is a call for African solutions to local conflicts. If Mobutu's Moroccan prop satisfies the proposed norm, Ethiopian troops landing to succor some friendly faction would be an *a fortiori* case.

Finally, there is the matter of naval competition in the Indian Ocean. The Soviet Union's sacrifice of its Somali facilities has not really allayed Western concern about Soviet naval activities. This or a successor government in Somalia might decide that the Soviets still have more to offer than the West and the conservative Arab states, an hypothesis Soviet propagandists have sedulously fostered since the expulsion of October, 1977. And so the Soviets may ultimately return to their facilities in Somalia. In addition, Ethiopia's recent reconquest of Eritrea's cities could open the province to Soviet use for naval and air operations. It is, therefore, no less necessary today than in 1976, at the time of this book's first edition, to examine both the character of the Soviet naval presence and its degree of dependence on facilities located in the African Horn.

Notes

1. See generally John Stockwell, *In Search of Enemies: A CIA Story* (New York: Norton, 1978).

2. *International Herald Tribune*, May 19, 1978.

3. Andrew Lycett, "The Sudan: Domestic Conciliation and External Dialogue," *Africa Report*, November-December, 1978, p. 9.

The Indian Ocean 8

The Indian Ocean is not a red sea. The Russians are there but with still problematical strategic consequence.

Soviet Interests

One body of expert opinion finds the main initial motive for the Soviet naval build-up, beginning in the mid-sixties, in a desire to lay the foundation for an active defense against the U.S. ballistic-missile-bearing submarines that might someday patrol the Indian Ocean.[1] For submarine-launched ballistic missiles (SLBMs) like Polaris A-3 and Poseidon,* with a range of roughly 3,000 nautical miles, the northwest quadrant of the Indian Ocean (the so-called Arabian Sea) offers coverage of potential targets in European Russia roughly equivalent to that achieved by missile-firing submarines deployed in the Mediterranean and the western approaches to the Eurasian land mass. Those missiles, together with the very low frequency communications stations operated by the United States at the two extremities of the ocean in western Australia and Ethiopia's coastal province of Eritrea and what appeared to be a third one programmed for Diego Garcia, made Indian Ocean patrols possible.

Other factors made them conceivably attractive. They would, for example, have widened the azimuth of potential attack on the Soviet Union, thus further complicating the problematical task of constructing a reasonably effective antiballistic missile (ABM) system. In actual fact, however, Indian Ocean patrols were not then and are not today a cost-effective means for achieving that or any other military objective. The northwest quadrant is simply too far away from the nearest U.S. submarine base in Guam.

---

* By the mid 1960s, these SLBMs were already in U.S. inventories.

Crew endurance, re-enlistment rates, and certain other factors set definite limits to the duration of a voyage. Hence, the comparatively longer time required for transit to and from the patrol area correspondingly reduces the length of time the submarine can remain on station. It thus follows that the farther the patrol area is from the nearest base, the greater the number of submarines required to assure that one is always in position to launch its missiles.

Indian Ocean patrols would be practical only if the United States could establish a submarine base with a proximity roughly comparable to Rota for Mediterranean patrols and Holy Loch for patrols off the northwestern rim of the Soviet Union. Theoretically, the only essential feature of a base is the "tender," an enormous ship—virtually a floating dry dock—staffed by the highly skilled technicians required to service a missile-launching submarine. But peacetime realities require the presence of housing as well as recreational and other facilities for dependents. Although offering the predictably benign political climate required to justify a large investment in fixed installations, a barren, claustrophobic pimple of land like Diego Garcia cannot, therefore, constitute a plausible missile-launching submarine base site. Some of the larger, more physically charming places in and around the Indian Ocean are governed by elites who deem neutrality or even a pro-Soviet tilt in East-West competition more consistent with their interests. Others are politically volatile. Still others, most notably South Africa, are pariahs to much of the world, including influential U.S. constituencies.

The evident high costs of an Indian Ocean patrol and the difficulties that would clearly attend any effort to reduce them have influenced some observers to deride the idea that the prospect of such patrols could have attracted Soviet concern. Implicit in the quiet ferocity of this recondite controversy is a larger debate over the meaning of the Soviet Union's efforts to establish a presence in the area. Those who prefer to construe the Soviet presence as a serious and immediate threat to Western interests are in general inclined to belittle the invocation of Soviet concern over SLBMs. The fantasts among these skeptics—some of whom are, as well, advocates of military collaboration with South Africa—prefer to envision a burgeoning threat to the sea lanes. Less whimsical analysts envision a Soviet plan to use naval power to erode Western influence through the classic means of encouraging friendly regimes and intimidating or facilitating the replacement of those deemed hostile.

Curiously enough, treating Soviet concern for potential U.S. SLBM patrols as an important explanation of the Soviet presence is quite compatible with the most jaundiced conception of Russian motives. Efforts to acquire the capacity to threaten our sea-based deterrent at some time in the future are not necessarily less ominous than the other theories of Soviet motivation enumerated above. In a certain tactical sense, antisubmarine warfare, is, of course, defensive. But in a strategic context, it may or may not be, depending upon the larger design of which it forms a part. Perhaps that is the problem, the fact that it *could be* defensive in intent. As a rhetorical weapon in our domestic debate over national security policy, the prospect of an attack on the West's sea lanes is flawed with none of those softening ambiguities. Hence the charm it exerts on such self-instructed authorities in the realm of Soviet military policy as Professor Daniel P. Moynihan.

Despite efforts to discount it, the antisubmarine hypothesis retains a plausible role in any comprehensive explanation of Soviet interests. Just as the shape of U.S. defense expenditures has sometimes been influenced decisively by worst-case projections of Soviet capabilities, the Soviets may have responded in this case to the technical feasibility of Indian Ocean patrols. They may not, after all, fully appreciate the way in which we tote up costs. Moreover, even if their analysts appreciated our probable assessments of cost effectiveness, the Russians could be laying the foundation for an unpredictable future.

It takes time to establish the political relations, the physical infrastructure, and the experience to operate effectively in a new environment. In the meantime, détente could collapse and with it the restraints on ABM deployment established by the first Strategic Arms Limitation Talks (SALT 1). There could, as well, be a major breakthrough in antisubmarine warfare which might provide additional incentives for the expansion of SLBM patrol areas. And for a variety of reasons, including the apparently relentless growth in economic ties between South Africa and the West, the United States might gradually discount the political costs of a submarine base in South Africa. In other words, the present inefficiency of Indian Ocean patrols would not make it irrational for the Russian navy to develop an antisubmarine capability in that area.

Whether or not it influenced the initial decision to deploy east of Suez, development of an antisubmarine capability now appears to be a significant part of the Russian mission there. During the worldwide naval exercise called OKEAN, conducted by the Russians in 1975, this seems to have been the only function assigned to their Indian Ocean squadron.

Whatever the initial motive for the comparatively modest presence the Russians have established in the Indian Ocean,* that presence has endowed them with the means to pursue a second interest: naval diplomacy.[2] Lacking foreign bases and a blue-water fleet and doctrinally committed to the use of naval power either in defense of the Russian coastline or in direct support of groand forces operating on the Eurasian land mass, throughout the fifties and the early sixties the Russians had left the field open to the navies of their Western

---

* For the past several years, this presence has generally been smaller than the flotilla maintained by France alone.

antagonists. But after careful preparation, moving from scattered, unprotected anchorages to well-endowed Arab bases, they joined the game through operations in the eastern Mediterranean in support of Arab friends. Following Colonel Qaddafi's coup in Libya, they were observed off the coast of that country, possibly, some analysts argue, to discourage a Western intervention in support of the deposed king. And nearer the end of the decade, by anchoring in Egyptian harbors during the war of attrition with Israel, they may have inhibited Israel's exploitation of its dominant military position.

Operations in the Mediterranean were soon extended to the Indian Ocean and the Atlantic littoral of Africa. When the government of Ghana seized two Russian fishing vessels and imprisoned their crews for alleged involvement in a rumored coup, Russian warships eventually took a leisurely cruise along the Ghanian coast in apparent support of conventional diplomatic protests. Whether or not they actually influenced the ultimate release of the crews is unclear.

The conflict over Bangladesh demonstrated Soviet determination to play in higher-stake games. Immediately following U.S. dispatch of carrier task force seventy-four toward the Bay of Bengal for the evident purpose of restraining the Indian government, the Russians responded with a dramatic increase in their own Indian Ocean force levels.

Clearly, the Western monopoly on naval diplomacy in the Indian Ocean has been broken. The question of whether that is a matter of much strategic consequence will shortly be examined.

Like the United States, the Soviet Union has interests in the Indian Ocean largely unrelated to superpower competition. The Russians depend far more heavily on the sea as a source of protein than do most Western states. Although less fertile than the Atlantic and the Pacific, the Indian Ocean is still an important operating area for Soviet trawlers, providing within recent years a fifth or more of their catch. Once upon a time, fishing was a peaceful occupation. It rarely required the ministrations of friendly gunboats. But today, in the face of burgeoning unilateral extensions of coastal-state claims to living resources, the occasions requiring naval escorts for fishing fleets have grown exponentially. And they are likely to expand at a yet more dramatic pace if a general agreement on littoral-state jurisdiction is not achieved in the context of the Law of the Sea negotiations. Such an agreement, moreover, may only slow the pace of gathering conflict; it will probably leave many issues (such as the period of phase-out for traditional users and the size of an optimal catch) for subsequent bilateral negotiations. The consensus supporting a contemporary agreement may, moreover, erode as national populations press ever more exigently against finite resources.

No one proposes that protection of its fishing interests is a major Soviet concern. Some analysts, noting the absence of any Soviet naval presence off the coasts of Latin America, where fishing is better and the littoral states more belligerent about extending their jurisdiction, argue that it figures not at all among Soviet interests.

While they may be right, the cited evidence is by no means compelling. The absence of securely friendly port facilities beyond Cuba, U.S. sensitivity to Soviet naval activities in the Western Hemisphere, and the danger of actually being forced to confront Latin navies (that have, after all, not been deterred even by the United States from bold assertions of exclusive fishing rights) all weigh heavily against the advantages of naval patrols in support of Soviet fishermen. Incentives in the Indian Ocean are radically different.

There is, in addition, the ocean's importance as a link in the sea route to Russia's Pacific coast and to important friendly governments, particularly in India and Vietnam. Between forty-five and fifty percent of Russian military and economic assistance now goes to Indian Ocean littoral states. For the movement of heavy equipment or oil either to such friends or to its own Asian territory, the sea route has no serious competition. To be sure, there is no present threat to that route. Nevertheless, if one conjures the long-term, worst-case scenarios so dear to the hearts of conventional strategists (in this instance, the growth of Chinese sea power), one can then visualize the argument for a protective presence probably advanced by Soviet admirals in budgetary competition with traditionally more favored branches of the Russian armed forces.

Beyond the Soviet leadership's interest in securing the country's shipping lanes looms the relentless competition with China for influence in the Afro-Asian world. The Chinese have the congenital advantage of being a colored race and the acquired advantage of a development model more engaging to idealists and, particularly in Africa, more plausibly relevant to the human condition. Moreover, having neither a blue-water fleet nor global military ambitions to service, the Chinese have no incentive to demand base rights as a condition for the extension of aid.

The Russians can attempt to overcome these advantages with potentially more bountiful aid, more advanced technology, and, thanks to their fleet, readily available muscle. Regimes can find balm in the prospect of a friendly cruiser appearing off the coast when coups are being hatched or a hostile neighbor is rattling its sabers. The Chinese can train Rhodesian guerrillas. But, unlike the Soviets, they cannot offer an on-the-spot deterrent to Rhodesian or South African intervention.

Soviet Strategic Superiority?

In the Indian Ocean area, the Russian navy suffers a double disadvantage vis-à-vis the West: overall, it has a greater need for, yet less-assured access to, littoral support facilities.

Any one of the carrier task forces the United States can deploy on extended patrol in the Indian Ocean represents air power capable of devastating any flotilla the Soviets can practicably deploy east of Suez in the near future without shore-based air support. The Soviets have only three carriers afloat. They are configured for helicopters and, perhaps, very-short-takeoff-and-landing planes with limited range and dubious ability to offset the offensive thrust of U.S. carrier-based aircraft. Moreover, until a far larger number of carriers enter service, the Soviet navy may be reluctant to deploy any carriers so far from the present focus of naval concern—the Mediterranean and the Atlantic approaches to European Russia.

Shore facilities also have a special urgency for the Russians because of their inferior amphibious support capability. Unlike the United States, they have only an extremely limited and thoroughly makeshift capacity for underway replenishment, plus a smaller overall service force. Furthermore, the twenty-five-percent-greater average size of U.S. ships in the destroyer-escort category probably translates into better habitability and larger on-board supplies with consequent gains in endurance. The Russians' profound dependence on surface-to-air and ship-to-ship missiles both for offensive and defensive operations, coupled with the absence of any on-board reload capacity for their anti-ship missiles (unlike comparable U.S. weapon systems), generates additional need for secure shore facilities where, among other things, missiles can be tested and stored.*

THE OLD SOMALI CONNECTION

Soviet facilities in the Somali Democratic Republic were not essential for bunkering and minor repairs, at least in times of low tension. For those limited purposes, the Russians could and can use other ports such as Aden in the People's Democratic Republic of Yemen (South Yemen), Umm Qasyr in Iraq, and, far to the south, Port Louis in Mauritius and Beira and Lourenco Marques in Mozambique. They can, moreover, use protected anchorages off the South Yemeni island of Socotra and the Maldive Islands for rendezvous and resupply. But only in Somalia did they have a complex of airfields capable of handling the largest planes in their inventory; communications facilities (which, if U.S. experience is any guide, are not yet fully replicable by satellites); a secure place for missile storage, testing, and loading; and barracks where crews could be rested or held in reserve.

WESTERN BASES

If Western facilities in the Indian Ocean are lumped together, which for certain contingencies is realistic, they constitute a far more sub-

---

* Anti-ship and anti-aircraft missiles lack the reliability required for combat effectiveness if they are not routinely disassembled and tested.

stantial infrastructure than the Russians have been able to assemble. The American base on Diego Garcia boasts a sophisticated communications facility and an 8,000-foot runway supporting reconnaissance patrols over most of the ocean. The runway will be extended to the 12,000 feet required for KC-135 aerial tankers, and the lagoon will be equipped for the anchorage, bunkering, and supply of a carrier and its support ships.

Just beyond the mouth of the Persian Gulf, on the Omani-owned island of Masirah, the British have been operating an air base capable of handling heavy bombers and the long-range P-3 Orion reconnaissance plane. Given the close defense cooperation between the United Kingdom and the United States, one may assume Masirah's availability to the latter on an informal basis as needed. However, with the British no longer able to mind the shop, the United States is now seeking to formalize its access through an agreement with the Omani sultan. That gentleman, a client jointly of the British and, until recently, Shah Mohammad Reza Pahlavi of Iran, who have sustained him in a harsh struggle with tribal insurgents supported by the South Yemenis, is likely to be accommodating. If it felt the need, the United States could also pick up the Royal Air Force staging base on Gan in the Maldive Islands.

Down at the Cape of Good Hope, Britain and South Africa have shared the modern naval base at Simonstown. National poverty seems to be accomplishing what Britain's conscience constituency never quite managed, namely, getting the United Kingdom out. Its departure will in no way affect the open invitation to the United States and other NATO countries to use South African facilities and to cooperate with the growing South African coastal defense force.

At the juncture of the Indian Ocean and the Red Sea there is Djibouti. With an excellent harbor, superior communications, and a well-developed airfield, it remains available to Western forces. This situation should endure as long as France and the conservative Arab states choose to subsidize the country's penniless government and to defend its borders. Ethiopia seems too dependent on the port to exercise the economic leverage which goes with Djibouti's heavy reliance on the transit of Ethiopian goods.

And then there are those not-trivial facilities in the Somali Democratic Republic—three military airfields and the port of Berbera—Soviet built, Somali owned, and now apparently available to the highest bidder in currencies of diplomatic, economic, and military support. A quiet auction for influence now proceeds with veiled offers from the still hopeful Russians and their NATO-Arab opponents.

A Soviet Blockade?

The threat of a Soviet blockade, heralded by Western tocsin ringers and the South African lobby, is credible if one accepts two proposi-

tions: first, that with their present or foreseeably available naval resources, the Russians might conceivably spring an effective blockade
outside the context of general war between the East and the West;
and, second, that an Indian Ocean blockade is a cost-effective way of
threatening the West's oil line. The first proposition is simply implausible. The second enjoys a comparable credibility.

The West has the resources to crack a blockade well before it could
seriously threaten European and Japanese oil reserves, which could
be supplemented on an emergency basis by off-take from West African and Western Hemisphere production. The large current excess
capacity in the world's tanker fleet assures the transport flexibility
required to effect a temporary change in source. Meanwhile, a normally heterogeneous agglomeration of states with a profound interest
in the unimpeded flow of Persian Gulf oil would coalesce to attack the
Soviet blockaders. Western air and sea power, operating from the various bases enumerated above and from the several carriers could be
deployed rapidly by the United States, supplemented at least by the
French fleet and probably the growing Saudi air force.

The Russians, on the other hand, would fight alone. Air strikes
would immediately eliminate any shore-based facilities they may have
acquired. Sudanese, Saudi, and especially Egyptian hostility, as well
as the Suez Canal's extreme vulnerability, would prevent the Soviets
from using the short Canal route (3,300 miles) either to reinforce its
Indian Ocean flotilla with elements drawn from the powerful Black
Sea naval base or to withdraw damaged combatants. The only way
back to European Russia would be around the Cape of Good Hope
(roughly 7,700 miles), a suicide route carrying Soviet ships far from
the effective range of Soviet air power and near the U.S. base at Diego
Garcia. Soviet efforts to reinforce from, or withdraw to, its Pacific
base complex would be pounded mercilessly by U.S. air and naval
power operating from, or at least backstopped by, U.S. bases in Japan,
Korea, Australia, and the Philippines.

Since a blockade could easily escalate to general war, the presence
of a substantial proportion of the Soviet navy in the Indian Ocean
rather than in the approaches to the Soviet Union would constitute
inconceivable strategic folly. In other words, unless they were to obtain a large quantitative and qualitative advantage in naval combat
vessels over the Western navies (a contingency for which there is no
present prospect and one well within U.S. capacity to avert), the Russians, if contemplating a blockade, would face an insoluble dilemma.
With grossly inadequate air cover, no capacity for rapid reinforce-
ment, and no hope of posing the kind of threat to Western interests
which could conceivably evoke panic-induced political concessions,
the Soviets must be presumed willing to take on the combined air and
naval might of the Western and Arab states, launched from a rich and
widely diffused base structure.

Assuming the Soviet leadership should suddenly seek the direct confrontation it has generally eschewed, there are more efficient and less strategically perilous means for interdicting Persian Gulf oil. The most obviously efficient means is an air or missile attack on the oil fields themselves, launched from Russian bases. A single day's raid could cripple production for months at lilliputian cost compared to the expenditure required to sustain a naval blockade. Despite anticipated exponential upgrading of Saudi air defense capabilities, the Russians can still sustain this option at far less cost than a projected interdiction campaign demands.

Another possibility is sabotage at the source. The large alien population required by the gulf states to operate the fields virtually precludes effective security measures. Iran's domestic convulsions may create comparable vulnerability.

A third possibility is naval interdiction in the Mediterranean and the North Atlantic. There would be numerous advantages over an Indian Ocean exercise: vastly superior air cover, short supply lines, nearby reinforcements, ready access to repair facilities, and the capacity to shift missions from interdiction to strategic defense without any significant time lapse.

In addition to its relative inefficiency, an Indian Ocean blockade, initiated before the outbreak of full-scale war between the Soviet and Western blocs, would be extraordinarily perilous. Freedom of passage is a nonnegotiable issue. This must be apparent to the Soviet leadership. Since Western acquiescence would be incredible, initiation of a blockade might be interpreted in Western capitals not as a probe but rather as a prelude to an attack in the European theater. The temptation, then, would be to essay a preemptive, disarming thrust against the various Soviet fleets.

For all of the above reasons, an Indian Ocean blockade would be strategic folly of the highest order. The Russians do not evince any temptation to flirt with this folly. If they envisioned an assault on the sea lanes either as an attractive option for coercion short of total war or as an important adjunct to a conventional war in Europe,* surely they would be turning out large numbers of cheap submarines bedizened with clusters of torpedoes. What they are actually doing each year is building a few very expensive and very sophisticated submarines.[3] They are fairly evenly divided between those that are ideally configured for attacks on carriers and those clearly designed to hunt down and kill missile-launching submarines. The evidently central concern to which this construction program responds is nuclear attack on the Soviet heartland.

---

* The Soviet forces in central Europe are deployed and equipped for a blitzkrieg, not a prolonged war with the NATO forces opposite them. Western Europe already possesses a six-month oil reserve which, if war broke out, could easily be stretched.

A Plausible Threat to Western Interests?

The blockade threat is implausible but is there any way in which an armed Soviet naval presence in the Indian Ocean could, in fact, imperil Western interests? An affirmative response seems implicit both in the sometimes frenzied press campaign to highlight the Soviet presence and also in the West's efforts over the years to preserve and strengthen the conservative regimes that dominate the Persian Gulf. Would the displacement of the Gulf's traditional rulers actually represent as serious a blow to Western interests as most people believe? Would an Arab equivalent of Mengistu or that other Horn Marxist, Siad Barre, inevitably behave differently in matters that most concern the West and particularly the United States?

The usual protection-of-investments concern is in this case almost obsolete, for the process of nationalizing Western oil concessions (with compensation far short of the discounted-stream-of-profits theoretically demanded by the United States) is well advanced and will soon be complete. There is, by the way, no correlation between the pace of oil nationalization in a given country and the ideological bent of its ruling elite. The conservative Kuwaitis, for instance, have completely nationalized Western holdings, while the Libyans apparently prefer to retain several Western companies as concessionaires.

Price? A government's position on how high to go how quickly seems much more a function of its immediate revenue needs than anything else. That great and good friend of the West, the Iranian Shah, whose revenues could not keep pace with his daydreams, did not always look with sympathy on Saudi calls for price restraint. OPEC (Organization of Petroleum Exporting Countries) governments differ not on whether but rather on how best to collect the golden eggs of the Western goose.

If radical governments in Saudi Arabia, Kuwait, and the Emirates came to power, they would inherit from their feudal predecessors the uneasy, often conflictual, yet powerfullyhsymbiotic relationship with the West—the uniquely great market for Arab oil and still very much the best source of that modern technology desired by Arab leaders of every ideological stripe. In one respect, however, a Marxist or Islamic socialist, or any other kind of government deemed radical by the West, would be less constrained to cooperate on existing terms. Today's governments rely on the West not only for markets and technology but also for security from both internal and external threats. They believe, perhaps rightly, that the very nature of their regimes precludes treating the Soviet Union as a potential alternative guardian of their interests. Thus, they have left themselves with no alternative to the West, even though it is the West that would become the gravest threat to their independence should the terms for the transfer of gulf oil become intolerable. Perhaps if a new Middle East war drove them to play the boycott card again they would coincidentally be driven to overcome their fear and loathing of communist power and, in their desperation, seek shelter under a Soviet security blanket. But for the time being they act as if they have to rely on the West alone.

Regimes of the Left would not feel this constraint, and they would, therefore, be freer to pursue objectives which the West (and particularly the United States) does not share. The odds are that they would produce less oil, the value of which will increase over time along with the gulf's capacity to absorb capital. Probably they would divert some of their arms purchases to the Soviet bloc, thus increasing the West's petro-dollar deficit. And almost surely they would more readily use the oil weapon to achieve political ends, including a Middle East settlement on terms that Israel now deems unacceptable.

Of course this is speculation. Only a fool would predict with great confidence the behavior of nontraditional regimes. Power and wealth breed caution, particularly where the wealth is precarious, dependent as it is now and will be for the foreseeable future on Western prosperity and Middle East peace. Both are preconditions for the political and military rejuvenation of the Arab world. The reality of interdependence imposes itself even on so obdurate a dreamer as Libya's Qaddafi, who, despite all his quarrels with the United States, prefers to buy Boeing planes.

I underline these constraints, not to suggest that the West should be indifferent to the prospect of political change in the gulf states, but rather to caution against the kind of blind hysteria that precludes the shrewd calculation of costs incident to efforts to prevent change and, where change nevertheless occurs, prevents quick and sensible accommodation to the new reality. If we act as if some Arab governments had alternatives to cooperation, we can only help them to believe wrongly that they do.

With that important caveat, I have no difficulty in affirming that any radical nationalists who may be slouching toward Riyadh to assume control do represent some added risk to Western interests in the Middle East. The Soviet naval presence in the Indian Ocean conceivably may enhance the prospect for the overthrow of existing governments on the Arab side of the gulf; Soviet ships might serve as a shield for radical insurgents or some newly installed radical regime threatened with a seaborne intervention mounted or organized by the West in conjunction with regional allies. The risk of direct engagement even with a very modest Soviet tripwire might possibly add a significant element to the deterrent value of Soviet forces based in the Soviet Union's southern extremities.

The Soviet navy could also deter a Western thrust against the oil fields themselves in case of an embargo sprung by the present rulers. The possibility of playing an interpositional role, deterring the use of Western naval force for Third World interventions, has been lost on neither the Soviet nor the American navies. Admiral S. G. Gorshkov, commander in chief of the Soviet navy, has trumpeted it with engag-

ing candor, presumably in the course of the kind of interservice budgetary squabbles so familiar to Pentagon aficionados. For their part,
Western navalists have cited it as justification for still greater investments in a surface fleet and a supporting base structure which might
allow American ships to reach their target before the Soviet tripwire
could be established or, of course, before the Soviets could themselves
intervene on behalf of friends.

Policy Implications

The Horn does not hold the key to the future of U.S.-Soviet naval
competition in the Indian Ocean. With the distance between Russia's
Black Sea base-complex and the Arabian Sea more than halved by the
reopening of the Suez Canal,* *peacetime* deployment is feasible for the
Soviets without *any* littoral support facilities, albeit with less logistical
elegance.
Loss of Somali facilities has not, in fact, reduced the Soviets to exclusive reliance on ship-based support. They have apparently shifted
their aerial reconnaissance and certain other support activities to
Aden, which has a far better natural port than Berbera and a good
air field. And they retain user rights at the two Iraqui ports of Umm
Qasr and Al Basrah, in addition to anchorages off the South Yemen
coast. Moreover, they can probably bunker, at least on an *ad hoc* basis
and at commercial terms, in Mauritius and Mozambique.

What they have retained does not entirely compensate for what
they have lost, particularly in terms of aerial reconnaissance and air
cover for their surface combatants. Their airbase near Mogadishu was
some 1,000 miles south of Aden. And the three Somali bases together
gave the Soviets a good deal more strategic flexibility and security. As
it is, Soviet facilities are isolated on the extreme northern periphery
of the Indian Ocean, in contrast to Western installations, which are
distributed comfortably throughout the ocean from Oman in the
north to Reunion in the south, with Diego Garcia in the middle and
Australia and Singapore just back of the ocean's eastern rim.

These deficiencies probably do not seriously affect the Soviet
navy's present missions. Now the Russians seem interested primarily
in gathering such marginal political capital as can putatively be acquired through showing the flag, in developing operational experience, and, possibly, in maintaining a potential tripwire. They may be
equally interested in signaling that they have the will and capacity to
match any escalation in Western activity. That signal is, of course, best
conveyed by shore facilities which can support a much enlarged fleet
deployment, as Diego Garcia will support a thrust of U.S. ships into

---

* From over 7,000 to roughly 3,300 miles.

the area. Facilities in Somalia served a comparable deterrent role for the USSR as well as facilitating the logistics of current operations and laying a foundation for the option of an enlarged presence. That is another facet of the loss they incurred and would like to recoup. As far as Indian Ocean operations are concerned, Eritrean bases would be of value primarily as insurance against access losses in Aden and Iraq, valuable insurance, to be sure, because relations with Iraq have become quite testy recently, because South Yemen is vulnerable to Saudi blandishments and conspiracies, and, more generally, because the Soviet Union's relations with Muslim (particularly Arab) states have a volatile history.

One way of inhibiting a provocative build-up of Soviet naval forces is to demonstrate the will and capacity to match, and, if necessary, exceed each Soviet accretion and thereby to preclude strategic gains. U.S. construction of a base on Diego Garcia and periodic Indian Ocean deployment of a carrier task force nicely served that end. Agreement, express or implied, on restraint in force deployment represents a less costly and abrasive alternative.

Initially the United States displayed little interest in seeking any kind of formal restraints. One explanation of our early indifference may have been the perceived obstacles to any successful negotiation. Among them were asymmetries between the interests, strategies, facilities, and weapon systems of the United States and the USSR which seemed to preclude acceptance of limits calculated in identical units of naval and air power. What, for instance, would be the Soviet equivalent of a U.S. nuclear carrier? Would it be two missile-armed cruisers? A squadron of fighter-bombers in Somalia? And so on. What, moreover, can equivalences between discrete weapon systems mean? The answer is that outside the context of particular missions, strategies, and contingencies, each of which may mandate a different "just balance," they mean very little at all.

The Strategic Arms Limitation Talks (SALT) have dealt primarily with a single contingency (nuclear war), a single strategy (deterrence), and a single common interest (avoiding nuclear war). They were preceded by years of clarifying analysis and debate. Yet a powerful political impetus flowing from the highest levels of government has been required to produce agreements, quickly subjected to unrelenting criticism. Agreement on a table of power equivalents mediating equitably among the asymmetries enumerated above in order to reach agreement on force deployments probably requires transcendance of larger and less well examined conceptual difficulties than those which have beset SALT. However, unlike advantages gained through serious errors in the calculus of deterrence, any advantage gained through an agreement on deployment restraints could easily be rectified. Nevertheless, given the public's strategic naivete and the even more complex calculations probably required in this case, such an agreement might be peculiarly vulnerable to the sort of vituperative attack raised against agreements on deterrence.

These obstacles were formidable; but no one claimed that they were insuperable. Inside the government, opposition to an agreement rested on other grounds.

Within the U.S. Navy, formal restraints on deployment appear to be regarded with the sort of unbuttoned enthusiasm one might reserve for a viper slithering into one's bed. This frank hostility is widely shared in the national security bureaucracy and, very likely, in its Soviet counterpart. Its source is not obscure. People who achieve positions of responsibility in most countries, but particularly in great powers, believe quite simply that the ultimate political arbiter is raw military power and that its demonstrable availability establishes the necessary background against which a state wages an effective diplomacy.

Naval power is seen to have two great virtues: it is easy to exhibit, and it can be employed worldwide and in doses carefully proportioned to the perceived requirements of each case. More precisely, it is by far the most effective means for intervention in the Third World.

As naval power has two great virtues, Indian Ocean deployment limitations would have two great vices: they would create a precedent for limiting deployment in other seas and threaten to erode the credibility of U.S. intervention in the Persian Gulf or in other parts of the littoral.

While defending the appropriation for Diego Garcia, one State Department expert summed up the underlying administration position with fetching candor: "We would want a naval presence in the Indian Ocean," he said, "even if the Russians were not there at all. We have interests there quite independent of our competitive relationship with the Soviets just as they have interests quite unrelated to us." As notional examples of specific contingencies requiring a naval presence, he cited guerrilla attacks on Israeli tankers passing through Bab el Mandeb and the eruption of hostilities between Iran and Iraq in which the United States, the principal armorer of the shah, would intervene to keep the peace.

Nothing was said about occupying the gulf. But one cannot help suspecting that that is a contingency lurking in some recess of the strategic mind when the virtues of a naval presence are extolled. As I have suggested, it may in fact be a major source of concern for the Soviet naval presence. The specter which may haunt is not an attack on the tankers or even Soviet interventions in the style of the 1965 U.S. occupation of the Dominican Republic but rather Soviet interposition in case the United States chooses this means to shore up the existing international economic order.

A force-limitation agreement might cover the geography as well as the dimensions of naval deployments. It might, for instance, declare the Persian Gulf out of bounds for both navies. That would, of course, leave the local traditionalists with a free hand to defend the status quo. On the other hand, combined with overall force limitations throughout the Indian Ocean, it would inhibit Western intervention in case of an oil embargo by the existing regimes. And it would have the precedential consequences cited above.

For Secretary of State Henry Kissinger, the Angolan civil war ruled out any immediate effort to test the seriousness of Soviet hints concerning their possible interest in a formal force-limitation agreement. Ever sensitive to the nuance of national image, he feared that a U.S. initiative might be construed as a sign of weakness or of indifference to Soviet activities in Africa.[4] Moreover, despite our disaster in Vietnam, like many other strategists, he apparently had not relinquished the belief that, in our transactions with the Third World, force is only the conduct of diplomacy by other means.

Though formal arrangements were neglected, both State and Defense Department officials implied that by 1975 there already was a tacit understanding on force limitations. The Russians stabilized the number and types of ships they were regularly deploying in the Indian Ocean. The United States, for its part, denied publicly any intention of establishing an Indian Ocean fleet and defended Diego Garcia only as a means of facilitating occasional patrols and as insurance in case of certain contingencies, including augmented and more aggressive Soviet operations.

Tacit arrangements are, of course, relatively more vulnerable than formal agreements to evasion through elastic interpretation and to wholesale annulment at the behest of new calculations of interest. Weighted with these generic deficiencies, informal rules of the game are generally even less effective than express understandings in restraining domestic demands for greater military expenditures.

Because their limits tend toward fuzziness and because they provide neither a public obligation nor the machinery to conciliate differences, tacit understandings are, in addition, relatively more likely to produce conflicting interpretations of the arrangement. The danger of conflicting interpretations is particularly acute in the present case where either side may be moved by the enumerated interests unrelated to superpower competition to raise its profile.

Perhaps it was an appreciation of these difficulties that moved the Carter administration very shortly after its formation to seek an understanding on Indian Ocean naval arms limitations as part of its overall package of proposed U.S.-USSR arms control agreements. Or perhaps it was motivated partially by pressure from Senate liberals who had unsuccessfully pressed Kissinger to explore Soviet attitudes and partiallyhby substantial evidence of Soviet interest reflected in a 1976 working document, tabled at the United Nations, in which the Soviet government stated that if all "foreign bases" were prohibited, it would "be prepared to seek, together with other powers, for ways to reduce, on a reciprocal basis, the military activities of non-littoral states on the Indian Ocean and directly adjacent regions."

In March, 1977, the two superpowers established a working group to explore the possibility of a formal arrangement. It has held four negotiating sessions without any evident result. Since naval activities continue to be stabilized at a rather low level in relation to the various interests of both parties, the leisurely pace should at this point be a source neither of surprise nor of particular concern. Still, one hopes the lack of a sense of urgency will not persist indefinitely, for an agreement on principles of restraint and, perhaps, on the establishment of a consultative mechanism is far more easily achieved in a time unmarked by high tension. Its achievement reduces the danger that events beyond the control of either power might again be blown out of proportion and might lead enthusiasts on both sides to press for a competitive escalation of forces and facilities.

Notes

1. See for example D. R. Cox, "Sea Power and Soviet Foreign Policy," *U.S. Naval Proceedings* 95 (June 1969) : 41 ff; T. B. Millar, "Soviet Policies South and East of Suez," *Foreign Affairs* 52 (October 1973) : 73; L. Martin, "The New Power Gap in the Indian Ocean," *Interplay* 3 (January 1969) : 37; O. M. Smolansky, "Soviet Entry into the Indian Ocean: An Analysis" in Michael MccGwire, ed., *Soviet Naval Developments* (New York: Praeger, 1973). p. 421.

2. See generally R. G. Weinland, "The Changing Mission of the Soviet Navy," *Survival* 14 (May/June 1972) : 131-2; Geoffrey Jukes, "The Indian Ocean in Soviet Naval Policy," *Adelphi Papers Number Eighty-seven* (London: International Institute of Strategic Studies, 1972), pp. 12-18; A. J. Cottrell and R. M. Burrell, "Soviet-U.S. Naval Competition in the Indian Ocean," *Orbis* 18 (Winter 1975) : 1123.

3. *Jane's Fighting Ships* (New York: Franklin Watts, Inc., 1975-76).

4. See *Congressional Record*, September 11, 1975, p. S15891 and May 6, 1976, p. S6626.

5. For a useful analysis of the issues that face any effort to achieve an Indian Ocean naval arms limitation see Richard Haass, "Naval Arms Limitation in the Indian Ocean," *Survival* 20 (1978): 50.

The Direction of Policy: Idealism and Self-Interest 9

The peoples of the Horn—Somalis, Amharas, Eritreans, Gallas, Afars, all and all alike—are the suffering Jobs of our present world, ripped by conflict, ravaged by nature, tormented by transient hope. In Ethiopia, revolution, its time come round at last, careens over living bodies towards uncertain ends. In the country's fleeting passage from American to Soviet clientage, Eritreans glimpsed the promise of victory. Today the vision recedes and dying is a way of life. In Somalia, filled with the widows and refugees of the Ogaden war, people go on dreaming, though now with little real hope, of one state, one people, a greater Somalia. And in the fledgling Republic of Djibouti? No doubt its present inhabitants wonder whether even the jackals will survive if the French fold up their various subventions and go home.

Yet the Horn has within itself the human materials for self-transformation. Unlike so many other Third World states, Ethiopia and Somalia are real nations with governments that function and leaders animated by ideals beyond or at least in addition to personal power and self-enrichment. As for Eritrea, Gerard Chaliand, the distinguished French journalist, rightly calls its leading force, the EPLF, "a remarkable organization . . . by far the most impressive revolutionary movement produced in Africa in the last two decades."[1]

Real peace, the peace of accommodation rather than temporary defeat, would open vistas of hope that are now closed. While, for their various purposes, both Soviets and Cubans appear eager to promote accommodation, both are clearly more concerned about preserving Ethiopia intact and retaining their places as chief advisers to its current masters. And thus far Mengistu and his allies offer their Somali and Eritrean opponents nothing but war or submission.

Mengistu himself seems hopelessly intransigent, having climbed to his present eminence over the bodies of competitors who tended to die as soon as they proposed a negotiated settlement with the Eritreans. Soviet arms and Cuban troops gave Mengistu a victory in the Ogaden, thereby vindicating his policy of war *à outrance*. At the penultimate moment Soviet arms and Cuban technical assistance thwarted an Eritrean victory. But Fidel Castro, once a benefactor of the EPLF, has so far refused to do more, holding his troops on leash while he exhorts the parties to compose their differences.

Eritrea

By force alone Mengistu probably cannot soon reestablish Ethiopian authority in Eritrea outside the cities and large towns and a few roads required for the movement of supplies and reinforcements. The war will therefore continue to bleed his troops and his treasury. Neither he nor any other now plausible leader will trade independence for peace. Urged on by Cubans and Soviet advisers, however, Mengistu or others who may yet succeed him might negotiate some sort of federal solution. The Eritreans, having seen victory elude them, seem prepared to compromise with the ideal of national independence.

Should the Eritrean war's outcome concern the United States? Of the various reasons Washington once paraded to justify American support for Ethiopia's war—maintaining base rights, sustaining credibility as an ally (even of partners pursuing doubtful ends by barbarous means), and preventing independence in Eritrea because it might adhere to the anti-Israeli cause—only the latter conceivably survives to influence the U.S. appraisal of alternative policies, and, from the beginning, that reason was featherweight in fact if not appearance, a matter more of dreamy metaphor—the Red Sea as an "Arab lake"—than of lucid strategy.

What of significance an independent, pro-Arab Eritrea could have added to Egyptian, Sudanese, Saudi, Yemeni, and Somali facilities available for Red Sea operations against Israeli commerce was a question perpetually in search of persuasive answers. If, as still seems possible this winter of 1978-79, Egypt makes peace with Israel and splits the Arab world, Eritrean facilities might appear more valuable to those forces in the Arab world determined to fight on. However, it is no longer clear whether independence or reintegration with Ethiopia is more likely to make Eritrean territory available to them.

Eritreans should detest Israel for aiding both Selassie and his successors. Ideologically the EPLF activists are natural cousins to the Palestinian Left. But it is sanctuary in the Sudan which guarantees their survival. And if, through some fratricidal explosion within the Ethiopian armed forces that would unleash anarchy at the center of the empire, the EPLF were eventually to win, Saudi dollars could finance reconstruction of their ruined land, and Saudi and Egyptian arms would offer the best insurance against Ethiopian *révanche*. An independent Eritrea would have other incentives for following Egypt's pacific lead, particularly the certainty of Israeli retaliation against Assab and Massawa. The mere threat of Eritrean involvement in any kind of armed conflict would deflect commerce to competing ports.

The consequences for Israel of Ethiopian control of Eritrea's coast are singularly obscure. Because of their assistance to the Eritreans and other anti-regime forces, both the Sudanese and the Saudis are regarded by the Dergue with intense hostility. But Iraq's intransigently anti-Israeli government also supports the Eritreans. On the one hand, Israel has been one of the handful of states willing to aid the Dergue; on the other, the Dergue's principal ally, the Soviet Union, is reckoned a main prop of those states that reject the Camp David Agreement.

Even if military facilities in Eritrea were a matter of much consequence for Israeli security, Israel's Western friends would be hard put to decide whether they should favor or oppose the Eritrean liberation struggle. In fact, those facilities have only a trivial potential for mischief. By sea and air, Israel can devastate any base along the Red Sea that might be used to harrass its commerce. For all of the above reasons, this residue of the old basis for U.S. antagonism to the Eritreans and, conversely, support for Ethiopian centralism should in no degree inform U.S. policy towards the Horn. What remains?

Rating the Horn's Strategic Value

Strategic marginality characterizes all of the Horn, not simply Eritrea, which I have emphasized here in order to lock up the "Red Sea fears" that periodically escape onto the agenda of Western concern. The Horn is too peculiar, too poor, and its principal actors are too preoccupied with provincial conflicts and aspirations to give the place a very high rank on any rational list of geopolitical priorities. But, for reasons sketched earlier, neither is it at the bottom. From a strictly geopolitical perspective it deserves a modest measure of Western attention and resources, but nothing on the scale of Soviet involvement.

The fact that the Soviets seem to calculate differently is in part a reflection of their own marginal position. Historical circumstances and Western diplomacy have denied them a central role in either Africa or the Middle East. Ethiopia gives them only a precarious fingerhold on the edge of both regions, not a field from which they can suddenly vault into prominence. In the Middle East, Syria, Iraq, Libya, and Algeria are incomparably more important. Even the People's Democratic Republic of Yemen has a leg up above Ethiopia. And in Africa, both Nigeria and the front-line states of the south—particularly Zambia, Mozambique, and Tanzania—have far more power to define the Soviet Union's African vocation—particularly in the immediate future—than Ethiopia or Somalia or both acting congruently on behalf of Soviet interests.

Lack of luxurious geopolitical alternatives is one explanation for Soviet investments in the Horn. Another is the sparsity of social revolutions. Neocapitalism in its protean forms reigns throughout most of the Third World. When you have very few ideological friends, you bang the drums loudly whenever another joins the club.

Aside from swelling their own investment over the past two years, the Soviet Union and its Cuban ally have coincidentally managed to reinflate Western notions about the Horn's significance. The Carter administration's decision to single out Ethiopia as one of three states tohbe formally punished for human rights delinquencies signalled a bear-market conception of the Horn's value. Then, as if the Soviet Union were an infallible analyst, Western concern scurried back to the Horn rather in the manner of a bull reacting to a red flag.

Normative Restraints

As noted earlier, this reactive escalation of anxiety was stimulated both by the effusions of American political adventurers like Senator Moynihan, apparently indefatigable in their search for American "defeats," and by the Carter administration's uneasy deference to their histrionics—deference implicit in its chaotic, self-defeating invocation of "standards" allegedly inhibiting foreign intervention. In developing new guidelines for U.S. policy in the Horn, the administration has another opportunity to reconsider the norms of intervention—whether conceived as legal standards or informal rules of the game—which it is prepared to support.

The traditional and still widely endorsed norms would preclude aid to any of the Horn's insurgents with the possible exception of the Eritreans, who arguably can and certainly do invoke Ethiopia's failure to comply with the original U.N. resolution as grounds for separation. Unfortunately, virtually every existing state tacitly recognized Ethiopia's suppression of Eritrean autonomy. Furthermore, the Eritreans have since failed to win even a hearing before the United Nations or the OAU, much less formal recognition as a "movement of national liberation." Nevertheless, for all the reasons developed earlier, Eritrea can be distinguished from other secessionist cases. And, given the almost genocidal impact of the war successive Ethiopian governments have waged, the United States and other states might also aid the Eritreans under the doctrine of humanitarian intervention, repudiated by the Third World but still embraced and periodically employed by Western states.

Since Ethiopia's formal legal right to occupy the Ogaden and Haud are a good deal less disputable (except with respect to the proper location of the border with Somalia, which was not clearly defined before Somali independence), traditional norms would inhibit U.S. military assistance that might facilitate the secession struggle supported by the Somali Democratic Republic. Economic aid, including assistance in succoring and resettling refugees of the Ogaden war would not, however, fall under the ban. And with its pronounced cant in favor of recognized governments struggling against rebels, the traditional rules also legitimate every form of U.S. assistance to Ethiopia.

The putative right of foreign states to aid governments in suppressing insurgents never went entirely unchallenged. Some scholars argued that foreign interventions violated national sovereignty since they occurred only when the legitimate government lacked sufficient indigenous support to triumph unaided.[2] In other words, intervention negated self-determination. The U.S. could pick up and shape this minor theme, without wholly rejecting the old normative dispensation, by conceding the propriety of arms transfers and arraigning only direct combat support in the form of fighting units or technical assistance at the operational level: for instance, servicing high-technology weapon systems. From this position, the United States could present a principled indictment of the Soviet-Cuban military presence in Ethiopia, without, as in the event of a blanket condemnation of Soviet-Cuban assistance to Ethiopia, seeming to challenge the principle of collective self-defense against external attacks.

Humanitarian Ends and Practical Means

Do these normative boundaries allow the United States room to pursue its strategic interests? Are they ideally configured for the defense of humanitarian values? Do strategic interests and humanitarian values coincide here?

If it were animated only by humanitarian sympathies, a government able to influence developments on the Horn would work to achieve the following goals: (1) Negotiated settlement of the Eritrean war, a peace without a victor and achieved at the earliest possible moment; (2) Negotiated settlement of the Somali-Ethiopian dispute on terms reflecting the nomads' economic imperative—the open border; (3) Local autonomy and equal opportunity for Ethiopia's ethnic minorities; (4) Resettlement of refugees from the Horn's various natural and man-made disasters; (5) Accelerated economic growth; (6) Rapid expansion of public services, particularly in the fields of health, agricultural research and credit, and vocational education; and (7) Respect for civil and political liberties. In short, peace, development, equity, due process, and participation.

Peace alone is probably a necessary but not a sufficient condition for approaching the other goals. The West, as a consequence of its original colonial manipulations and its subsequent relinquishment after World War II of Eritrea and Somali-inhabited territories to Ethiopian sovereignty, carries a heavy responsibility for today's conflicts; however, it can play only a subordinate role in resolving them.

As a result of its patronage, the United States once might have pressed Addis towards compromise. Instead, it built the Emperor's armies, endowed him with unqualified diplomatic support, and thus encouraged his harsh intransigence. Soviet aid to Somalia, for its part, may have encouraged Somali obduracy, though that is hard to tell since the Emperor never tested it with a serious offer.

With the reversal of patrons and clients, now it is the Soviet Union, together with the Cuban government, which possesses leverage over Ethiopia, still the central actor in this region's endless bloody dramas, while the United States has by force of circumstance acquired a potential influence over the Somalis and, indirectly, the Eritreans. More has happened, however, than a mere reversal of roles. The Somalis have experienced the chastening discipline of failure. The Eritreans also have seen victory jerked away as they reached for it; but they have still acquired a military and political stature not even imagined in the days when the United States was complicit in the Emperor's campaign to destroy them. Ethiopia's government is, on the one hand, more powerful than in the Emperor's day—the army doubled, backed by a huge militia, and far more heavily armed—and, on the othzr hand, more precarious, because its enemies have multiplied, its place in regional diplomacy has greatly diminished, and its internal unity threatened as it has not been since the 19th century. Meanwhile all three actors have begun to build new societies guided by a radical socialist ideology (in the Somali case, the new society is heavily alloyed with Islamic values).

Ethiopia's revolution is the single change most relevant to peace. The Amhara-dominated, centrally-controlled, intensely hierarchic imperial order could not by its nature have left much breathing room for other cultures and religions. Nor could it have offered much hope or scope to the growing elite of secular modernizers. Its joints were too old and brittlely interdependent. One could not yield much of substance, the Emperor feared, without splintering the whole fragile structure.

It did not yield, it could not yield, but it could be and was smashed. The new, still emerging order rests on principles of legitimacy—equal rights, social justice, religious freedom—which actually require for their fruition a society free of the intolerance that ignited the Eritrean war and united Ethiopia's Somalis into a permanent fifth column.

Ethnic and regional rivalries have not been banished. And it is by no means certain that the revolution will not quickly rigidify into rule by and for parochial interests. But this will surely occur at the expense of that legitimacy which so facilitates government and thus releases resources for investment, development, and diplomacy.

You cannot federate incompatible elements and expect federation to survive. Either they will redivide or one unit will absorb the others. That is why the U.N. decision to join a democratic Eritrea with a feudal and imperial Ethiopia was transparently hypocritical. Now that

Somalia, Ethiopia, and Eritrea have become more like each other, the notion of some sort of federal solution seems less fanciful, although the differences among them remain formidable. Those differences helped frustrate Fidel Castro's mediation* and continue to fuel the Eritrean conflict. But the conditions for settlement through an agreement which jettisons conventionally rigid notions of territorial sovereignty in favor of a more supple and functional architecture of political authority are markedly more propitious.

Having lost their valiant bid to liberate the Ogaden and seen their armed forces ground up by overwhelming opposition, the Somalis have acquired a far greater incentive to explore solutions short of a greater Somalia. And because they fought well, have retained their national cohesion, and, with Arab and Western help, could soon become again a dangerous military adversary, they are not without leverage of their own, leverage which is increased by the continuing insurgency in southern and eastern Ethiopia.

As the Ethiopian victory improves the prospects for settlement on the Somali front, so the stalemate enhances the prospect for an Eritrean settlement.

The surest way to make oneself an object of scorn among hardened diplomats is to propose terms of settlement for an interstate dispute which require more than incremental change in the behavior of the antagonists. It is hard to arraign their cynicism, forged as it so obviously is on the anvil of experience. If history is any guide, most states most of the time would rather fight than change. And the hardest change of all to contemplate in this era of resurgent nationalism, sanctioned by the charter and practice of the United Nations, is one involving the very definition of the state.

Nevertheless, there are occasions when, through some extraordinary conjunction of circumstances, states are propelled out of their normal behavioral orbits. Though always unique, the circumstantial pattern undoubtedly includes in its constituents a sensation of newly released, momentous, and transient possibilities. That describes the state of the Horn today.

The ideal settlement is simply the one that all the actors will accept. From the vantage point of today, surrounded by volatile and uncertain factors including the precise equilibrium of forces at the time negotiations might commence, one can only suggest the rough outline of agreements that might satisfy the bedrock requirements of Eritreans, Somalis, and Ethiopians.

To date, peace has always beaten futilely on the high barrier of classic nationalist ideals: one people (however accidental and recent their sense of identity), one state, equal to all and with all the diplomatic trappings. In fact, both Somali and Eritrean claims have strong

---

* Another reason for Castro's failure, according to some sources, was his failure to come armed with a detailed and balanced compromise proposal.

historical and moral foundations. In a just world, the Ogaden would be in Somali hands and Eritrea would be free. Historical forces, proceeding in their own implacable way, have made it otherwise. With Western and Arab help, Somalis and Eritreans can go on pressing their claims, bleeding Ethiopia and hoping for that elusive collapse of central authority in Addis which could open the way to victory. Is that slender possibility worth the awful human price?

Peace means bowing to the fact of Ethiopian primacy and its resolution to fight forever rather than to allow secession. What might Ethiopia yield in return? The Eritreans need more than a modest degree of local autonomy. Still able to carry on a savage guerrilla war, already having paid an unimaginable price, they will demand freedom to develop their social revolution without interference from Addis. They will demand internal self-government and some solid guarantees that they will not again be betrayed.

One way to mitigate their fear of betrayal is an external guarantee by states with the interest and means to enforce a peace settlement. Ideally such a guarantee would be buttressed by a trip-wire force in place like the Turkish force in Cyprus, a precedent certain to provoke Ethiopian resistance. Several Arab states, particularly Egypt and Saudi Arabia, satisfy the criteria of interest and capability; but it is hard to imagine any Ethiopian government countenancing their armed presence on the Horn.

What an Ethiopian government seriously committed to compromise might and certainly should accept is an arrangement under which the only Ethiopian troops allowed in Eritrea after the settlement (without prior permission from Eritrean authorities) would be a division recruited from the Eritrean liberation movements. The best long-term supplement to internal arrangements is an Ethiopian entente with the principal Arab Red Sea states. Unless the march towards a Middle-East settlement falls short of its goal, a peaceful Red Sea will be an economic and strategic imperative for Ethiopians and Arabs alike. The roots of an entente can also grow out of the mutual capacity of Arabs and Ethiopians to injure each other: Ethiopia by throwing tinder on southern Sudan's smouldering embers and assisting plots against the Saudis; the Arabs by inflaming and arming Moslem nationalism throughout the Horn.

A formal federation would be the best juridical guarantee of autonomy. By joining, Somalia would donate much needed balance to the Eritrean-Addis relationship. Eritrean admission to the United Nations, following the precedent of the Ukraine and Byelorussia, would symbolpze and thus help stabilize elements of equality in the federal relationship.

Within the framework of at first probably a very nominal federal structure, what might the Somali Democratic Republic hope to gain? Possibly some minor, face-saving border adjustments; but the primary potential gain would be a much more secure and autonomous existence for the Ogaden nomads. Of course there would have to be open borders. If, in addition, as part of a broad demilitarization of the frontier area, Ethiopia would agree not to station troops in the Ogaden, to staff the courts and the administration and the police with ethnic Somalis, and to localize most taxing authority and the bulk of decisions affecting education and other state services, then President Barre could not so readily be charged with betraying his compatriots by relinquishing demands for their secession.

Friction over the possible exploitation of oil and gas resources could be resolved through the designation of a joint development area on both sides of the frontier to the depth of a prescribed number of miles. Title to all oil and gas reserves would be assigned to a public corporation, established by treaty, in which the two states would hold equal shares. This arrangement would not constitute a unilateral Ethiopian concession. The geological formations on the Somali side of the provisional border are not notably different from those in the Ogaden. Such reserves as there may be seem as likely to be found on one side of the frontier as on the other. An agreement on joint development would, in addition, assure access to the sea along the most economic route for a pipeline. Finally, it should be noted that the now most promising exploration area inside Ethiopia is located in that part of the Ogaden where Somalia has the strongest legal and historic claims to a favorable adjustment.

What goods might the Dergue find in the kind of settlement I have outlined? Though short, successful wars help to smother internal disputes and legitimate those who win them, long draining stalemates have very much the opposite effect. By coming to terms with its principal adversaries, the Dergue probably could reduce other threats to the level of nuisances. Then it could get on with the great tasks of revolutionary social development. Peace would release enormous human and material resources. It would, for instance, permit efficient use of all available ports, including those on the Somali coast. Together the former antagonists could expand rail and road facilities to link up the various parts of this massive territory and tie them more effectively into international commercial channels. A peaceful Horn would draw increased financial assistance from the World Bank and bilateral aid programs and could attract foreign investment, particularly to explore for and develop mineral resources.

A federated Horn would immediately acquire increased prominence in African politics, for it would deploy the most impressive military forces north of South Africa and would be administered and led by men who have demonstrated a capacity to govern that has few parallels in Africa. In addition, Somalia would link it to the aid programs of Arab neighbors. And the end of the Eritrean conflict would facilitate a mutually beneficial détente with the Sudan.

Presumably the Russians and Cubans still favor a peaceful settlement—through federalization or any other means the parties find acceptable. Both before and after the Ogaden war they reiterated their desire to reconcile the antagonists. Cuba's apparent refusal to commit its ground forces to the Eritrean campaign and its public espousal of a negotiated settlement evidences a determination to influence events by means short of a threatened break with Mengistu.

The United States and its allies also can influence developments on the Horn. The main Eritrean liberation movements now seem convinced that they have little hope of winning in the foreseeable future. Mengistu, buoyed by his reconquest of Eritrea's towns and cities, still seems bullish. Acting in concert with concerned Arab governments, Washington could moderate his hopes of a final, decisive victory, if it would orchestrate for the Eritreans a steady flow of modern arms and a continuing sanctuary in the Sudan, protected if need be by Egyptian troops. The administration would not have to become directly involved. Arab governments have the necessary means to prevent an Eritrean defeat. Washington's role would be to encourage and coordinate such an Arab effort—which must include additional political and military support for Sudan's President Numeri to block an Ethiopian riposte—while simultaneously holding the Eritreans to a conciliatory course and assuring Mengistu that the Arabs also would endorse the kind of settlement his Cuban patrons have urged.

Similarly in the case of Somalia, the United States, Saudi Arabia, Egypt, and other sympathetic parties could create a momentum towards settlement by initiating a rearmament program at a pace and on a scale sufficient to enhance Somali leverage without reinflating Somali dreams. Such a program would have to be publicly conditioned, not on a flat Somali disavowal of intent to aid Ethiopian insurgents, but on a declared willingness to initiate negotiations without prior conditions and an implied willingness to settle for an open, slightly revised border and local autonomy.

If the Carter administration were simply to write off the region, Mengistu and his colleagues would be less likely to pursue negotiated settlements. If, on the other hand, the United States were to undertake a massive rearmament of the Somali armed forces and to encourage unqualified support for the Eritreans, the inhabitants of the Horn would cease even to imagine an end to war.

Americans do not easily imagine a nice correspondence of U.S. and Soviet interests anywhere in the world. Assuming that the greatest single humanitarian contribution the United States can make in this region is to propel the parties towards a form of settlement endorsed by states whose presence on the Horn it has furiously condemned, is that contribution consistent with American strategic interests? Or do those interests command one of the two alternative policies: competing without restraint for influence over the Dergue or seeking its destruction by financing, arming, and coordinating its many opponents?

The Dergue would no doubt welcome an avid competition for its favor. With equal certainty one can predict that the Soviets would sulk. But what would the United States gain? A reduced risk that the Ethiopians would trade base rights for Soviet aid or in other ways collaborate in Soviet adventures? Those are gains worth securing at a price corresponding to the Horn's modest strategic value. One may doubt, however, that support of Ethiopian belligerence is the most efficient means at our disposal. Assistance in war-making is the Soviet Union's most impressive asset. Why compete on its terms, when in time of peace it can match development assistance from the United States and its allies only by a relatively much more onerous investment?

Why then do the Soviets and Cubans want peace? In part, perhaps, because they do not expect capitalist Western or neocapitalist Arab states to compete in assisting an avowedly radical government. The U.S. track record is miserable but, one hopes, not immutable. We cannot teach the Ethiopians how to manage a centrally planned economy on the Soviet model. We can, however, teach them a great deal about increasing agricultural production. And in the process we might and certainly should attempt to convince Ethiopia's revolutionaries that rigid collectivism, Soviet style, is a recipe for failure. Even the more rabid of our congressional cold warriors might be intrigued by the prospect of peaceful competition to influence the shape of Ethiopian rural development, while practically no one at all who resides on Capitol Hill will, however insistent the strategic arguments, tolerate U.S. complicity in the extermination of the Dergue's various opponents.

If we were to assume that either the ideological petrification of American policy-makers or the ideological zeal of Ethiopian ones predetermines an intimate, long-term alliance between Ethiopia and its Marxist patrons, the second policy—attempting to manage the Dergue's destruction—might begin to charm ruthless strategic minds, if only Addis's masters revealed greater signs of weakness. But so far they have shown an impressive capability to contain their own, the army's, and the whole country's centrifugal forces, while cuffing about every challenger for the levers of central power. In the sophistication of its urban and rural reforms, as well as in its marshalling and deployment of force, one sees capacities which, supported by Soviet and Cuban arms, now seem likely to result in the Dergue dominating most of the Horn unless Washington is prepared to intervene at a level quite unjustified by the region's limited importance and the alternative ways of fostering its nonalignment. Moreover, as long as Soviets and Cubans are prepared to match Western and conservative-Arab arms aid, Western proxies might succeed in making most of Eritrea uninhabitable and in draining resources otherwise available for development, without disabling the Dergue or preventing the Soviet Union from acquiring air and naval facilities. In any event, neither Congress nor public opinion is likely to countenance intense U.S.

involvement in a major insurgency until the stakes appear higher and other alternatives are foreclosed. In short, these alternative lines of policy compete ineffectively on both strategic and humanitarian grounds with the mix of limited cooperation and conditional opposition initially outlined.

To describe any degree of cooperation with the Ethiopian government as superior from a humanitarian perspective may seem flatly contradictory with my account of its brutality. Obviously—at least one hopes it is obvious—I am not proposing that the immense social reforms already achieved by Mengistu and his colleagues somehow balance or even obscure the concomitant bloodshed. How nice it would be if the breakers of Ethiopia's feudal order were lovable, kind, altogether gentle sorts of people able to reshape a rotten society by the elegance of their arguments or the beauty of their language or the charismatic force of their personalities. In the real world (a less pretty place) the United States faces a group of very rough customers with a demonstrably low tolerance for opposition. That is by no means the sole explanation for the slaughter. The masters of Addis are not paranoid. They have real enemies who also espouse arresting ideals and defend them with guns.

This Ethiopian government has done much that is awful and also much that is good. The issue of policy is not how to assess the moral balance of its deeds. The past is relevant only to the extent it is instructive. One describes the achievements of the Dergue not to absolve it but to suggest that it has some purposes with which we can sympathize. If all its ends and means were despicable as in the case of South Africa's government or Uganda's Amin, then cooperation could not promote humane ends. Cooperation would be equally repugnant if the present regime could be replaced with a plainly more attractive alternative without still greater costs in human suffering.

In the Horn today poverty remains the main cause of misery and death. Unlike poverty in many other Third World countries, particularly in those of Latin America, poverty in the Horn is the condition, not merely of the lower classes, but of practically the entire society. Poverty, in other words, is more a consequence of failures in production than of distribution. War is the second great killer. For the time being, the policy I have urged for the United States and its allies seems the alternative most likely to counter those scourges.*

Is it compatible with the classic and still conventional view of the legal limits of intervention in civil wars? Probably not. If polled, the great majority of states would doubtless refuse to regard Eritrea as an

---

* However, if fratricidal struggle within the Ethiopian Armed Forces led to the collapse of central authority, the United States would have to reassess its position. At that juncture, the primary concern of the United States would probably have to be a possible Soviet-Cuban effort to impose new leaders on the Ethiopian people.

exceptional case justifying external assistance. Probably they would also arraign any aid to Somalia that in turn facilitated continued Somali support of Ethiopian insurgents. Some may think that this apparent incompatibility establishes a presumption against my recommendations. Others will find in it good reason to reconsider the proper limits of intervention.

Notes

1. Gerard Chaliand, "The Horn of Africa's Dilemma," *Foreign Policy* 30 (Spring, 1978): 126.

2. See, for example, William Edward Hall, *A Treatise on International Law*, 8th edition (Oxford: Clarendon Press, 1924), p. 346. On the law governing intervention in civil armed conflicts, see generally, Tom Farer, "The Regulation of Foreign Intervention in Civil Armed Conflict," *Hague Academy Recueil des Cours*, Vol. II (Leyden: Sijthoff, 1974), pp. 297–404.

Bibliography

Abir, Mordechai. "The Contentious Horn of Africa." *Conflict Studies* 23 (June 1972).

——————. "Red Sea Politics" in *Conflicts in Africa. Adelphi Papers Number Ninety-three.* London: The International Institute for Strategic Studies, 1972.

——————. "The Reopening of the Suez Canal—Strategic Aspects." *Israel Defense Army Quarterly,* May 1974.

——————. "Sharm al-Sheikh—Bab al-Mandeb: The Strategic Balance and Israel's Southern Approaches." *Jerusalem Papers on Peace Problems.* Jerusalem: The Hebrew University, 1974.

Atkins, Harry. *A Geography of Ethiopia.* Addis Ababa: Sim Printing Press, 1970.

Bell, J. Bowyer. "Bab El Mandeb, Strategic Troublespot." *Orbis* 16 (Winter 1973).

——————. "Endemic Insurgency and International Order: The Eritrea Experience." *Orbis* 18 (Summer 1974).

——————. *The Horn of Africa: Strategic Magnet in the Seventies.* New York: Crane Russak & Co., 1973.

——————. "Strategic Implications of Soviet Presence in Somalia." *Orbis* 19 (Summer 1975).

Burrell, R. M. "The USSR and the Indian Ocean." *Soviet Analyst,* March 11, 1974.

Campbell, John Franklin. "Background to the Eritrean Conflict." *Africa Report* 16 (May 1971).

Castagno, A. A. "Interview with Mohamed Siad Barre." *Africa Report* 16 (December 1971).

——————. "Somalia Goes Military." *Africa Report* 15 (February 1970).

Clapham, C. "Ethiopia and Somalia" in *Conflicts in Africa. Adelphi Papers Number Ninety-three.* London: The International Institute for Strategic Studies, 1972.

Cohen, John M. "Effects of Green Revolution Strategies on Tenants and Small-scale Landowners in the Chilalo Region of Ethiopia." *The Journal of Developing Areas* 9 (April 1975).

——————. "Ethiopia After Haile Selassie: The Government Land Factor." *African Affairs* 72 (October 1973).

_____ and Peter H. Koehn. "Rural and Urban Land Reform in Ethiopia." *African Law Studies* 14 (1977).

_____, Arthur A. Goldsmith and John W. Mellor. "Rural Development Issues Following Ethiopian Land Reform." *Africa Today* 23 (April-June 1976).

Contini, Jeanne. "The Illiterate Poets of Somalia." *Reporter,* March 14, 1963.

Cottrell, Alvin J. and R. M. Burrell. "Soviet-U.S. Naval Competition in the Indian Ocean." *Orbis* 18 (Winter 1974).

Cox, David R. "Sea Power and Soviet Foreign Policy." *U.S. Naval Institute Proceedings* 95 (June 1969).

Decraene, Philippe. "Scientific Socialism—African Style." *Africa Report* 20 (May-June 1975).

Democratic Republic of Somalia. *Memorandum on French Somaliland to the U.N. Special Committee on the Situation with Regard to the Implementation of the Declaration on the Granting of Independence to Colonial Territories and Peoples.* Ministry of Foreign Affairs, June 1, 1965.

Drysdale, John. *The Somali Dispute.* New York: Praeger, 1964.

Enahoro, Peter. "Eritrea's War of Secession." *Africa,* March 1975.

"Ethiopia: Land War." *Africa,* December 1975.

"Ethiopia: The Military Regime." *Africa Confidential* 15 (September 20, 1974).

"Ethiopian Tikden." *Africa,* April 1975.

Farer, Tom J. "Ethiopia: Soviet Strategy and Western Fears." *Africa Report* 23 (November-December 1978).

Great Britain, Colonial Office. *Kenya: Report of the Northern Frontier District Commission* (CMND, 1900). London: HMSO, 1962.

Greenfield, Richard. *Ethiopia: A New Political History.* New York: Praeger, 1965.

Halliday, Fred. "The Fighting in Eritrea." *New Left Review* 67 (May-June 1971).

Harbeson, John W. "Socialism, Traditions, and Revolutionary Politics in Contemporary Ethiopia." *Canadian Journal of African Studies* 11:2 (1978).

International Institute for Strategic Studies. *The Military Balance 1975–1976.* London: The International Institute for Strategic Studies, 1975.

_____. *Strategic Survey 1977.* London: The International Institute for Strategic Studies, 1978.

Jaffe, Andrew. "Haile Selassie's Remarkable Reign." *Africa Report* 16 (May 1971).

Jane's Fighting Ships. New York: Franklin Watts, Inc., 1975–76.

Jukes, Geoffrey. *The Indian Ocean in Soviet Naval Policy. Adelphi Papers Number Eighty-Seven.* London: The International Institute for Strategic Studies, 1972.

Kaplan, Irving *et al. Area Handbook for Ethiopia.* Washington, D.C.: American University Foreign Area Studies, 1971.

Legum, Colin. "Ethiopia Looks for Reformers." *Observer Foreign News Service,* July 5, 1974.

――――――. "Ethiopia's Soldiers Ready to Fill Power Vacuum." *Observer Foreign News Service,* July 3, 1974.

――――――. "Ethiopia's Army Split by Feuds." *Observer Foreign News Service, July 4, 1974.*

――――――. "Ethiopia's Soldiers Ready to Fill Power Vacuum." *Observer Foreign News Service,* July 3, 1974.

―――――― and Bill Lee. *Conflict in the Horn of Africa.* New York: Africana Publishing Co., 1977.

Levine, Donald. *Greater Ethiopia.* Chicago: University of Chicago Press, 1965.

――――――. "The Roots of Ethiopia's Nationhood." *Africa Report* 16 (May 1971).

――――――. *Wax and Gold.* Chicago: University of Chicago Press, 1965.

Lewis, I. M. *The Modern History of Somaliland.* New York: Praeger, 1965.

――――――. "The Referendum in French Somaliland: Aftermath and Prospects in the Somali Dispute." *World Today* 23 (July 23, 1967).

Lycett, Andrew. "The Sudan: Domestic Conciliation and External Dialogue." *Africa Report* 23 (November-December 1978).

Manning, Robert. "Diego Garcia: The Pentagon Trump Card." *Far Eastern Economic Review* 90 (November 7, 1975).

Matatu, Godwin. "Interview with Mohamed Said." *Africa,* April 1975.

MccGwire, Michael, ed. *Soviet Naval Developments: Capability and Context.* New York: Praeger, 1973.

McConnell, James M. and Anne M. Kelly. "Super-Power Naval Diplomacy: Lessons of the Indo-Pakistani Crisis 1971." *Survival* 15 (November-December 1973).

Marks, Thomas A. "Djibouti: France's Strategic Toehold in Africa." *African Affairs* 73 (January 1974).

Martin, L. "The New Power Gap in the Indian Ocean." *Interplay* 3 (January 1969).

Matthies, Volker. "The Horn of Africa and International Relations." *Intereconomics* 12 (December 1974).

Meister, Jurg. "Diego Garcia: Outpost in the Indian Ocean." *Swiss Review of World Affairs,* April 1974.

The Military Balance 1975-1976. London: The International Institute for Strategic Studies, 1975.

Millar, T. B. *The Indian and Pacific Oceans: Some Strategic Considerations. Adelphi Papers Number Fifty-Seven.* London: The International Institute for Strategic Studies, 1972.

——————. "Soviet Policies South and East of Suez." *Foreign Affairs* 49 (October 1970).

Moorehead, Alan. *The Blue Nile.* New York: Harper & Row, 1962.

Mousset, Paul. "Referendum à Djibouti." *Revue des Deux Mondes,* April 15, 1967.

Oudes, Bruce. "The Lion of Judah and the Lambs of Washington." *Africa Report* 20 (May-June 1975).

Pankhurst, Richard K. *State and Land in Ethiopian History.* Addis Ababa: Institute of Ethiopian Studies, 1966.

Perham, Dame Margerie. *The Government of Ethiopia.* London: Faber & Faber, 1969.

"Reopening the Suez Canal." *The Petroleum Economist* 41 (December 1974).

Robbs, P. "Battle for the Red Sea." *Africa Report* 20 (March-April 1975).

Samuels, Michael A. "The Horn of Africa." *The Washington Review of Strategic and International Studies* 3, Special Supplement (May 1978).

Schroeder, Richard C. "Indian Ocean Policy." *Editorial Research Reports,* March 10, 1970.

Shepherd, Jack. *The Politics of Starvation.* New York: Carnegie Endowment for International Peace, 1975.

Shilling, Nancy A. "Problems of Political Development in a Ministate: The French Territory of the Afars and Issas." *Journal of Developing Areas* 7 (July 1973).

Singh, K. R. *Politics of the Indian Ocean.* New Delhi: Thompson Press Ltd., 1974.

Spencer, John. "Haile Selassie: Triumph and Tragedy." *Orbis* 18 (Winter 1975).

Thomas, Hugh S. "Not-so Vital Suez Canal." *New York Times Magazine,* March 17, 1974.

Thompson, Virginia and Richard Adloff. *Djibouti and the Horn of Africa.* Stanford, California: Stanford University Press, 1968.

Touval, Saadia. *Somali Nationalism.* Cambridge, Massachusetts: Harvard University Press, 1963.

Trevaskis, G. K. N. *Eritrea, A Colony in Transition.* London: Oxford University Press, 1960.

United Nations, Conference on Trade and Development, 1973. *The Economic Effects of the Closure of the Suez Canal* (TD/B/C.4/104/ Rev. 1).

United Nations, General Assembly, Ad Hoc Committee on the Indian Ocean, *Declaration of the Indian Ocean as a Zone of Peace* (A/AC 159/1), May 3, 1974.

United Nations, General Assembly, *Report of the U.N. Commission for Eritrea* (Fifth Session, Supplement Number Eight-A/1285), 1950.

United Nations, General Assembly, *Resolution 390 A (V): Final Report of the United Nations Commission in Eritrea* (Seventh Session, Supplement Number Fifteen A/2188), 1950.

Unna, Warren. "Diego Garcia." *New Republic,* March 9, 1974.

U.S. Congress, House, *Hearings on the Proposed Expansion of U.S. Military Facilities in the Indian Ocean Before the Subcommittee on the Near East and South Asia of the House Committee on Foreign Affairs,* 93rd Cong., 2nd sess., 1974.

Weinland, R. G. "The Changing Mission of the Soviet Navy." *Survival* 14 (May-June 1972).

Whitaker, B., ed. *The Fourth World.* New York: Schocken Books, 1972.

Africa Confidential

Africa Contemporary Record

Africa Research Bulletin

Horn of Africa

Index

Abate, Atnafu (Lt. Col.), 42, 60

Absentee ownership of land, 51. *See also* Ethiopia; Land reform

Aden, 35, 154-55

Addis: Italian occupation, 82; kebeles, 59-60; land ownership, 59; strike-threat, *1975*, 61-62.

Adowa, 16, 75

Afar clan, 64-65, 100-107 *passim. See also* Djibouti

Aklilu Habte-Wold (Prime Minister), 20

Ali, Ibrahim Sultan: Eritrean Democratic Front, 32-33; Muslim League and emancipation, 27; Tegray tribes and, 30

Amharas, 12, 164

Amharic language, 25n, 32, 99

Andermichael, Immanuel, 40

Andom, Aman Michael (Gen.), 23, 41, 62

Anglo-French agreement of *1888*, 74

Anglo-Italian protocol, *1894*, 75-76

Angolan conflict, 137

Arab League: Djibouti membership, 105; Somalian accession, 117

Arab nations, Eritrean support, 34, 43, 46-47

Armed Forces Coordinating Committee. *See* Dergue

Armed forces, Ethiopia, 18. *See also* Second Division

Arms limitation, U.S. and Soviet, 154-58

Assimilation, Ethiopian peoples, 12-13, 99

Asmara: mutiny, *1974*, 19; strike, *1958*, 33

Associations: peasants, 54-57; self-help, old regime, 60; urban neighborhood (kebeles), 59-60

Barre, Mohammed Siad (Pres.), 5-6, 111-14 *passim*, 122-23, 126

Big Four, 29-30, 85

Blockade, Indian Ocean, 149-51

"Bloody Saturday," 41

British Somaliland Protectorate: Anglo-French agreement of *1888*, 74; border negotiations, 76-77; grazing lands, 88-89, 98; independence, 90; Italian invasion, 82

Brussels General Act, 74

Carter administration, 6, 122, 127, 162, 168

Castro, Fidel, 122-23, 160, 165

Central Cooperative Society, 60

China: Ethiopian diplomatic ties, 37; foreign aid to Somalia, 117

Christianity, 14-15, 26, 99. *See also* Eritrean Christians

Colonialism: British occupation of Egypt, 73; British occupation of Somalia, 72-89; French interests in Horn, 74; Italian, 26, 26n, 74, 81-82; Western responsibility, 163. *See also* Great Britain

Commercial farming, 51-52. *See also* Land reform

Constitutional reform: Dergue proposal for constitutional monarch, 22; Eritrea, 31-32; Kenya, 94-95; Second Division manifesto, 19

Cooperatives, urban, 59-60

Coptic Church, 26, 99

Cuba: Dergue, support of Eritrean attack, 48; detente and Ogaden war, 137-38; Ethiopian influence